URBAN

INTENSITIES

PETER G. ROWE
HAR YE KAN

U R
B
A
N

CONTEMPORARY
HOUSING TYPES
AND TERRITORIES

I N
T E N
S
I
T I E S

BIRKHÄUSER
BASEL

For Layla,

my new companion in life.

P. G. R.

For my parents, sister, and Wayne,

with much love and gratitude.

H. Y. K.

CONTENTS

INTRODUCTION

This book deals with housing in the service of creating conditions of urban intensity. The projects used as central examples in each chapter date from about 1990 to the present, with a focus on contemporary circumstances.[1] As used here, 'urban intensity' is to be understood as a function, simultaneously of density, diversity, and connectivity in clearly urban circumstances. Moreover, it is the interaction among these three properties of urbanity that brings vitality, vigor, and a certain keenness to the reception of a place, or at least this possibility. Not that constant hub-bub is entirely necessary or even desirable for dwelling, which must also have its quieter moments, but some measure of choice in the matter is truly a *sine qua non* of urban life. More specifically, in this context, 'density' refers to dwelling density, although it does not by itself guarantee either dynamism or healthy intensity in a city. Too much can and does result in overcrowding, dilapidation, and eventual urban decay. Too little often leaves dwelling environments entirely bereft of the chance of important kinds of social interaction and association. Density is also sometimes striven for as a good in itself, with various degrees of it enshrined in urban policies, plans, and regulations. Nominally, higher densities, at least up to some point, are often regarded as virtuous in

the pursuit, for instance, of aspects of good environmental performance and quality of life. Nevertheless, density is also simply an outcome of a wider entanglement of market forces, regulatory provisions, resource availabilities, locational opportunities, and cultural proclivities.[2] That being said, most examples discussed here are either within the bounds of prevailing dwelling density in specific locales or somewhat above those levels, acknowledging, if anything, the virtue of being so, *ceteris paribus*, from a broader social perspective.

'Diversity' in this context is manifested in several ways. First, at the level of specific housing complexes, it refers to the additional magnitude and range of non-residential uses that are included. This appears to be warranted from the standpoint of nearby support of an urban dwelling lifestyle, as well as employment and other local benefits of mixed use at a relatively fine grain of accommodation. In the service of smaller environmental footprints, for instance, there is something to be said in favor of a combination of dwelling density and a local mixing of use. Second, diversity here refers to variety in the different kinds of dwelling units within a specific housing complex and at the same time variety in the provision, or not, of flexibility within those units for accommodating different day-to-day, occasional, or life-cycle aspects of occupation and use. In principle, anyway, various valences or modes of inhabiting dwelling space can be adopted, ranging through bi-polar dimensions like flexible versus specialized occupation, diverse versus repetitious units, and emptied-out versus partitioned spaces. Generally though, recent development in these regards shows a trend towards poly-functional space in place of arrangements of particularized mono-functional spaces.[3] Third, diversity seen here on the demand side of housing provision refers to fluctuations and rises, generally, in household formation of different types, pushing the need on the supply side for diversity in unit types, as well as poly-functional arrangements.

In these regards, the First Demographic Transition, as it is referred to, concerns the original decline in fertility and mortality witnessed in Western countries from the eighteenth and nineteenth centuries onwards and during the second half of the twentieth century elsewhere in the world. The Second Demographic Transition, by contrast, emerged roughly from the 1960s onwards in well-developed countries. This was sustained by sub-replacement rates of fertility, a multitude of living arrangements, little stationary population, aging effects, rises in divorce rates, declines in remarriage, rising cohabitation and extra-marital fertility, declining household sizes, and rises in individual autonomy alongside of weakening social cohesion, especially around traditional families.[4] By the 1980s going into the 1990s, all OECD countries, for instance, experienced radical changes in their demographic profiles and living arrangements of their populations. This was particularly marked in France, Germany, and the United Kingdom.[5] Statistics showing the relationship to householder for household population in the United States make much the same point from the 1980s onwards, through fairly dramatic shifts across the board.[6] With some recent stabilization, this increased diversity nevertheless seems likely to continue for some time to come. It is also why the turning point of 1990, or thereabouts, was chosen for discussion here of contemporary circumstances.

'Connectivity', in this context, refers to two aspects. The first is proximity and ease of access to other parts of a housing complex, including support functions and non-residential uses, but also to the provision of places and occasions for 'neighboring' among dwellers in the same residential environment, should that be deemed desirable. Second, it also refers to the manner in which complexes are situated in broader urban contexts, especially with regard to wider transportation access, neighborhood community facilities, stores, public open space amenities, and the like. Again, there is something to be said in favor of an urbanity that virtuously combines dwelling density and social diversity, or their possibilities, alongside of proximity and access to a range of other available forms of discretionary use and amenity as well as employment. Measures of such connectivity can vary, but all involve walkable proximities and numbers, or relative occurrences, of available nearby non-residential activities, as well as to transit, along with the sheer quality of the walking experience itself. This, in turn, argues for a degree of embeddedness in a city, or other urban context, and a scale of embeddedness that is inviting, largely pleasurable, and civic in character.

'Housing type' is used variously in accordance with commonplace descriptors with regard to occupancy, massing, and scale, like 'single-family attached dwelling'; 'mid-density, low-rise dwelling'; 'high-density, high-rise housing', and so on. It also embraces quasi-architectural designations like 'row houses', 'apartment towers', 'slab blocks', and 'perimeter blocks', pointing to dominant kinds of buildings in use for housing. Or, it covers descriptors by way of building rise and access, like 'mid-rise, walk-up buildings'; 'mid-rise, elevator-served buildings'; 'high-rise, gallery-access structures', and so on. At root, 'type' here is an abstract shorthand designation of bundles of salient features of housing, with regard to discriminable artifactual qualities around which numerous examples congeal separately from other groupings. In short, 'housing types' and 'typal qualities' are broadly recognizable and generally agreed upon without too much confusion.

'Territory' is used here in two senses. The first refers to a particular physical context, environment, or kind of property circumstance like urban blocks, superblocks, or sites of former infrastructural engagements such as railroads or port facilities. The second refers to a particular sphere of action, as in conserving indigenous characteristics in housing or taking care of a particular population. Also at work is the premise that territories, in both senses of the term, are shaped by housing insofar as housing contributes to the making of a particular territory, as in the shaping of urban blocks and the making of submultiple or infill arrangements. Conversely, territories are also seen to shape housing in, for instance, the occurrence of tall buildings in places with high land values, or through both the opportunities and constraints presented by so-called brownfield sites such as those once used for infrastructural developments. More important here, however, given the primary focus on 'urban intensity', is the twinning of the two forms of terminology and the combination of both housing types and territories. This, in turn and in effect, provides a certain focus or specific emphasis to the examples of housing under discussion in each chapter. "Urban Block Shapers", for example, engages with low-to-mid-rise buildings, mostly comprised of housing, deployed in the service of inscribing or otherwise making distinct urban blocks within cities. By contrast, "Indigenous Reinterpretations" is about forms of housing that attempt to reify local, time-honored layouts and expressive manners of building in otherwise contemporary urban circumstances. Such categories, however, are often far from being exclusionary. There are, for example, rather obvious overlaps among them. The Byker Wall in Newcastle-upon-Tyne, for instance, was originally about the accommodation of infrastructure but now is also a 'big building' and something of a 'submultiple' in the language of this volume. Likewise, the *superquadra* of Brasilia can be viewed as "Superblock Configurations" and as "Housing and Landscapes". Indeed, in many of the more complex project examples, several categories of 'type' and 'territory' are invariably engaged. After all, urban intensity can and must mirror a wide array and ensemble of building and contextual or territorial circumstances, ambiences, and emphases.

What follows are nine chapters, each dealing with a particular typal and territorial category, beginning with "Urban Block Shapers", "Housing and Landscapes", "Superblock Configurations", and so on.

This is by no means intended to be an exhaustive list of such regimes but rather one that captures important aspects and directions in contemporary housing. Examples are drawn from different cultural settings with emphasis on Europe, North America, and East Asia, although also including Latin America, North Africa, and the Middle East. The centerpieces of each chapter are several contemporary projects. Also incorporated, however, are discussions of earlier precedents and concepts pertinent to a particular category of housing. The periods of these precedents vary. For instance, in discussing infill projects, the row houses of several American cities date back into the late eighteenth and nineteenth centuries. Big buildings as submultiples, by contrast, are largely post-World War II phenomena. Tall towers, to take a third example, date essentially from the early twentieth century for housing use, while housing of special populations, to take yet another example, dates well back into the nineteenth century with almshouses and the like. In all, 28 specific contemporary projects are discussed in some detail, within the more general discussion ranging over some 100 examples. Graphic presentation, beyond photographic images, consists of contextual depictions of the central case studies emphasizing various urban dimensions, followed by data sheets for each that depict critical dimensional qualities, the diversity of unit types, alongside of typical household formations and mixing of other uses. Internal arrangements within the projects, emphasizing various aspects of functionality, openness, pre-determination in layout, and so on, are also included. Finally, a concluding chapter re-addresses the issue of urban intensity more generally and across all the examples discussed. Presentation is also made of other metrics such as density to building rise, and diversity in functional use. The claim that contemporary urban housing, seen generally since 1990 or thereabouts, follows and embodies a turning point in its form, appearance, and urban disposition is also taken up in the affirmative. This is done through both an examination and discussion of prevalent trends in contemporary housing seen against more constant features, as well as in an empirically analytical manner using the three measures of urban intensity.

U R B A N

B
L
O
C
K

S H A P E R S

El Silencio

From antiquity, groupings of buildings have defined public spaces. In the context of this book, however, the term 'urban block shapers' fundamentally involves a conscious reciprocity whereby buildings comprised of an ensemble of units define streets, roads, plazas, and most other public spaces of a district plan and are defined by characteristics of that plan in turn. Further, these buildings are generally of two types. The first are linear or sequential arrangements sometimes referred to as 'bar buildings' facing, defining, and being defined by streets, roads, and other aspects of public infrastructure, while the second are 'perimeter blocks' comprised of linear arrangements of units defining and being defined by streets and public open spaces on one side and interior courts and garden spaces on the other. Certainly during the early days of the modern era, around the turn into the twentieth century, the plans to which the urban block shapers conformed were influenced by several planning emphases. The first of these involved layout and regulation of light and air requirements for healthy habitation of

rooms and other indoor and outdoor spaces in buildings. As much as anything, this was driven by tenement legislation in places like New York City, as well as elsewhere. Somewhat later, prescriptions derived from the likes of Walter Gropius' study of *zeilenbau* or bar building organizations in 1928 to 1931, also came into play, focusing on optimal spacing between buildings. There, for example, a 27-meter spacing was recommended between typical walk-up bar buildings on the order of 16 meters tall. Parenthetically, this also corresponded to the desired nominal width of relatively major streets at the time. In addition, concerns for minimal housing space standards were pursued, ranging from CIAM's 14 square meters per person to slightly less in some American stipulations.[1]

A second planning emphasis was on rational layout and, in particular, a hierarchical arrangement of streets and other elements of urban vehicular circulation. In addition, by the late nineteenth and early twentieth centuries, such functional considerations also became embroidered with well-mannered urban

10

place making, incorporating axial arrangements of buildings and public spaces, spacious civic plazas, accommodations of public parks, and the like. This inflection, in turn, generally derived from at least the first modern planned city in the mid-eighteenth century and subsequent neoclassical urban interventions, including the City Beautiful Movement in America. On the other hand, by the early twentieth century, rational aspects of plans were beginning to gain an upper hand even as straightforward gridiron layouts were sometimes seen to be too archaic. In any event, within this planning and building milieu, urban block shapers were low- to mid-rise walk-up assemblages of residential units for the most part, sometimes together with other non-residential uses. Most commonplace in Europe and to some extent the Americas, these housing layouts began largely as expansions of existing urban circumstances around, for instance, Italian, Dutch, and German cities in the throes of dealing with housing production to accommodate pressures of industrialization and modernization, as well as *de novo* development in countryside sites near urban peripheries. Then, as time and circumstances moved on up into the contemporary era, deployment of urban block shapers was to be found in a variety of redevelopment circumstances, ranging through slum clearance to former brownfield sites.

PRECEDENTS:
FROM PLAN ZUID TO THE MEANDER

An epitome of early modern usage of urban block shapers occurred in the Netherlands during the early part of the twentieth century. At the time, housing circumstances in Holland were often squalid and poorly serviced. Such conditions were exacerbated further by overcrowding due to rapidly increasing urban labor forces in search of opportunities in major cities like Amsterdam and Rotterdam. In 1900, for instance, fully 25 percent of all housing units had only one room and the demand for new housing was reckoned to be around 90,000 to 100,000 units or near 10 percent.[2] One of the most notable urban expansions involving urban block shapers was Amsterdam's Plan Zuid, the Plan for the South Amsterdam district, first commissioned to Hendrik Berlage around 1901 by the city's Office of Public Works, also coinciding with the 1901 National Housing Law. His subsequent plan of 1904, replete with wide roads, generous public open space, and a certain strong monumentality was, however, deemed unfeasible. Returning to the drawing board in 1914, the plan that appeared in 1917, with narrower streets, a less grandiose accompaniment of public open space and larger building blocks, was accepted by the city authorities and put into effect. This plan divided the relatively seamless transition of Amsterdam's existing urban fabric to the south into several components or subdistricts, with an overall aim of accommodating several thousand residents.[3] Within these components, a clear hierarchy of wide stately streets down to smaller side streets was envisaged, together with civic plazas, neighborhood squares, public parks including a large one on the southern perimeter, and several other spatial parentheses in the form of canals. As mentioned, the building blocks tended to be long and were seen by Berlage as being predominantly comprised of bar buildings and narrow perimeter blocks inhabited by people of all social classes, departing from price segregation in this regard and in the reliance on small, often single private units. There, housing blocks were taken up, in turn, by the architects of what became known as the Amsterdam School, such as Michel de Klerk and Piet Kramer, materializing

Weisse Stadt

Kiefhoek

uncommon flourishes of brickwork across well-composed façades with articulate expressions of fenestration, balconies, and places of vertical access. More often than not, uniform building lines were tightly held, defining street edges, with tower-like and other inflections at corners of prominent street crossings. Overall, the architecture was in the service of urban place and fabric making, but also with a subsidiary or secondary mode of expression for specific blocks in the overall composition. De Klerk also went on to design the Eigen Haard complex in West Amsterdam, among other projects, dating from 1914 to 1921, or thereabouts.[4]

Elsewhere in Holland and particularly in Rotterdam, priorities also turned towards housing and urban expansion. As a major port and before the era of more complete mechanization of port activities, the city was undergoing significant expansion of its labor force and of its population. Between 1900 and 1920, for instance, the population rose from 312,000 to 500,000 inhabitants. During this time, with the use of its expropriation power, the City of Rotterdam then acquired 29.5 hectares of land in 1918 on the south side of the River Maas in close proximity to expanding port facilities.[5] Among other projects and drainage improvements by way of *wetering* or drainage canals, the Kiefhoek housing estate by Rotterdam's then city architect – J. J. P. Oud – stands out certainly as an accomplished example of urban block shaping using primarily housing. Completed between 1925 and 1929, the project is modest, providing for 300

units of worker housing in small but well-organized basic two-storey units of 61.5 square meters of floor area on small 7.5-meter-deep by 4.1-meter-wide footprints, alongside of a couple of playgrounds, two shops, a central heating plant, and a church – the Hertsteld Apostolische. Essentially, the bar buildings that make up most of the complex are uniform rows of two-storey units, each with individual gardens on the backsides. Internally, the arrangement of streets and some public open space, with few points of entry or exit, gives the complex an inward orientation, no doubt to foster a strong sense of community. Within each block, there was room for the personalization of dwelling space through further 'tenant fitout', even though this was clearly an attempt to establish a strong collective image. In this last regard, unlike the earlier projects mentioned in connection with the Amsterdam School, the urban architectural expression at Kiefhoek was comprised of taut modernist façades reflective of the frugal times and the application of modern materials and techniques of building in a conspicuous version of the Dutch New Objectivity, similar to the Neue Sachlichkeit prevailing elsewhere at much the same time.[6]

In Germany during the post-World War I Weimar Republic, overcrowded and run-down conditions in cities like Berlin were pushing new developments to the outskirts and into the neighboring countryside in order to lower costs. One such project was the Berlin Britz estate, south of the city proper, constructed between 1925 and 1932. The context of

Eigen Haard

the Britz estate was literally agricultural fields with a few local water bodies and it was a case of making something largely out of nothing, with the prolific use of primarily residential block shaping structures. Under the planning and architectural authorship of Martin Wagner and Bruno Taut, the Berlin Britz estate was large, at some 21,374 dwelling units mainly in the form of three- to four-storey apartments, often conformed to found local features like the well-known 'horseshoe block' partially enclosing an extensive green plaza with a lake in its midst.[7] Within this area were also 679 single-family units arrayed in linear arrangements of two-storey attached units with private back gardens. Clearly, deformations from a regular east-west linear alignment of units were to imbue the project with its own particular sense of place and also to create a central spine, as it were, of related though different public open spaces. The facilities of the apartment complexes and particularly the one enframing the horseshoe-shaped space were punctuated by deep reveals of private balconies, capped above by a single row of maisonette units with little to no window openings, further emphasizing the coherent walled-in definition of the public open space. Elsewhere, the urban-architectural expression, especially in Bruno Taut's hands, aligns closely with the Neue Sachlichkeit and the new realism and objectivity of the times in Germany with regard to economy, functionality, materials, and construction technique. Another project in Berlin of a similar ilk, though far smaller at the neighborhood scale of 1,286 dwelling units, was the Weisse Stadt by Bruno Ahrends,

Otto Salvisberg, and Ludwig Lesser as the landscape architect.[8] Built between 1929 and 1931, it was also fabricated largely in the countryside to the northeast of the central city. Again, relatively big apartment buildings rising to four storeys were arranged on site with wide communal courts in between used for allotment gardens and other recreational purposes.

Moving on in time and geography, one notable urban block-shaping project from Latin America was El Silencio in Caracas, Venezuela, of 1942 to 1945 by Carlos Raúl Villanueva.[9] As in the Dutch cases, it was to be an integral part of the city's expansion and was conceptualized as a terminating end to the Avenida Central Plan for Caracas, stretching from its site at the foot of the hillside of El Calvario to Bellas Artes Plaza some kilometers to the east. At the time of construction, the 9.5-hectare site was occupied by slum conditions of a makeshift squatter settlement, prone to damaging flooding by a water course – barrancas – crossing the area from high up on the northern side of the east-west running valley within which the city was constructed. The basic plan of El Silencio enframes part of the Avenida Central axis and the Fuente Las Toninas Plaza, where it terminates against El Calvario, in seven related though distinctive building massings. The number of dwelling units was 845, effectively constituting a distinctive community or neighborhood essentially for a lower-income market. It was not literally constructed to rehouse the squatters displaced by the project although some, under the auspices of the Banco Obrero, the client for the project,

El Silencio

Berlin Britz

Meander © Mirande Phernambucq

did make such a move. Among the seven building massings, four are perimeter blocks with spacious central courts, while the other three are linear blocks, or bar buildings, shaped to the topography and local circumstances of the site. Rising from four to seven storeys in height, the taller apartment buildings, with elevators and shops on the ground floor, terminate the central axis, while the lower buildings comprise the urban block structure of the basic gridiron, laid out in the Avenida Central Plan. There are some 400 shops provided for in the project at the ground level, along with some accommodation of industry and local crafts. The dwelling units, in comparison to the European examples, are larger, ranging from 51 percent at three bedrooms, 30 percent at four bedrooms, and 19 percent at two-bedroom apartments. Ample community open space is also provided in the complex, which is comprised of only 32 percent of building, although the overall density is high, at close to 9,000 dwelling units per square kilometer. Again, the urban-architectural expression is modernist in an orthodox sense, although inflected, even playfully, with ground-level loggias sporting local traditional figural motifs and with both open and closed balconies animating well-composed façades.

Returning to Holland in contemporary times and to positions and debates about place making dating back into the late nineteenth century, there is the Meander in Amsterdam of 1995 by Leon Krier. Comprised of 204 dwelling units, a school, a community library, shops, restaurants, and subsidized space for young entrepreneurs, the project was built on a brownfield site beside a canal, formerly occupied by industry.[10] Within this mix of uses, the dwelling units tend to be on the upper floors of the predominantly five-storey structures. Aptly named, the complex of what are essentially bar buildings and three circular

towers in plan, literally winds in through the site and is certainly post-modern in its stylistic inclinations. However, rather than being primarily neoclassical in the manner in which an otherwise rational layout is inflected like in the earlier Dutch plans, formal aspects of the scheme seem to be more rooted in principles espoused by Camillo Sitte around 1889 and his critique of late nineteenth-century urbanism and moving back even to a pre-modern irregularity yet concern for place making.[11] Also present is a return to the lavish brickwork and façade articulation, within the main frame of the bar buildings, found in the earlier Amsterdam School.

CONTEMPORARY CASES: BUILDING IN BARCELONA AND LOS ANGELES

The two contemporary urban block shapers case studies examined are Villa Olímpica and La Maquinista, both of which are located in Barcelona. The former is located right by the coast and the latter is situated further inland right along the TGV high-speed railway line connecting the city to France. From its early days as a Roman colony, Barcelona has evolved from a walled, medieval fortress town into a major metropolitan center in the Western Mediterranean both economically and politically. The composition of the city's urban fabric bears witness to its transformations, and one of its hallmarks is the 113.3 meters by 113.3 meters orthogonal grid interdicted by perimeter blocks rising up to six storeys above grade in the Eixample district. A legacy of Ildefons Cerdà's 1859 Pla d'Eixample, or Expansion Plan, largely imposed upon the Barcelona City Council by the central government in Madrid, the blocks with their distinctive 45 degree chamfered corners were built up over time, and accommodate an intensity and diversity of uses as well as a range of architectural expressions within them while still maintaining a high degree of urban coherence. In the 1980s, Barcelona experienced a second *renaixença*, or rebirth. Much like the first Catalan cultural revival dating back to the 1830s that saw the city undergo a metamorphosis into one of the most dynamic centers of modernist art and architecture in Europe, this 'second wind' of change led to a profusion of urban-architectural projects which rejuvenated the city after it broke free from the chains of dictatorial rule. By the time democratic governance was restored in 1978, Barcelona had deteriorated physically. Living conditions were poor and there was a lack of public services supporting a population then of around 1.75 million.[12] Efforts to reclaim the city and to make it more livable materialized through an urban renewal program launched in 1980 with a focus on urban public space projects. Drawing on the General Metropolitan Plan proposed in 1976 that called for the "reconstruction and harmonization of [existing] urban space" and with a view towards projects rather than plans, the program implemented various projects across all the districts with the aim of enhancing the overall quality of the city.[13]

Against this backdrop of urban regeneration, key sites were identified based on their strategic location and potential to assume a metropolitan significance. These included the industrial sectors of Poblenou and Sant Andreu that were later redeveloped into Villa Olímpica and a part of which became the La Maquinista neighborhood respectively. The impetus to carry out the urban renewal project at Poblenou was further strengthened with Barcelona's successful bid for the 1992 Olympic Games. Slated to be a new residential neighborhood that would be used to accommodate the athletes during the games, the industrial sector of Poblenou was then in a state of dilapidation and comprised a mixture of abandoned factories and squatter housing, warehouses, car parks, a water treatment plant, the women's prison, and dumping grounds. With active railroad lines and a highway traversing the entire site, the city was effectively cut off from what had then deteriorated into an undesirable waterfront. The site's redevelopment was thus of utmost importance as this would

allow it to become the first project to re-open the city to the sea, and create a new modern seafront residential neighborhood.

The Villa Olímpica urban design project was entrusted to MBM, a team comprising Josep Martorell, Oriol Bohigas, David Mackay, and Albert Puigdomènech. This was not unexpected as Bohigas had played a major role in the city's planning and urban design, having served then as the Director of Public Works. The basic plan proposed by MBM was composed of five strips: first, the stretch of beaches and protective seawall; followed by a 30-meter-wide seafront promenade; a third strip of coastal activities that would be a linear accumulation of activities and higher density programs; a fourth strip of infrastructural linkage comprising the sunken Ronda Litoral as a section of the broader metropolitan system of ring roads and expressways that is crossed by plazas and pedestrian bridges; and finally, a fifth strip closest inland known as the urban nucleus incorporating the mixed-use residential typologies within an extension of the grid-block morphology. The dimensions of the Cerdà grid were maintained in the urban nucleus, with several of the blocks to be approached as variants of Cerdà's original proposal, while others were agglomerated into multiples of three or four constituting superblocks or maxi-grids that would allow for "a more radical application of new typologies and new urban layouts".[14] In determining the urban design guidelines for the project, MBM emphasized the perimeter in these blocks and established consistent building heights and setbacks that would still facilitate a range of architectural expressions.

After winning the Olympic bid, the Ajuntament de Barcelona organized the work through several public and quasi-public companies, known as Societats Anònimes (SA), including the Villa Olímpica Societat Anònima which had two subsidiaries - the Nova Icària SA (NISA) and the Port Olímpic de Barcelona SA (POBASA) - that had private capital commitments of 60 and 50 percent. These SAs are similar to 'special district' authorities that appeared in Barcelona as early as the 1840s and, as public companies, were allowed special technical and managerial teams to be formed for a public work project on a temporary basis.[15] The POBASA oversaw the development of the

Olympic Port component adjacent to the waterfront, including the axial arrangements of the two 44-storey towers and the square quay with docking and sailing facilities set off to one side. The two skyscrapers anchoring the site are the Torre Mapfre office building by Iñigo Ortiz and Enrique de León, outwardly defined by the horizontal bands, and the Les Arts Hotel sheathed in criss-cross structural bracing by Bruce Graham and SOM, with the commercial complex and iconic 'fish' sculpture by Frank Gehry around its base.

The core of the project showcasing the urban-architectural operations of housing in the trope of urban block shapers is the urban nucleus that accommodated the athletes during the games and residential units for the locals after the event. Overseen by the development company NISA, the urban nucleus comprised a total of 1,976 dwelling units, covering an area of 14.9 hectares that also incorporated other uses such as commerce and offices.[16] Rising around seven storeys above ground, these residential blocks are a composition of both modern linear apartment buildings and traditional perimeter block types, much akin to the form in the Eixample. Unlike the built-up and infill conditions emblematic of the Eixample, the courtyards of these blocks are much more open, containing a range of gardens and hardscape plazas. Architects who were past recipients of the Barcelona FAD award in recognition of design excellence were commissioned to undertake the design for each and in some instances parts of the housing complexes, resulting in a variety of architectural expressions.[17]

Two exceptional projects that stand out within this rich architectural variety of apartment complexes are MBM's Can Folch Housing and Elías Torres and José Antonio Martinez Lapeña's housing complex along Carrer de Salvador Espriu. The former is located on the western edge of the urban nucleus while the latter serves as an anchor for the eastern corner. In contrast to the other projects that somewhat preserve yet also re-interpret the classical form of the

VILLA OLÍMPICA

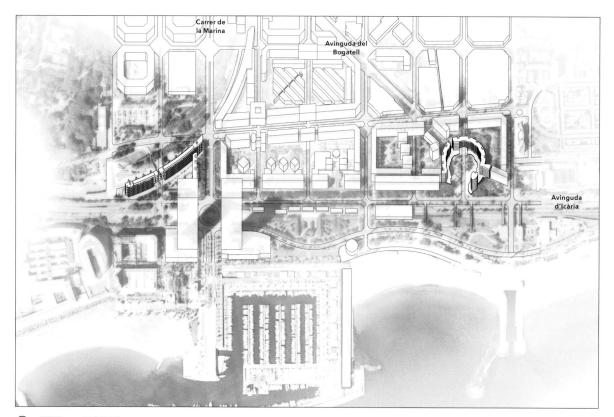

URBAN BLOCK SHAPERS

Eixample, these two complexes respond creatively to their unique site conditions, allowing the design of the buildings to work in concert with their contexts, as well as enhance the definition of the streetscapes. The Can Folch Housing was redeveloped on the site of the old Folch factory, whose magnificent brick chimney was conserved as a nod to the area's industrial past. The great 235-meter-long curving building with its concave façade facing the Carles I Park derived its form from the old railway line that used to cut across the streets with a wide sweeping arc. Spanning across the Carrer de Ramon Trias Fargas that leads directly to the waterfront, the building turns into an arcade just above the street, allowing the longer façade to continue virtually uninterrupted. At the same time, this also lends emphasis to the contour of the Carrer de Mouscou, while the north-south orientation of the building provides direct sunlight all day, with views to both the sea and the park. To break the monotony of this continuous façade, the alternate bands of grey bricks and windows are broken regularly by shafts of bay windows.

Overall, the perimeters of the Can Folch Housing block and the surrounding streets are well-defined, interposed with a number of sightlines cutting through into the interior public space and encouraging a higher degree of urban porosity and street-level activity. Along Carrer de la Marina, the six-storey complex is demarcated by a brown brick building perched above a strongly rhythmic arcade with arches that open up to views of the sunken shopping plaza. Intended to be a mixed-use project with parking in the basement, the complex houses 151 units, 90 of which were sold at market rate, and the remaining 60 were social housing.[18] The units are composed typically of duplexes and three-bedroom apartments of no more than 13 meters in depth. With a total built area of 34,022 square meters on a site of just 9,923 square meters, the project has one of the highest building intensities among the complexes developed in the urban nucleus with nearly 70 percent given over to residential purposes, 25 percent for parking, and the remaining five percent for commercial use.[19]

VILLA OLÍMPICA - CAN FOLCH HOUSING

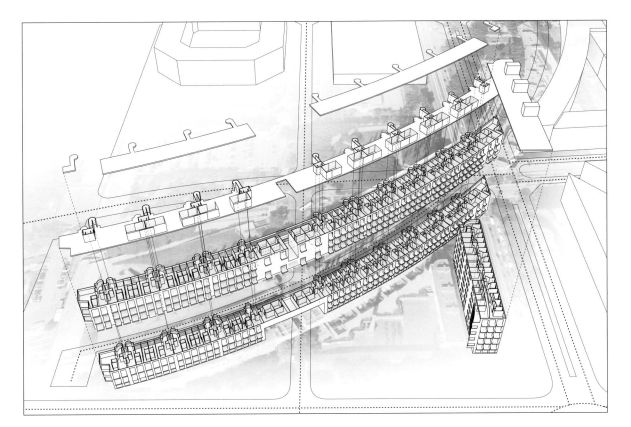

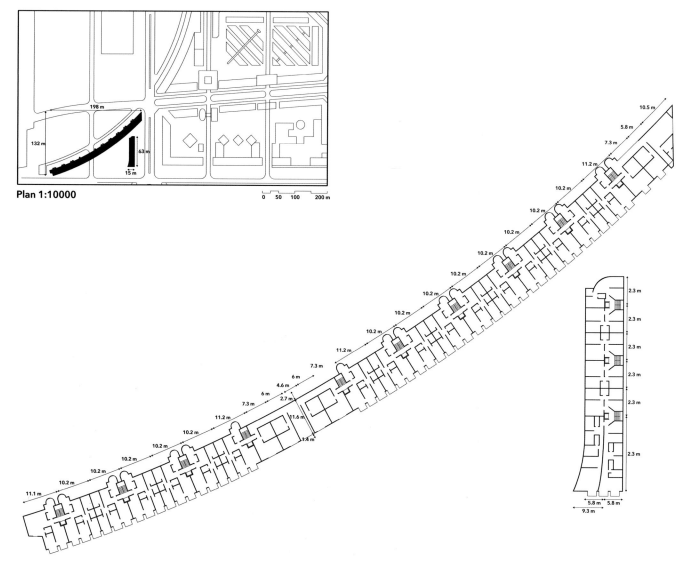

Plan 1:10000

0   50   100   200 m

Plan 1:1000

0   5   10   20 m

Key

■ Housing Units
▫ Entrance/Parking

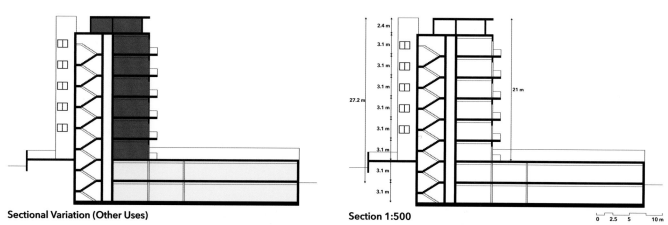

Sectional Variation (Other Uses)

Section 1:500

0   2.5   5   10 m

URBAN BLOCK SHAPERS

Household Types
Unit Types 1:600

Key
- Bedroom/Living
- Kitchen
- Bathroom

Unit Type Locations

3 BR
122 sq m
6 units

1 BR
73 sq m
6 units

3 BR
138 sq m
6 units

2 BR
85 sq m
24 units

3 BR
117 sq m
98 units

2 BR
102 sq m
6 units

4 BR
152 sq m
14 units

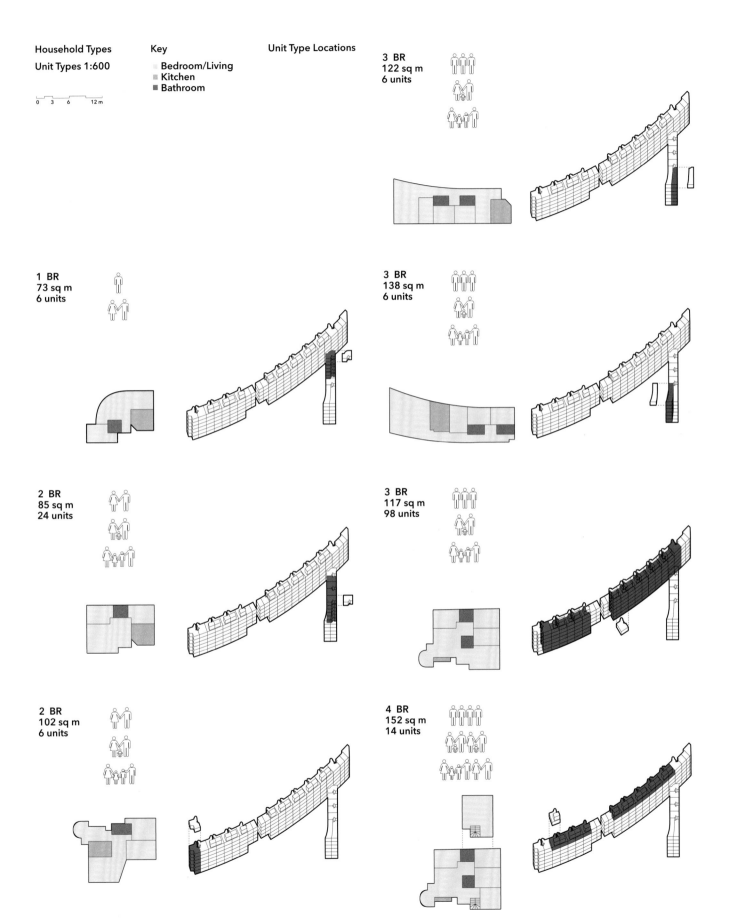

URBAN BLOCK SHAPERS

The other project of interest is the <u>138 Villa Olímpica Apartments</u> by Torres & Lapeña along Carrer de Salvador Espriu, distinguished by its prominent circular plaza created by the housing within this seemingly typical perimeter block. The housing complex was laid out as a break in the façade of the street, providing a termination to the diagonal street, Avenida Bogatell, extending through the project via the two pedestrian ramps leading up to the terraced plaza. By deviating from the original block plan, this complex by Torres & Lapeña not only offers a change to the morphology of the block, but also opens up and literally frames a view to the sea. Occupying a site of 1.03 hectares, the project also has a high building intensity with a total built area of 34,911 square meters. Slightly more than half of the built area is taken up by the 138 dwelling units, while 38 percent is given over to parking, and another eight percent is for commercial use on the ground floor encircling the hardscape plaza dotted with palm trees.

Carrer de Joan Oliver itself passes under the block that forms a large gateway, much akin to the arcade in the Can Folch Housing by MBM. Raised above grade, the circular block is seven storeys tall while the solitary, crowning tower in the shape of a prow of a ship marking the terminus of the diagonal rises 10 storeys in height. The dwelling units are generally commodious, composed of three- or four-bedroom types, with two units sharing a common access core. In maintaining the coherence of the scheme, Torres & Lapeña have chosen a warm, brown brick palette for the entire complex that resonates with the rest of the seaward façades of the apartment complexes along Carrer de Salvador Espriu. Within the central court, the building façades are splayed in and out slightly, incorporating sliding screens generating a dynamic surface enhanced by the light at different times of the day. This playful surface variation is reflected similarly in the floor plans, revealing a building depth ranging from 11 to 13 meters.

VILLA OLÍMPICA - 138 VILLA OLÍMPICA APARTMENTS

Carrer de
Salvador Espriu

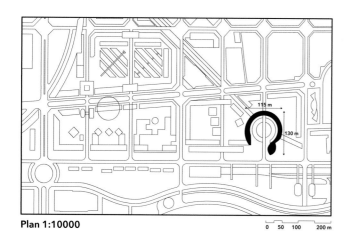

Plan 1:10000

0   50   100   200 m

Household Types
Unit Types 1:750

Key
Bedroom/Living
Kitchen
Bathroom

0   3.75   7.5   15 m

Unit Type Locations

3 BR
102 sq m
102 units

3 BR
112 sq m
6 units

3 BR
117 sq m
10 units

3 BR
134 sq m
6 units

4 BR
128 sq m
10 units

4 BR
175 sq m
6 units

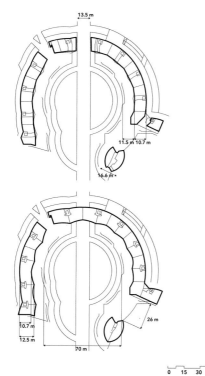

Plan 1:3000

0   15   30   60 m

Key
■ Housing Units
■ Entrance/Storage

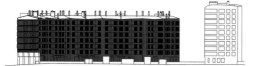

Sectional Variation (Other Uses)

Section 1:3000

0   15   30   60 m

URBAN BLOCK SHAPERS

La Maquinista was completed in 2002, a decade after Villa Olímpica, and is located in the district of Sant Andreu further inland and to the north of Barcelona's city center. The neighborhood was a former railway and industrial zone for the manufacturing of tractors and wagons, and unlike the regular Cerdà grid that defined Barcelona's Eixample and an extension of that block-like fabric to the Villa Olímpica waterfront, here there are unevenly shaped lots that resulted from Sant Andreu's industrial past. From the outset, La Maquinista was conceived of not only as a residential project, but a major urban project as part of the city's broader initiative to transform the area into a residential and mixed-use development for lower-middle income groups after the Olympic Games. Located near the La Sagrera high-speed rail station slated for completion in 2016, the project will be one of several neighborhoods connected by a 4.5-kilometer-long park covering the rail yard.[20] The project was developed by the Inmobiliaria Colonial, one of the leading real estate companies in Spain, and BAU-Barcelona led by Joan Busquets was commissioned to design the urban project.

LA MAQUINISTA

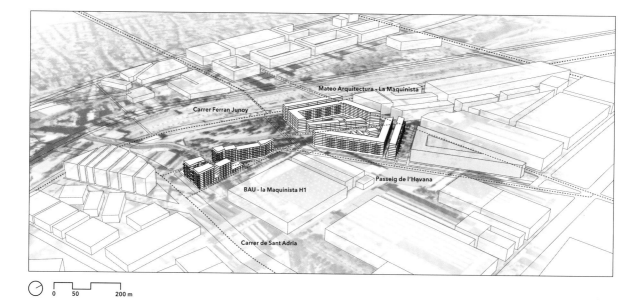

The overall urban scheme is composed of four blocks with different shapes and non-orthogonal intersection angles, resulting in a path of irregular shape with intermediate residential densities. In coming up with the comprehensive plan, including the architectural guidelines and open space planning, BAU-Barcelona took into consideration variables such as the relationship to the broader Sant Andreu neighborhood, connections to public transport, sun exposure, and the access to the sprawling, open-air La Maquinista Shopping Mall located across Carrer Sao Paulo. Urban parameters such as a height limit of 26.85 meters were imposed by the Barcelona Metropolitan Master Plan, and conventional materials were stipulated to reinforce the coherence of the plan as a holistic urban project while still providing adequate freedom to diversify the architectural form. The layout of the buildings is shaped by the geometry of the blocks and the definition of the civic axes, and the decision was made to design open blocks with adequate open spaces dedicated to private and/or collective gardens. Of the four residential blocks, the focus of the following examination will be on Block H-1 designed by BAU-Barcelona and Blocks H-2 and H-3 by MAP Arquitectos under Josep Lluís Mateo.

The plan by MAP Arquitectos for the H-2 and H-3 Blocks was to have taller, continuous perimeter blocks surrounding low-rise bars in the center, as predetermined in the urban design guidelines. The perimeter buildings are fairly conventional, and are double-layered on the west and east sides of the block separated by a void of nearly eight meters. These 'sandwich' buildings have a depth of approximately 10 meters, while the singular bar continuations that wrap around the north and south sides of the block range from around 12 to 13 meters. Passages are created along the major streets providing access into the courts, while a sense of intimacy is still maintained by the enclosure of apartment buildings containing 120 dwelling units. The central void with the garden/pool facilities constitutes the structuring device of the scheme, continuing underneath the inner band of the perimeter block that has been raised on the *pilotis*, and into the eight-meter-wide void rising upwards forming a vertical patio of sorts. By creating this vertical patio wedged between the double-layered perimeter buildings, the project not only increases its building intensity, but also benefits from the cross-ventilation and improved daylight levels. At the upper levels, bridges linked by stairs cross the void at every floor and connect the units and

corridors to each lift tower. The number of dwelling units sharing access landings is kept to a minimum, reinforcing the level of privacy, and typically, a lift lobby leads to just two apartments.

In the nine-storey-tall parallel perimeter buildings, the floor plans are mirrored on each side, and each unit efficiently accommodates three bedrooms, two bathrooms, and built-in storage. Apart from these three-bedroom units, the complex also offers a range of smaller one- and two-bedroom units, as well as duplexes in the low-rise bars fronting the pedestrianized Passatge Posoltega bisecting the H-2 and H-3 Blocks. Access to the perimeter 'sandwich' buildings is marked by colorful island-like lobby entrances on the ground floors, interspersed with lightly vegetated patches extending the lawn into the vertical patio. The brown brick façades are kept relatively simple, punctuated by sheltered terraces as well as open-air balconies that add a touch of lightness to the project's compact mass. Given its immediate adjacency to Barcelona's largest open-air shopping mall designed by Manuel de Solà-Morales, the need for commercial and retail programs on site, as was the case of the Villa Olímpica blocks or the mixed-use fabric of the Eixample, was completely eliminated.

LA MAQUINISTA H-2 & H-3

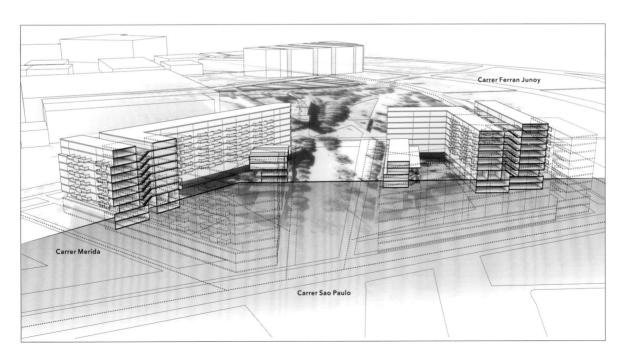

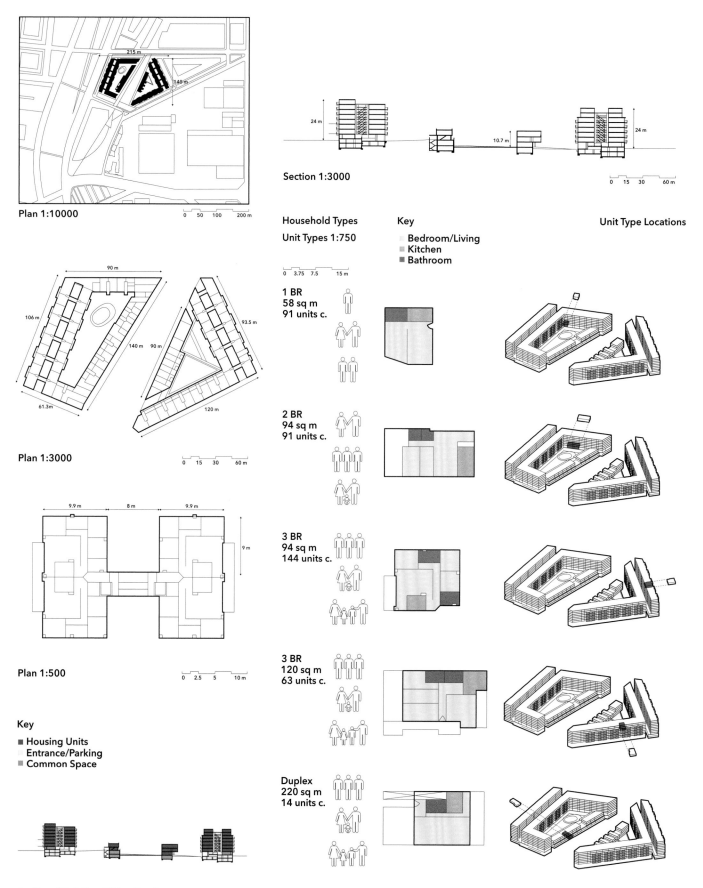

Plan 1:10000

215 m

140 m

0 50 100 200 m

Plan 1:3000

90 m

106 m

140 m   90 m

93.5 m

61.3 m

120 m

0 15 30 60 m

Plan 1:500

9.9 m   8 m   9.9 m

9 m

0 2.5 5 10 m

Key

■ Housing Units
■ Entrance/Parking
■ Common Space

Sectional Variation (Other Uses)

Section 1:3000

24 m

10.7 m

24 m

0 15 30 60 m

Household Types
Unit Types 1:750

0 3.75 7.5 15 m

Key

■ Bedroom/Living
■ Kitchen
■ Bathroom

Unit Type Locations

1 BR
58 sq m
91 units c.

2 BR
94 sq m
91 units c.

3 BR
94 sq m
144 units c.

3 BR
120 sq m
63 units c.

Duplex
220 sq m
14 units c.

URBAN BLOCK SHAPERS

Located across the street from the H-2 and H-3 Blocks is the H-1 Block by BAU-Barcelona. Occupying a relatively narrow wedge, this narrow eight to nine-storey brick building is right next to the Parc de La Maquinista. With 146 dwellings and 10 retail units, Block H-1 has a built area of 16,300 m² and a floor area ratio (FAR) of 3.13. The site plan opted for an open block typology, so as to provide access to the internal collective garden. The depth of each block is approximately 12 meters, and again is ideal for improving cross-ventilation within each unit that is open on one or two façades. The whole perimeter of each block is elevated on a plinth which is made possible by allowing the underground car park to rise up to one meter above street level, upon which ground floor shops, some collective garden terraces, and some special dwellings are located. Besides creating more defined garden spaces through this elevation, this spatial operation also allows

for greater privacy for the domestic spaces above. The layouts of the residential units vary in size from two- to four-bedroom units, including dwellings such as duplex units or units with large terraces on the top of the elevated podium. This diversity in unit types corresponded in large part to BAU-Barcelona's objective of providing "typological diversity despite [this] being a residential sector with rather homogeneous demands".[21] Access to the apartment units is provided through distinctive lobby entrances located along the inner court, typically with two units sharing a single lift landing. Unlike the manicured lawns in the MAP project, the internal collective garden here is in the vein of a Mediterranean hardscape court with planters lining the lobby entrances. Again, the use of bricks in earthen colors engenders a sense of coherence with the other three blocks designed by two different architectural firms.

LA MAQUINISTA H-1

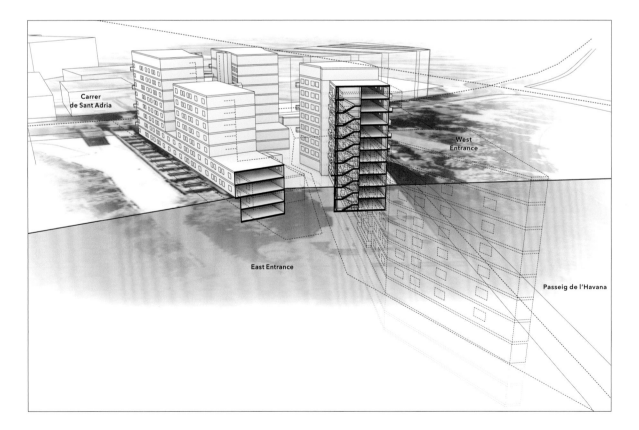

URBAN BLOCK SHAPERS

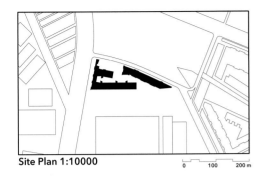

Site Plan 1:10000

0   100   200 m

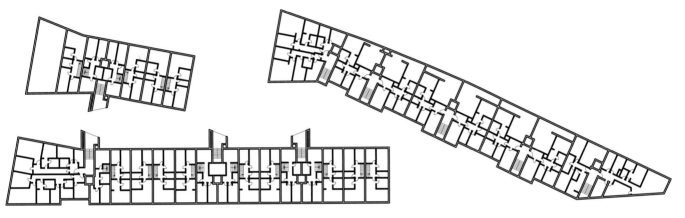

Plan 1:750

0   7.5   15 m

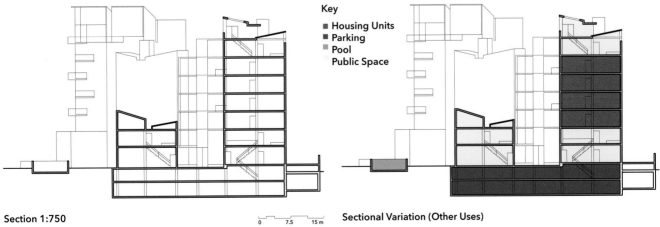

Section 1:750

0   7.5   15 m

Key

■ Housing Units
■ Parking
■ Pool
  Public Space

Sectional Variation (Other Uses)

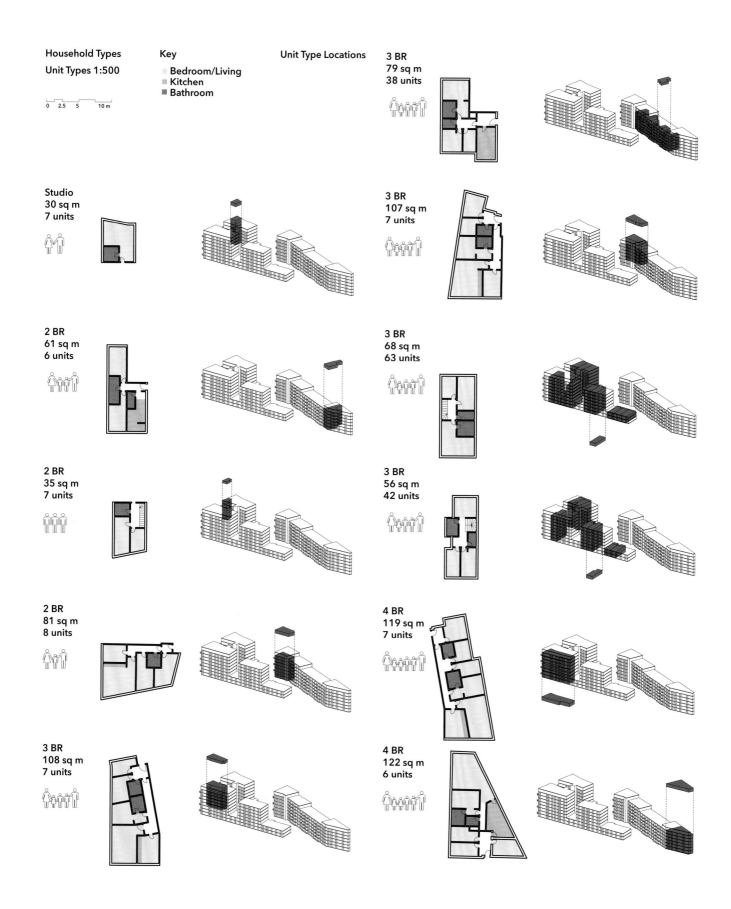

Household Types
Unit Types 1:500

0 2.5 5   10 m

Key
Bedroom/Living
Kitchen
Bathroom

Unit Type Locations

Studio
30 sq m
7 units

2 BR
61 sq m
6 units

2 BR
35 sq m
7 units

2 BR
81 sq m
8 units

3 BR
108 sq m
7 units

3 BR
79 sq m
38 units

3 BR
107 sq m
7 units

3 BR
68 sq m
63 units

3 BR
56 sq m
42 units

4 BR
119 sq m
7 units

4 BR
122 sq m
6 units

Moving away from the European context where urban block shapers commonly occur, instances of this approach towards housing and urban design can also be found in North America albeit in the form of individual row houses that collectively line the edges of blocks in cities like New York City, Boston, and San Francisco. A notable project that is inserted into a subdivided block, giving shape to both the block as well as its own lot, is the Harold Way Apartments in Hollywood, California, completed in 2003. Designed by Koning Eizenberg Architecture for the Hollywood Community Housing Corporation, this affordable housing project sits on the corner of a block, occupying a site area of 0.24 hectares. Given the demand for economy due to the limited funding, as well as other code requirements such as the allocation of 25 percent open space area and setbacks, the architects achieved their desired density by fitting in 51 units within a configuration of two parallel bars sandwiching a thin zigzag building in the center. The longer edges of the four-storey-tall parallel bars define both the major artery of North Western Avenue and the boundary with the adjacent lot, while the shorter edges facing Harold Way reveal the tripartite arrangement interspersed with two pedestrian courtyards. While the two parallel stucco-clad bars frame the site, the central block clad in cement board and wood battens steps down in elevation towards the back, opening up views to Hollywood Hills to the north. The unusual composition of this central zigzag building not only injects some rhythm and sequence to the project from the interior, defining the outdoor external access balconies with bridges linking the residents directly to the paired entrances of their apartments, it also carves out the big courtyard for the children's play area and the barbecue hubs for the community, thereby activating the site and lending an urban feel to the project. Together with the landscaping at the end of the vista, as well as other amenities like the provision of a community room and a laundry area, the architects pay much attention to these "little things" that help to "make life sweeter".[22] Each building is no more than 10 meters deep, creating this courtyard space where all apartments receive adequate light and cross-ventilation, effectively eliminating the need for air-conditioning. In total, the scheme offers a variety of unit types, including 17 one-bedroom units, 19 two-bedroom units, and 15 three-bedroom maisonettes.

HAROLD WAY APARTMENTS

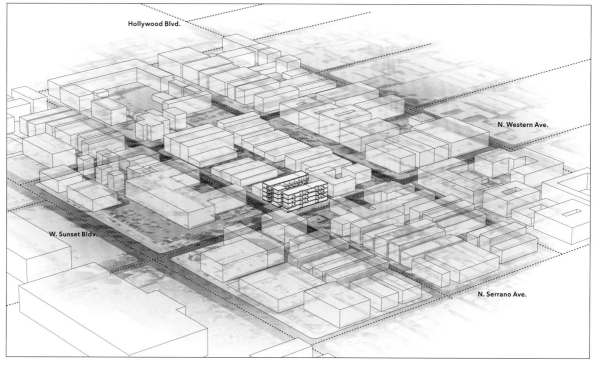

URBAN BLOCK SHAPERS

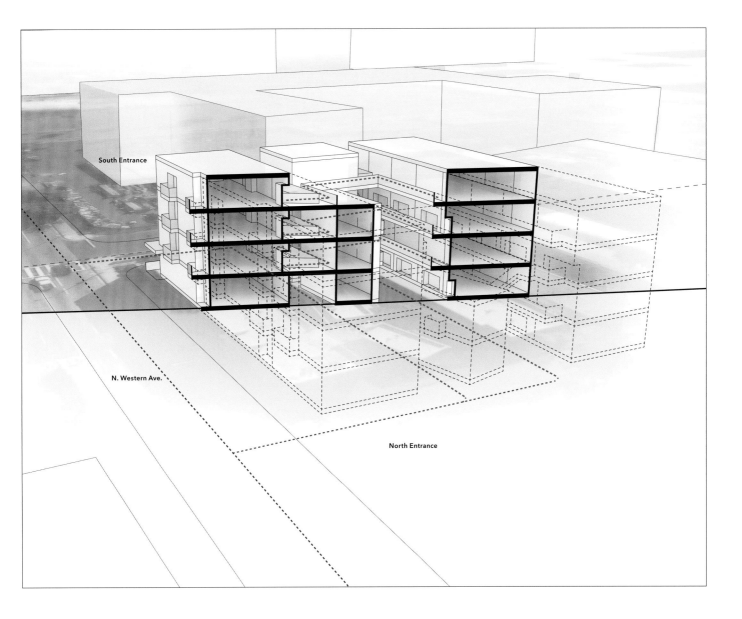

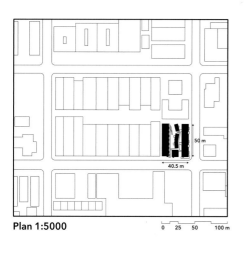

Plan 1:5000

0   25   50   100 m

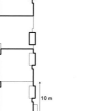

Plan 1:1000

0   5   10   20 m

Key

- Housing Units
- Entrance/Parking
- Common Space

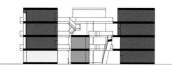

Sectional Variation (Other Uses)

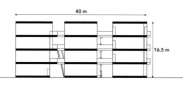

Section 1:1000

0   5   10   20 m

Household Types

Unit Types 1:500

Key

- Bedroom/Living
- Kitchen
- Bathroom

0   2.5   5   10 m

1BR
53 sq m
2 units

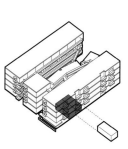

Unit Type Locations

1BR
66 sq m
3 units

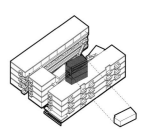

1BR
56 sq m
3 units

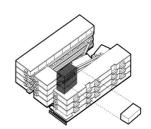

2 BR
106 sq m
22 units

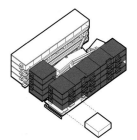

Maisonette
138 sq m
16 units

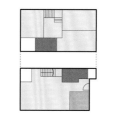

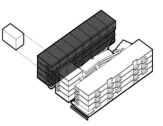

CONVERGENCES AND CONTEXTS

Urban block shapers of the kind under discussion consist either of linear housing blocks of bar buildings and row houses, or perimeter block organizations of similar forms with courts or private yards in between. The planar shapes of the linear blocks are malleable either to local topographic or other existing circumstances and to roadway conditions and adjacent urban structures. Overall, a reciprocal relationship with a setting obtains, including with willful re-shaping of urban spaces to form 'urban rooms'. The horizontal serial arrangement of units within blocks is largely repetitive, although often not entirely and especially at corner conditions. Vertical variation can be apparent, also early on in the use of the type, with double-storeyed maisonette units on the top floors, reducing the length of stairways serving units. As with other housing types, accommodation of a diversity of living conditions became more apparent into the contemporary period, away from the exigencies of the sheer production of dwelling units. Despecialization of ground floors into shops has been fostered, including through the use of loggias, arcades, and other sidewalk circumstances. Again, this is more evident nowadays for urban redevelopment than earlier on during times simply of urban expansion.

Dimensionally, urban block shapers are usually from three to seven storeys in height, or nominally five-storey walk-up structures, nowadays often also with elevator service. Early on, nominal depths of units were on the order of nine meters with widths of six meters, although sometimes reaching as low as 7.5 meters by 4.1 meters in pursuit of minimum space standards. Later on, more contemporary dimensions range from 10 to 16 meters in depth and five to 10 meters in width, although nominal dimensions of 12 meters in depth by seven meters in width also seem to prevail. Most projects are not radical with respect to the manner in which flexibility within a unit is provided, although allowance for tenant fit-out and an absence of partitioned spaces can also be present. Spacing between blocks for roadways and communal open spaces varies, but are usually on the order of 25 or so meters. Exceptions include conjunction of parallel blocks through open patio and walkway devices. Common courtyard spaces, especially landscaped gardens, often proved to be problematic in the absence of strong communal management, in many cases resulting in privatization of courtyards by adjacent units. Indeed, provision of private outdoor spaces at the level of the court, sometimes raised in height to accommodate parking and services below as well as balconies and terraces within buildings, has become commonplace and almost *de rigueur*, along with rooftop accommodation of space for non-residential, leisure-time activities.

Urban architectural expression varies both in the manner of the times and in the degrees of variation. Nevertheless, within the basic, overall oblong format of apartments, a more localized pattern of building articulation and surface openings, as well as patterning, is often deployed. This, in turn, serves to individuate units and other spatial components like entrances and stairways, as well as giving particular visual identity to particular blocks within a larger ensemble. Finally, urban block shapers of the kind under discussion can serve the need for diversity in unit types reasonably well, in addition to despecialization away from residential use, particularly in ground floor circumstances, as well as elsewhere if loft-like, flexible, and convertible spaces are provided. Dwelling diversities vary, typically by building height as depths are relatively constant. Local densities of around 150 dwelling units per hectare are certainly obtainable, or more generally on the order of 10,000 to 12,000 people per square kilometer.

HOUSING

A
N
D

LAND

SCAPES

Garbatella

At a certain level of generality, it is impossible not to think of housing and the landscapes in which they are placed or created, especially when landscape is regarded more or less synonymously with a literal or virtual setting, milieu, or context. Used more narrowly here, 'housing and landscapes' typifies ensembles of both terms within which a particular status, category, or kind of landscape relationship is of primary importance. Early on in the modern era, for instance, the relationship was often equated with a bucolic, rural setting that was deemed to be healthful in facilitating recuperation from livelihoods that otherwise involved industrial and related toil. In effect, it was a merger of 'town and countryside' that was the appropriate physical and spiritual repose for human habitation and, in one way or another, one that was embraced by those interested and active in reforming the working, social, and material conditions of the industrial era. Albert Brisbane, for instance, in his promotion of Fourier's concept of the *phalan-*

stère in America of the 1840s, conceived of his phalanxes as both city and country in an era of rapid and disorienting urban expansion and increasing nostalgia for nature.[1] Later, the Cadbury brothers in England of the 1890s endeavored to make it easy at Bournville for workingmen to own their own homes in the form of a garden village. This was quickly followed by Ebenezer Howard whose Garden City was to marry town and country together and from "this joyous union", it was believed, would spring "a new hope, a new life, and a new civilization".[2]

Certainly after the Garden City Movement got underway, the subject of the landscape in housing became both more conspicuous and varied. The Garden Cities Aniene and Garbatella in Rome, for example, were less a case of urban-rural merger, particularly of an Italian small-town variety, as they were housing in a garden setting and a somewhat exotic one at that.[3] At Sunnyside, New York, another well-known Garden City application, landscapes and buildings were juxtaposed next to each other in more or less comparable volumes, and at Radburn, New Jersey, houses certainly became clustered in gardens comprised of unfenced private domains closely associated with a broader, less-manicured landscape of vegetated areas traversed by pedestrian paths and trails, including other recreational venues.[4] Indeed, looking across houses and landscapes in America's suburban evolution, sentiment has shifted noticeably from dwelling with a landscape in earlier eras, to dwelling in a landscape as a source of leisure-time activity in, say, the 1950s and 60s to more mindful engagement in contemporary times, particularly as the size and use for active pursuits have tapered off. In short, the ensemble relationship between housing, particularly when viewed as dwelling, with consciously and construed landscapes is both malleable and can change almost episodically with the times. Furthermore, this contrivance is part and parcel of particular contemporary forms or types of housing.

PRECEDENTS: FROM ACTIVE MERGERS TO OBJECTS OF CONTEMPLATION

A project that epitomized the idea of appropriate physical and spiritual repose for human habitation, alongside of multiple engagements with landscape, was Römerstadt on the then outskirts of Frankfurt am Main in Germany and constructed between 1927 and 1928 during Ernst May's term as *Stadtbaurat* or 'City Architect'.[5] Indeed, it was also prominently part of the broader Garden City Movement, being built and managed by the Gardenstadt AG, a public property development company. Located next to the flood-prone Nidda River to the north of central Frankfurt in the city's Niddatal area, Römerstadt was also intended from the outset to be a joint-use project where its lengthy embankments and allotment gardens formed part of a flood-control improvement beside the rectification of the river channel. Originally conceived in 1914, this plan came to fruition largely under Max Bromme, part of Ernst May's team, after the First World War and several floods in 1920 and 1926, respectively. The larger project also engaged with several other contemporary housing projects, such as Praunheim and Westhausen.[6] In this regard, Römerstadt clearly engages with a larger city-scale landscape and one in which it served an explicit utilitarian purpose rather than simply being located generically in a countryside setting. The rounded *faux* fortifications of the embankment were also intended to recall a Roman encampment thought to formerly occupy the site, along with the name of the housing project itself. In addition to this larger landscape and its project-related landscape gardens for individual use by inhabitants, Römerstadt also incorporated private gardens directly associated particularly with two-storey terrace housing that comprised about half of the

Römerstadt

Tiburtino

Radburn, New Jersey

Tuscolano

overall project, along with several community parks, including well-vegetated and secluded areas on top of the *faux* fortification along the length of the flood-control embankment. Leberecht Migge was the landscape architect behind most of these proposals.[7] When seen in cross-section, the gardens associated with both the terrace housing and the larger apartment blocks clearly enjoyed a spatial reciprocity with the housing as external extensions. Overall, the project was comprised of 1,182 dwelling units housing a population on the order of from 3,000 to 4,000 inhabitants and well supported, as a more or less complete neighborhood, with community services, shops, an elementary school, and a community hall. Among the overall complement of dwellings, the terrace houses were of 75 to 88 square meters in area, often with useable basements, while the four-storey apartment blocks were of similar areas and largely in the form of three storeys of separate units plus additional maisonettes on the top floors. In fact, an overall intention behind the housing, both in and within specific landscapes, was to constitute what May referred to as a *neue wohnkultur*, or new dwelling culture, and "as places to recuperate from daily labors". More specifically, "the minimal housing units and gardens were seen to be part of a spiritual revolution and return to basics", where "simplicity in the building realm would produce a new mental attitude" and one that was "more flexible, simpler, and more joyful".[8]

Moving forward and particularly into the era of mass urban immigration in Italy after the Second World War, two schemes provided through INA

CASA, a government-sponsored affordable housing program dating from the 1950s, presented two further relationships between housing and landscape. The first was Tiburtino, authored largely by Ludivico Quaroni and Mario Ridolfi on an 8.8-hectare sloping site towards Rome's eastern periphery. Composed of 771 dwelling units and housing a neighborhood-sized population of around 4,000 inhabitants, the target population was lower-income immigrants to Rome from rural areas in neighboring provinces and from the *mezzogiorno* in the south.[9] Working with the topography, the general layout was in the form of irregular attachments of three- to five-storey walk-up units with ample balconies and pitched roofs. This seriation of units, set beside winding streets and among paved and vegetated landscapes, was formally very different from what was and became the more normal *palazzine* arrangements of housing. From research and documentation of dwellings in rural villages and towns, primarily by Ridolfi, a 'shape grammar' was developed that served as a guideline for specific architectural elements of the project. The results were clearly sympathetic to the informal and *ad hoc* configurations and architectural inflections to be found in countryside villages and towns familiar to the new immigrants. Indeed, this familiarity was clearly intentional and a driving force behind the otherwise contemporary scheme.[10] Overall and in combination with garden terraces alongside of small, well-vegetated, and paved plazas as well as interstitial spaces, a picturesque vernacular developed with the look of a small Italian town amid otherwise modern materials and construction techniques.

In the other scheme in Rome at Tuscolano, largely under the direction of Saverio Muratori, a more modernist array of housing blocks with a strong formal order was constructed, although also with incorporation of vernacular materials, window elements, and roofs. However, as a part of this complex, although otherwise adjacent to it and dating slightly later from 1953, was Adalberto Libera's mat building and apartment block ensemble, presenting quite another way of engaging housing and landscape.[11] With one element comprised of single-storey courtyard houses, accessed along narrow lanes, a strong 'inside-outside' arrangement of building and outdoor space was introduced in a clear domestication of landscape. Although with few, if any, precedents, the mat of courtyard housing, close by the Felice Aqueduct, harkened back to much earlier Roman residential quarters. The second element of the overall scheme, housing some 1,000 inhabitants all told, was a four-storey apartment building on *pilotis* and with a continuous banding of wide cantilevered balconies bringing landscape yet again into the adjacent housing units. This block, in turn, was also used in conjunction with the exterior wall of the adjacent courtyard houses to frame a relatively spacious park-plaza, entered into from a band of single-storey shops along another edge. In essence, two very different kinds of landscape, particularly along a public-private spectrum, were provided: one highly integrated with housing and domestication, with the other arranged more formally in the tradition of Italian public urban landscapes.[12]

Another modern commonplace of housing and landscape is 'slabs and towers in a park', envisaged early on by the likes of Le Corbusier and in many ways a logical outgrowth of a search for a balanced attachment between housing and greenery, light, and open air. A notable project in this regard, and also from the 1950s was Roehampton Lane, built on the outskirts of London by the London County Council Housing Division and project architects such as John Partridge, Whitfield Lewis, and Sir Leslie Martin. In an effort to decentralize London's post-war circumstances, Roehampton was located in a rolling country setting of 40.5 hectares along a 1.3-kilometer-long frontage. Around 35 percent of some 1,900 dwelling units were provided in high-rise point blocks, symmetrically disposed around a central service core, rising 12 storeys in height and accommodating two- and three-bedroom flats.[13] A further 30 percent of the units were in stacked maisonette configurations in slab blocks on *pilotis* and clearly floating, as it were, above the ground plane of the parkland setting. These configurations, along with the high-rise point towers, afforded broad panoramic views of the surrounding countryside. Most of the remainder of the housing was provided in the form of terrace housing along small lanes, in contrast to the more expansive parkland setting, although again not divorced in locational sentiment from the English countryside.

Another more iconic arrangement of 'slabs in a park' can be found in Lucio Costa's *superquadras*, or superblocks, of Brasilia, dating from 1956. Stretching in a wide arc in plan, like the wings of an airplane, the interconnected configuration of *superquadras*, each comprised of around 600 dwelling units and housing a population of 3,000 or so people,

Superquadra

Roehampton Lane

was consistent with 'neighborhood theory' at the time. This arc, in turn, was seen by Costa to exist perpendicular to a monumental axis of larger public buildings and all in a bucolic setting.[14] After all, the natural habitat of Brasilia, set inland and away from the Brazilian coast, was a forested area. The underlying arrangement of slab blocks in the *superquadras* varied considerably from one to another, but all embraced well-landscaped adjacent areas used for recreational and leisure-time activities. Each slab was usually six storeys in height, elevator-served, and raised on *pilotis* on top of a paved slab. The footprint of each apartment block was nominally 80 meters in length by 12 meters in width, accommodating around 220 inhabitants each, going back again to critical dimensions for dwelling units to be well-served by light and air. Various configurations of recessed balconies and *brise soleil* were used to mediate solar insolation to the dwelling units and the strips between the *superquadras,* usually accommodating community facilities like schools and playgrounds, as well as strip malls for shopping. The resulting ensembles of well-ordered 'slabs in a park', almost literally floating over a well-vegetated and managed setting, has been well received by inhabitants and is relatively dense, at some 340 people per hectare.[15]

CONTEMPORARY CASES: HOUSES AND NEW GROUNDS

With its low-lying geography highly susceptible to floods, the Netherlands is one of the few countries where human intervention has profoundly shaped the landscape. Even with a relatively flat terrain, there is a variety of landscapes ranging from the agricultural and town landscapes in Groningen, polders and inland seas along the North Sea coast, castles and lakes of the Vecht region, harbors and canals, major trading ports, to the lush meadows and iconic windmills that have become emblematic of the country's landscape. The two projects of interest here, De Citadel in Almere and Schots 1 & 2 in Groningen, present novel, contemporary approaches towards the integration of housing and landscapes. They illustrate how housing not only engages the broader built or natural landscapes that they are in, but also how

landscapes are activated materially and metaphorically within housing. Completed in 2006 and 2003 respectively, De Citadel and Schots 1 & 2 are representative of a historic shift in Dutch housing that occurred in 1995 when all state housing subsidies were rescinded, leaving the provision of housing primarily to the market. A related directive that was equally influential was the government's Fourth Spatial Planning Report (1988) and its later supplement published in 1993 that called for the production of low-density housing, and more specifically, 800,000 of such dwelling units to be constructed between 1995 and 2005 in neighborhoods close to existing cities.[16] This prompted housing associations, which were semi-public institutions with strong government ties, to become financially independent development agencies.[17] With the move towards marketization, architects were also increasingly expected to cater to the demand for individual expression and growing social diversity, and to the desire for functionally integrated programs.

Designed by Christian de Portzamparc, De Citadel is located in Almere – the newest city in the Netherlands, built on polders less than 20 kilometers away from Amsterdam. As one of the main cities in the Amsterdam metropolitan area, Almere is also part of the Randstad conurbation, the urban region in the shape of a crescent linking The Hague, Rotterdam, Utrecht, and Amsterdam that collectively encircles a green area known as the Green Heart. Unlike other metropolitan areas in Europe, there is no dominant core within this polycentric area. Instead, functions are spread out across the four largest Dutch cities as well as several medium-sized cities between them. In Amsterdam, a growing population due to immigration flows from the Mediterranean, and especially from the former Dutch colony of Suriname in the 1970s and 1980s,[18] prompted the government to develop the *groeikernen* or growth center of Almere to increase the housing stock with some state funding.[19] Akin to the new town strategy adopted in the United Kingdom, the aim was to create a complementary core within commuting distance to the larger metropolitan centers, thereby relieving the pressures in the major cities and encroachment on the Green Heart. Almere was therefore initially conceived of as a residential suburb comprising several semi-separate nuclei or districts and without a need for a large-scale commercial center. By 1991, however, this bedroom community function was no longer viable as the population had expanded to 100,000; so the municipality of Almere decided to create a fully-fledged city center in 1994.[20]

Almere's city center, located in the district of Almere Stad, was designed by OMA which proposed a radical approach of vertically integrating public space, retail, leisure, and residential uses on top of the existing infrastructure in a compact and dense manner. In addition, OMA's winning scheme in 1999 sought to recreate a medieval atmosphere by deviating from the orthogonal grid structure; the urban blocks were intentionally displaced at odd angles and a curved ground plane was introduced. Through a series of negotiations with the developers - Blauwhoed Eurowoningen and M.A.B., which specialized in housing and inner-city projects respectively - the finalized master plan also ensured the continuity of the grid across the blocks and the ground plane, and the creation of a vista allowing views to the water. Within this public-private development of commercial, cultural, entertainment/leisure, and housing projects, a cast of international architects were assembled to undertake various parts of the scheme, such as Kazuyo Sejima for a new theater and arts center, William Alsop for the Almere Urban Entertainment Center, OMA for a new cinema at Block 6, De Architekten Cie, René van Zuuk, and Claus en Kaan for housing along the waterfront, transforming this new city center into a showcase of architectural pieces. In particular, Block 1 situated right at the heart of this plan was entrusted to Christian de Portzamparc.

Occupying a full block measuring 130 meters by 130 meters, the project has a total built area of 45,000 square meters, and is divided into four sections by pedestrian paths that preserve the underlying integrity of the urban grid as well as OMA's proposed layout. In keeping with OMA's intention, De Citadel is a relatively dense project, at 29 dwelling units per hectare or approximately 100 people per hectare. Physically, the curved ground plane cuts through the project, separating the underground world of public transit, automobiles, and parking from the two floors of commercial activities experienced at the street level. Floating immediately above this plinth of shops and leisure programs is the world of habitation, with terraced housing bordering a central garden of sorts. Collectively, this stratification of programs in conformance to OMA's urban design guidelines creates a massive 'citadel' or fortress complex, reminiscent of the medieval castles and fortresses in the neighboring Vecht region, rising above the verdant countryside. Here, landscape is not just evoked by this parallel with the famous Vecht scenery, but presents itself almost quite literally as a cut through the layers of the earth: emerging from the caverns and networks of the underground to a porous stratum of activity that is symbolically demarcated from the living world above by a highly articulated façade. The façade pattern, derived from traditional Siennese brickwork, represents a tectonically extruded 'bedrock' undergirding the artificial 'ground' plane above. Apart from these gestures, another design feature alluding to the rivers and significance of water in the Dutch landscape is the array of black and white mosaic tiles in sinuous curves, laid on the interior plazas and courts within the shopping blocks.

At the pedestrianized shopping street level, the four main circulation routes widen towards the intersection, creating a plaza and nexus of activity while simultaneously, in de Portzamparc's words, "avoid[ing] the wall effect".[21] Every unit faces onto the pedestrian areas, clad in a double-storey structure of steel and glass that might seem repetitive but in fact allows for creative storefront displays, distinguishing one from another. Rising above the corner at this intersection is a six-storey residential tower supported on stilts - the only landmark in the undulating meadow - surrounded by two- to three-storey townhouses, in the vein of Dutch row houses' local modern block typology familiar to the place. The townhouses are distinguished by a palette of solid white, brown, or yellow wash, and are stepped in and out along the edge of the access path, creating a dynamic façade underscoring the playfulness and vibrancy of this young city. There are 46 of these townhouse units in eight different unit types, while the six-storey tower contains another six identical units, each occupying an entire floor.

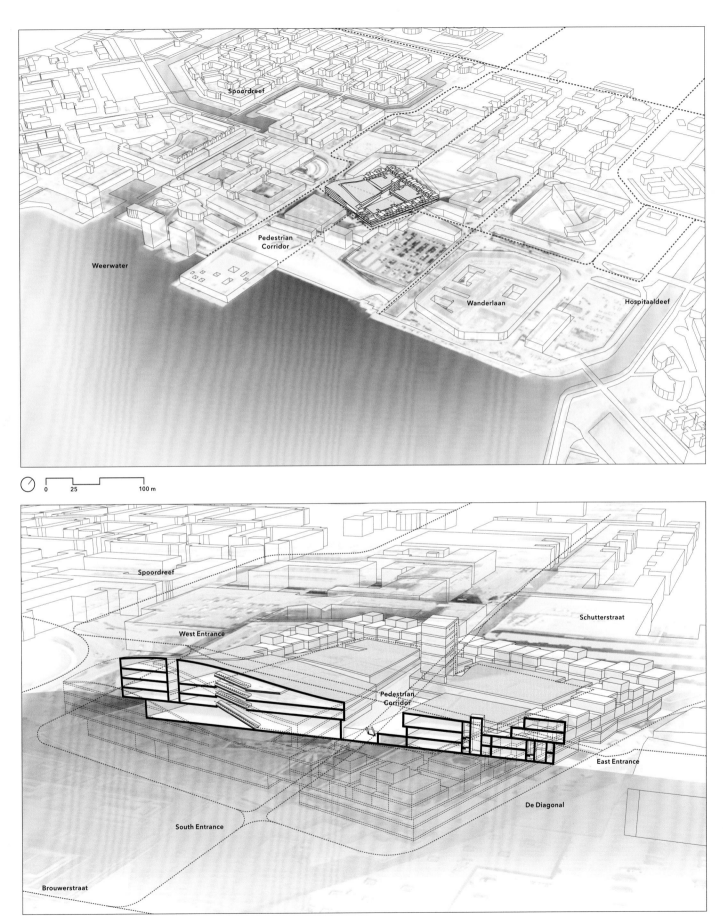

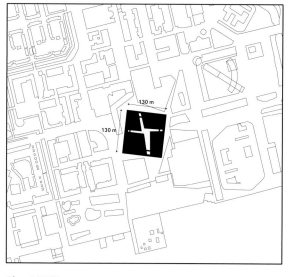

Plan 1:7500

130 m
130 m

0 50 100 200m

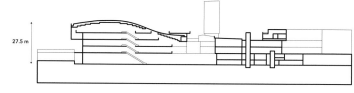

Section 1:1500

27.5 m

0 10 20 40m

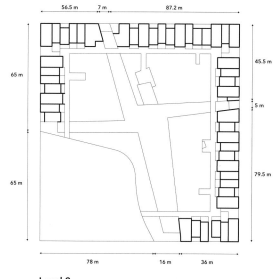

56.5 m 7 m 87.2 m
65 m
65 m
45.5 m
5 m
79.5 m
78 m 16 m 36 m

Level 2

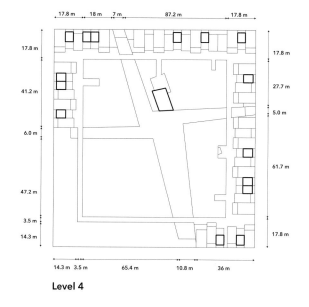

17.8 m 18 m 7 m 87.2 m 17.8 m
17.8 m 17.8 m
41.2 m 27.7 m
6.0 m 5.0 m
47.2 m 61.7 m
3.5 m
14.3 m 17.8 m
14.3 m 3.5 m 65.4 m 10.8 m 36 m

Level 4

Plan 1:1500

0 10 20 40m

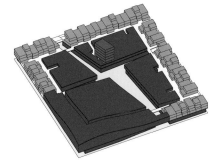

Key

■ Apartment Type
■ Terrace Type
■ Commercial
□ Entrance Parking

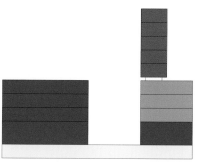

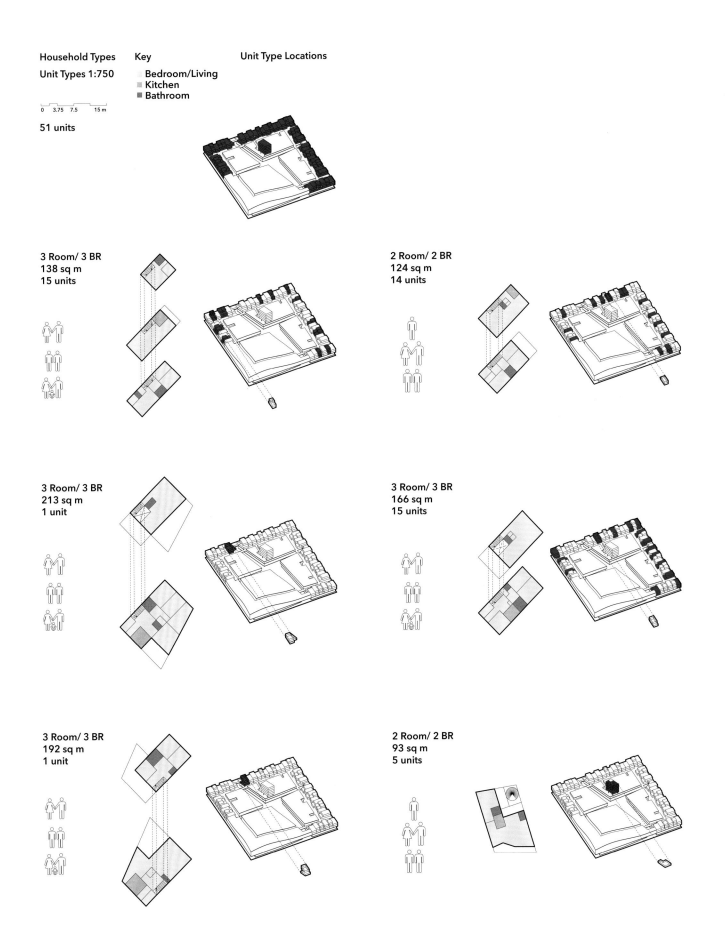

Household Types
Unit Types 1:750

Key
Bedroom/Living
Kitchen
Bathroom

Unit Type Locations

0   3.75 7.5   15 m

51 units

3 Room/ 3 BR
138 sq m
15 units

2 Room/ 2 BR
124 sq m
14 units

3 Room/ 3 BR
213 sq m
1 unit

3 Room/ 3 BR
166 sq m
15 units

3 Room/ 3 BR
192 sq m
1 unit

2 Room/ 2 BR
93 sq m
5 units

DE CITADEL

HOUSING AND LANDSCAPES

All 52 dwelling units are 100 percent owned and constitute 8,000 square meters in built area, and are typically occupied by young families. Access to the central meadow and the bridges crossing the four sectors is restricted to the residents, while public access to this green space is confined to a cantilevered deck serviced by a café offering views to the meadow and a brief respite from the retail activities below. Looking out to the meadow from within one of the apartments, one is literally transported to a bucolic world akin to the pastoral Dutch countryside, recreating a landscape to be admired rather than for functional use.

Further north in the historic city of Groningen, the Schots 1 & 2 project presents a slightly different engagement between housing and landscapes. Located in the CiBoGa terrain, an urban renewal project comprising Circus, Boden, and Gasterrein at the edge of downtown Groningen, Schots 1 & 2 are among 13 *schotsen* – compact residential blocks with collective internal courtyards – in the master plan proposed by S333. Covering an area of 14 hectares, the CiBoGa terrain was a former industrial site sandwiched between the Noorderplantzoen city park and the Oosterhamrikkanaal waterway. The master plan, which was undertaken in 1996 and slated to be completed in 2014, aimed to connect these two landscape elements through the mixed-use neighborhood, including capping the polluted ground with underground parking, re-using the industrial buildings for public programs, creating 900 residential units that would support a live/work environment, introducing retail and collective services on site, and, more importantly, establishing a "strong, clear identity for the landscape and public spaces".[22] Following their work on the master plan, S333 was commissioned in 1998 to design the first phase of this redevelopment project – Schots 1 & 2.

In contrast to De Citadel, which was undertaken by a private real estate developer in a public-private partnership, Schots 1 & 2 was taken on by a development consortium of private organizations including ING Vastgoed, Amstelland Onkwikkeling, Bouwbedrijf Moes BV, and Amvest Vastgoed, together with Groningen's largest housing association, Nijestee Vastgoed, which supplies some 13,000 rental housing units in the city.[23] Given this social agenda, 30 percent of the 149 rental units in the project were thus designated as social housing. From the outset, S333 pursued two key strategies: first, they sought to elevate the role of context, nature, and urban ecology in re-evaluating, re-interpreting, and re-organizing dense urban neighborhoods; and second, they attempted to create a "multi-layering of activities and landscape", somewhat similar to the stratification at De Citadel, to offer a compelling alternative to the traditional urban block typology.[24] In essence, landscape and ecology were central to the design considerations and outcomes in this project. Besides treating and sealing the previously polluted ground with underground parking, S333 also had to work within the municipality's regulation for a car-free zone throughout the site, where parking is capped at a ratio of one parking space for every two dwelling units. Further, apart from creating a landscape link between the city park and the canal, the site is also conceived of as a buffer or transition zone between the historic city fabric to the south, and the twentieth-century housing types to the north, where the *schots*, or literally 'ice floes', float within this open landscape.

Schots 1 & 2 have distinct site conditions that have had an influence on their resultant forms. Schots 1 is located at the intersection of two main streets – Boterdiep and Korreweg – and occupies a single urban block. Schots 2 is separated from Schots 1 by a pedestrianized shopping street in between, and sits in a much larger urban block that has also retained some of the existing, one- to two-storey Dutch row houses along the eastern and northern edges. As such, this two-part 'megaform' extends itself horizontally while working to densify existing fabric, beginning with a three-storey limb of terraced houses on the eastern side of Schots 2 that slopes up towards four storeys as it wraps around the corner before it folds along the western edge adjoining the southern terraced limb that likewise starts off as a two-storey limb of terraced houses that rises up to three storeys as it wraps around the western edge, defining the shopping street together with the four-storey limb that it meets seamlessly. Across the lively ground-floor public realm that is created by the shopping and community amenities, Schots 1 continues the building topography with a three-storey bar mirroring the pedestrianized façade for Schots 2 that breaks at a key moment where it adjoins a C-shaped limb and ascends into an eight-storey tower. To accommodate the awkward site, the two building limbs similarly twist and turn in ways that continue to define the perimeter of the block. Like the three-storey bar that it grafts upon, the four-storey C-shaped structure fronting the arterial street of Boterdiep has two additional eight-storey 'outgrowths', effectively demarcating the 'peaks' within what the architects have termed as a "volumetric landscape".[25]

The notion of landscape is also incorporated through the provision of an array of functional outdoor spaces, such as courtyards, collective roof gardens, vertical gardens, patios, and winter gardens. The gravel-covered courtyards are shaped by the arms of housing and shops embracing these internal collective spaces that remain accessible to the public, albeit through discrete openings that maintain a degree of intimacy within them. Few trees are planted within the sprawling, terraced courtyard of Schots 2, generating a space that seeks to bring nature into human habitation but is easily maintained for a high degree of use and pedestrian traffic. In fact, the communal courtyard in Schots 2 has become a popular recreational spot for the residents, with the gravel appreciated for its practicality in the rainy weather as compared to a surface of grass and mud. Gravel is also used as a roof surface material across the S-shaped limb of Schots 2, and the four-storey bridge of the C-shaped component in Schots 1, juxtaposed with patches of green on the collective roof gardens. These landscape surfaces thus act as green roofs for the city, with watering systems integrated into the building. With the eight-storey abutments on Schots 1, the vertical surface afforded by the increased building height also offered an opportunity for greening in the form of climbers such as ivy.

With regard to its façades, Schots 1 is clad entirely in glass with varying levels of transparency to endow it with more of an urban character, while Schots 2 is clad with western red-cedar boarding, punctuated only by full-length glass doors and windows. Despite the contrasting materials, the 'megaform' projects a coherent form not only through the play with volumes, but also the adoption of a common design principle where the façades for both sections would comprise an irregular alternation of openings and closed areas, thereby concealing the individual units from the exterior. To inject a sense of warmth to Schots 1, the fibre-cement panels on the walls of the access areas were painted red, offering a contrast to the green glazed façades of the dwellings, creating the impression of a pixelated surface with the irregular sequence of openings and glazed glass panels. Together, Schots 1 & 2 offer a diversity of accommodations for a range of household types, including families with children, couples, the elderly, and students. This is reflected in the assortment of unit types, with three- to four-room single-storey apartments in Schots 1 and Schots 2 on the order of 87 to 135 square meters and 80 to 90 square meters respectively, and seven different types of terraced houses in Schots 2, ranging from two- to four-storey units accommodating five to seven rooms on the order of 90 to 158 square meters. Overall, the program is varied and apart from the 105 apartments and 44 houses, the project also includes one medical center, two supermarkets, eight shops, 300 parking spaces, and a plethora of landscape spaces. Clearly, apart from the emphasis on social and programmatic diversity, there is also a high intensity of use and density on the order of 114 dwelling units per hectare within this 1.3-hectare site.

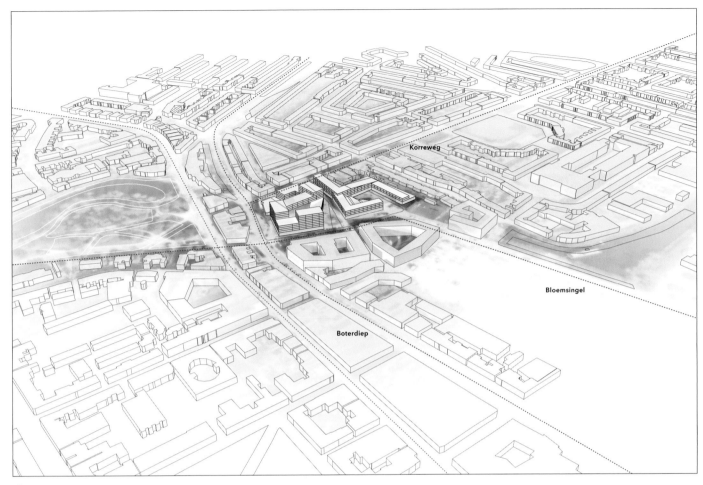

Korreweg

Bloemsingel

Boterdiep

0   25   100 m

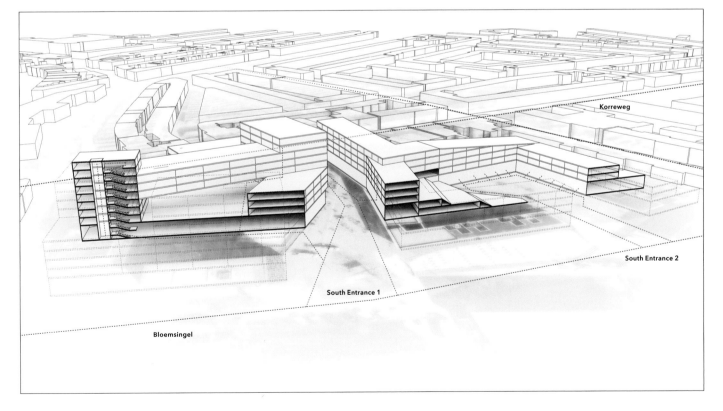

Korreweg

South Entrance 2

South Entrance 1

Bloemsingel

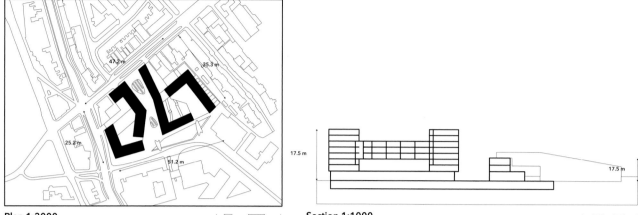

Plan 1:3000

Section 1:1000

0 25 50 100 m

0 5 10 25 m

Key

- ■ Apartment Type
- □ Terrace Type
- ■ Retail
- ■ Parking

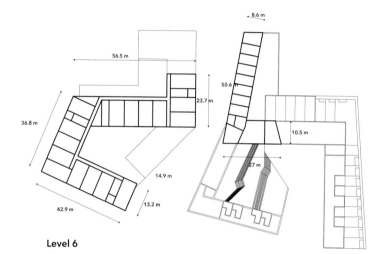

Level 6

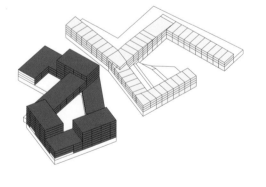

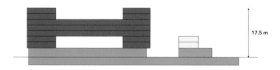

Sectional Variation (Other Uses)

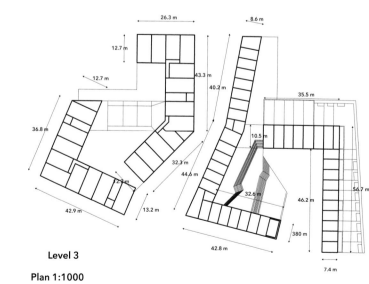

Level 3

Plan 1:1000

HOUSING AND LANDSCAPES

Unit Types 1:500
Household Types

Bedroom/Living
Kitchen
Bathroom

149 units

Unit Type Locations

Unit Type Locations

5 Room/ 2 BR
156 sq m
8 units

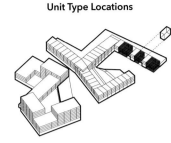

4 Room/ 1 BR
80~90 sq m
106 units

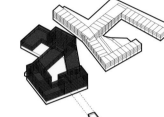

5 Room/ 2 BR
130 sq m
4 units

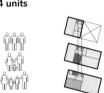
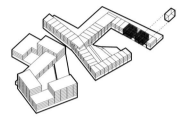

4 Room/ 1 BR
90~158 sq m
5 units

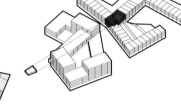

5 Room/ 2 BR
137 sq m
10 units

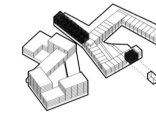

5 Room/ 2 BR
132 sq m
6 units

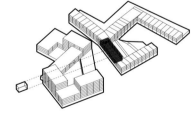

7 Room/ 2 BR
174 sq m
4 units

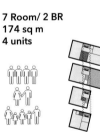
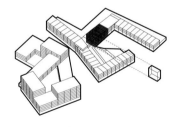

5 Room/ 2 BR/ Roof Garden
187 sq m
3 units

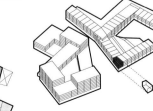

7 Room/ 2 BR
140 sq m
3 units

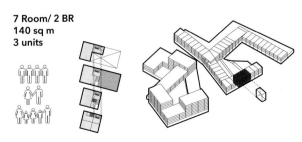

Particular ensembles of houses and landscapes can be and have been used in national and regional circumstances to re-make and re-state terms of reference for modern mass housing, away from prevailing conditions. One such circumstance can be found in the broader Seoul Metropolitan area of South Korea, otherwise dominated by housing in the form of high-rise 'towers in a park', at least since they gained popular traction from the 1960s onwards. A project of note in the reaction to prevailing circumstances is Sanun Maeul in the Pangyo new area, dating from 2005 to 2010.[26] This project is by the newly formed Land and Housing Corporation, a merger between the Korean Housing Corporation and Korean Land, both public companies engaged in property development and yet nowadays finding it difficult to compete in markets dominated by private entities. Designed by Kunwon, the project had two large objectives. One was to provide for and demonstrate the efficacy of more diversified publicly-sponsored housing. The other was to help make the Land and Housing Corporation more profitable and assist in defraying its large public debt.

In a not uncommon trend elsewhere in the world, as South Koreans have become wealthier, the diversity of now active demand for housing has intensified away from the otherwise normal, high-rise apartments of modest size and accoutrements. At Sanun Maeul, the response was lower-density, multiple-unit housing and community center provision with a distinctive landscape setting. The project is comprised of 208 dwelling units on a six-hectare site on a relatively steep hillside, with units ranging in size from 131 to 208 square meters. Unlike many earlier housing projects in and around Seoul, the project cleverly engages with its site and internal spatial arrangements to establish meaningful connections with landscape in three different ways. The first is the building complex in its broader landscape of a hillside with a characteristic mountainous backdrop. The second involves buildings with landscapes in the form of outdoor terraces and newly-created grounds. The third is in the form of landscapes adjacent to buildings, both in a normal vegetated manner, as well as in the provision of unusual hardscapes and water gardens.

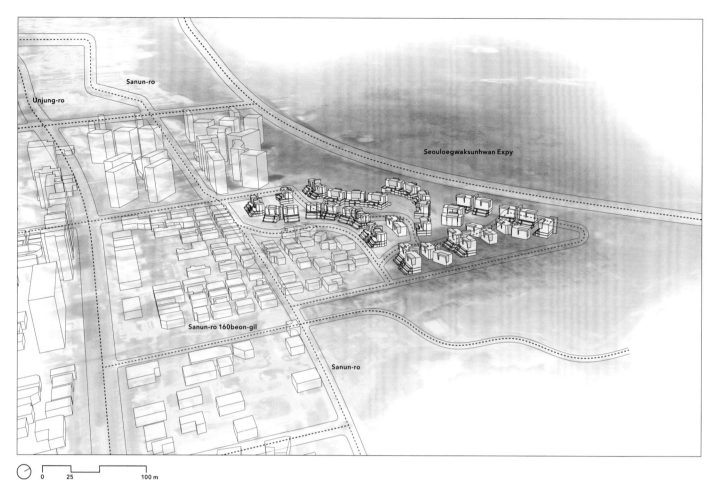

Unjung-ro

Sanun-ro

Seouloegwaksunhwan Expy

Sanun-ro 160beon-gil

Sanun-ro

0   25   100 m

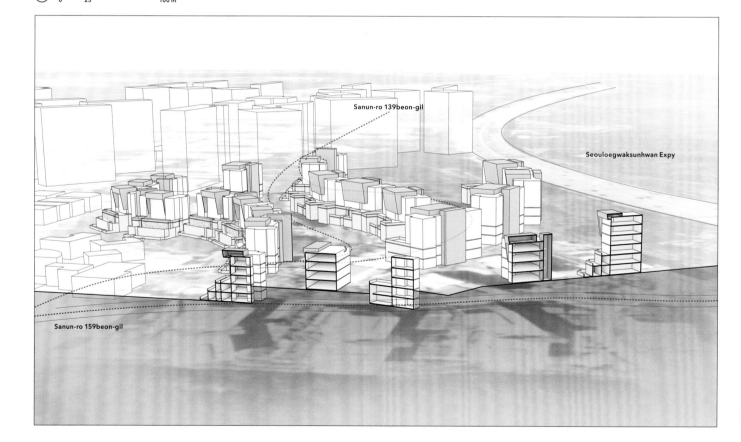

Sanun-ro 139beon-gil

Seouloegwaksunhwan Expy

Sanun-ro 159beon-gil

HOUSING AND LANDSCAPES

Critical Dimensions

Site Plan 1:5000

380 m
260 m
137 m
297 m
100 m

0　25　50　100 m

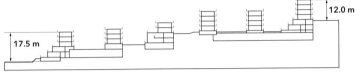

Section A-A' 1:2000

17.5 m
12.0 m

0　20　40 m

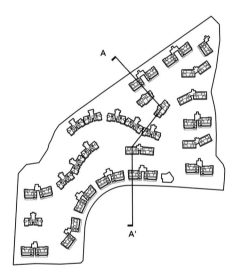

A
A'

Plan 1:5000

0　25　50　100 m

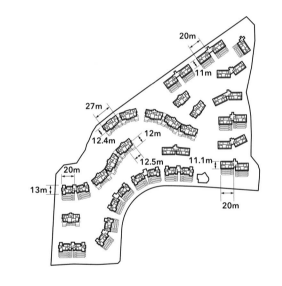

Plan 1:5000

20m
11m
27m
12.4m
12m
12.5m
11.1m
20m
13m
20m

0　25　50　100 m

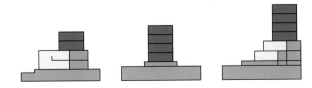

■ Apartment Type
□ Terrace Type
■ PIT
■ Parking

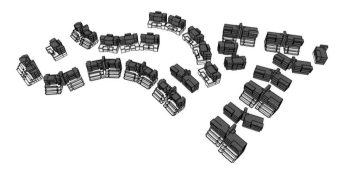

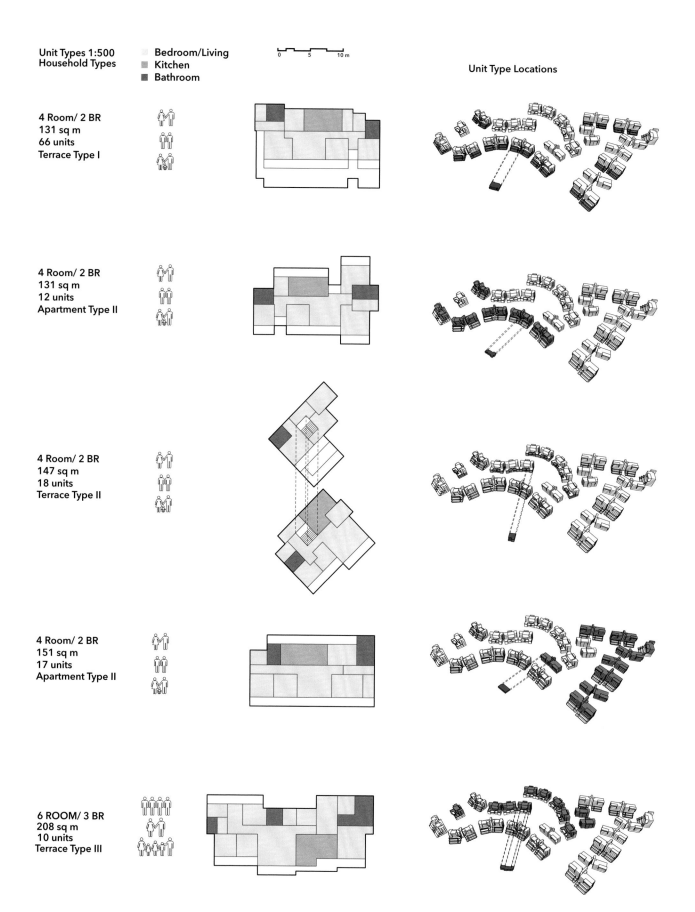

Unit Types 1:500
Household Types

Bedroom/Living
Kitchen
Bathroom

0   5   10 m

Unit Type Locations

4 Room/ 2 BR
131 sq m
66 units
Terrace Type I

4 Room/ 2 BR
131 sq m
12 units
Apartment Type II

4 Room/ 2 BR
147 sq m
18 units
Terrace Type II

4 Room/ 2 BR
151 sq m
17 units
Apartment Type II

6 ROOM/ 3 BR
208 sq m
10 units
Terrace Type III

TRENDS, CONSISTENCIES, AND CONTEXTS

Various valences emerge in the inevitable ensemble of housing and landscape. Contrary to other tendencies towards higher densities in this volume, although not necessarily higher intensity, many of the projects in this chapter have been about relieving overcrowding in urban circumstances or, more specifically, towards bettering the relationship between housing and its immediate surroundings, especially with regard to the ready availability of light, air, vegetated open space and leisure-time, as well as recreational opportunities. At root, or so it seems, this bettered relationship, along with accommodating people in more familiar or desirable and distinctive ways, has propelled the building of housing in landscapes into different relationships and colorations of emphasis. When it comes to the impact of connections and adjacencies – fundamental aspects of urban intensity – the less quotidian arrangement and sharp juxtaposition encountered in contemporary projects like De Citadel and Schots are pronounced and more so than in the past when both literal and metaphorical naturalization devoid of surprise was an aim. Along the way, the relationship between housing and landscape has gone from 'town and country mergers', to 'dwelling in a garden setting',

to 'building with landscape' in a direct reciprocal manner, to 'slabs and towers in a park', and then on to embracing sentiments of a vernacular picturesque, outright domestication, and on to 'landscapes both of and for the mind'.

Along the way, these valences and sentiments have been conjured up largely by relatively direct design operations, all focused on striking a particular relationship between building and landscape in an ensemble of dwelling. Included among these operations are conditions of juxtaposition where building is placed into a landscaped setting, or set adjacent to a landscape setting, as in, say, Sunnyside, New York, or where landscape is superimposed within a constructed setting in the case of courtyard housing and to some extent in the cases featured here in Almere and Groningen. This juxtaposition, in turn, can serve to physically or expressively integrate housing with landscape in a particular manner as at Tiburtino, or be about less connected yet proximal spatial reciprocity at, say, Greenbelt, Maryland, or in the first phase of Tuscolano. It can also involve and serve utilitarian needs, as at Römerstadt, as well as those that are more cerebral in inclination and sentiment, as in the later contemporary projects. Finally, it can also vary in spatial and other qualities within a single project, as at Sanun Maeul in South Korea.

S U P E R B L O C K

Stuyvesant Town

C O N F I G U R A T I O N S

First and foremost, 'superblock configurations' involve purposeful appropriation of broader territories than is the norm in an urban area for a single enterprise, or involve development on large single land parcels as mega-plots. They are relatively common in parts of East Asia in the post-Second World War period and somewhat earlier in the former Soviet Union, although not unknown in the hands of some institutions in the Western world.[1] More specifically, superblocks have been a common arrangement for housing combined with places of employment and community services defining singular state-owned organizations, or *danwei*, in China together with similar situations in the former Soviet Union. But they are also manifested in earlier times, as well as in government-sponsored and privately-provided housing today in other places like South Korea, and in the context of new town developments in and around places like the Seoul Metropolitan Region. In Japan, superblocks have been more the exception than the rule for development in cities like Tokyo, although very apparent as large plots on reclaimed lands in

Tokyo Bay during contemporary times in areas like Koto-ku. They are also apparent in what might be regarded as exhibition projects, such as at Fukuoka, where a superblock arrangement is used to delimit and emphasize specific projects within its boundaries.

Superblocks range in scale usually from something at or above 200 meters by 200 meters in surficial area and usually the equivalent of multiple expression of smaller existing block structures, if they exist. New York University, for instance, a well-established institution, embraces several superblock arrangements within New York City, effectively aggregating several of the smaller blocks from the 1811 Commissioner's Plan for the city. However, this is not always a modern condition, extending to the large blocks of, say, Berlin, and the *höfe* and *mietshäuser* to be found there, where the large blocks were penetrated by accessible courts and pedestrian, as well as limited vehicular, connections in a more or less organic manner.[2] By contrast, East Asian and Soviet superblocks and mega-plots have been typically comprised of 'slabs and towers in a park', bordered by large thorough-fares in contrast to discontinuities introduced into a smaller block structure as in, say, New York City. Exceptions also occurred in both China and Japan with larger blocks in cities like Shanghai and Tokyo, and the assemblage of smaller areas of *lilong* and *roji* lane environments bounded on the outside by shop-houses or similar commercial establishments.[3] In fact, in certain respects, particularly with reference to entry and egress, as well as distinct outer edges and more informal interior arrangements of building and open space, these Eastern dwelling circumstances are similar to those in Berlin and other old parts of Europe.

PRECEDENTS: FROM MASS HOUSING TO A NEW URBAN LIFESTYLE

From the middle to late 1930s and into the 1940s housing authorities and private developers in the United States began to address the need for mass housing, especially in places like New York City where demand was rapidly rising. Superblock devel-opments entailing the aggregation of existing urban blocks into much larger parcels became favored sites, along with a prevalence of 'slab and tower in the park' configurations of buildings and landscapes where an economy of scale provided a ready answer to the efficiency of mass housing production. These config-urations could also provide well-landscaped settings with associated health and welfare benefits, or so it was claimed. Furthermore, the broad singular hous-ing domains could be easily made relatively safe for pedestrian movement and leisure, as well as outside intrusions. A conspicuous example began in 1943 with Stuyvesant Town on New York City's Lower East Side, although not completed until 1949 because of delaying controversy over its scale, alleged monot-ony and racist exclusivity in its originally intended use for white middle-class families. The project was built by the Metropolitan Life Insurance Company through legislation allowing insurance companies at the time to make direct investments in moderate-rate rental housing.[4] It involved demolition of an 18-block area on the order of 630 meters by 400 meters and was comprised of 35 thirteen-storey brick buildings with a site coverage of only 23 percent, leaving

ample space for verdant landscape amid the panopti-con-like site organization and its central oval-shaped park space. Designed by a team of architects under Gilmore D. Clark, lower commercial buildings and parking structures partially enclosed and secured the project's street edges, with any vehicular access limited to eight entry points. Stuyvesant Town, along with neighboring Peter Cooper Village, appealed to numerous tenants well into the contemporary era.[5] Public housing along similar lines was also con-structed, including Brownsville Houses in Brooklyn of 1949, set at 45 degrees to the existing gridiron around Blarke Avenue, and Farragut Houses of 1952, also in Brooklyn and the last project in New York City to use radiating asterisk plan forms for its towers. Although not necessarily in New York City, many of the 'tower in the park' projects of this era and espe-cially in public housing fell into disfavor and were torn down, perhaps most famously at Pruitt-Igoe in St. Louis.

At much the same time, if a little later on, super-block and mega-plot configurations became com-monplace, as alluded to earlier, in the spatial con-figuration of China's *danwei*, or work units. Again, it was an economic and efficient way of meeting needs in the case for housing along with specific places of employment and provision of a wide array of community services on a single site. It was also a place where there could be high conformance between the physical embodiment of a new socialist model and its community organization and produc-tion. Depending upon their value in China's new hier-archy of industrialization, which generally favored heavier industry in what was termed 'the primary production of the means of production', *danwei* varied in size and in the quality and range of spatial provisions. The Changchun No. 1 Automobile Com-pany that began in the early 1950s, for instance, was large, being comprised of around 20 mega-plots on an otherwise un-urbanized site of around 400 meters by 270 meters each, surrounded by wide tree-lined thoroughfares.[6] Within these plots, neighborhoods were constructed modeled after the Soviet *kvartal* as perimeter-block schemes, with schools, kindergar-tens, and other social services at the center, ringed by rows of three- to five-storey walk-up apartments. Overall, the architecture mirrored the prevailing

Caoyang

Changchun No. 1 Automobile Company

doctrine of 'socialist content and Chinese form', incorporating traditional-looking upturned roofs and corner towers in a monumental manner. Provision of larger work-unit facilities like gymnasia and clinics was also involved in an opulent social-realist style of building.

Elsewhere in China, superblock and mega-plot residential districts were also constructed, often averaging 400 meters by 400 meters or more each in size. Although not a *danwei* in the sense of being associated with a particular production unit, Caoyang in the Putuo District of Shanghai, for example, housed and otherwise provided for urban workers from its site on the then western outskirts of the city.[7] Begun in 1951 and completed as late as 1984, Caoyang was made of 32,000 dwelling units with an eventual population of 107,200 inhabitants, as well as a full complement of community services and non-residential uses including department stores, a hospital, cultural centers, and a post office. It was truly a town within the city. Indeed, it was this degree of self-containment, higher even than in Soviet applications of similar models, that lent a coarse-grained and cellular distribution of communities to Chinese cities at the time, in relative isolation from one another. Even if certainly not unprecedented, given for instance the bannermen compounds fenced off within the walls of the Qing Dynasty in Beijing or the corporate compounds later on in Shanghai of the 1930s, the relative lack of accessible proximity to other parts of the city and the sheer scale of many of the communist residential districts and work units was certainly different in degree, if not in kind. On its 180-hectare site, Caoyang

was phased in nine substantial subdistricts, each conformed to its topography, often involving the use of canals and a small river as armatures of a well-landscaped environment. Designed by the Shanghai Institute of Architects and in particular early on by Wang Dingzeng, who returned from studying abroad in the United States, the initial housing was provided in the form of two- and three-storey slab units with pitched roofs, radiating out into the landscape from more central facilities, in a manner reminiscent of Greenbelt, Maryland, built earlier in 1935 on U.S. federal land. Many of the early apartments at Caoyang were self-contained with regard to bathroom and cooking facilities, unusual in comparison to the 'sleep-type' units that predominated elsewhere in China. Subsequent housing took different forms and became denser as the years went by, including high-rise towers. Certainly during the life of this project in the late 1950s, a debate broke out over the use of perimeter block arrangements within the superblocks in China or use of uniform arrays of slab blocks arranged in parallel rows facing north-south. Finally, this issue was resolved in favor of the parallel block schemes for reasons of solar efficiency and lessening of disturbance to residents from outside thoroughfares, amid an increasing need for frugality in building as China's economic fortunes faded. As a consequence, 'function, form, and appearance only when circumstances allow', replaced the earlier more opulent 'Socialist content and Chinese form' in architecture.

Many of the characteristics of these earlier projects like Caoyang have been perpetuated into the contemporary era in China, especially in outlying

Sanlinyuan

Bundang

areas of cities. Sanlinyuan in the Pudong New District of Shanghai, for instance, was constructed mainly to re-settle people from the deconcentration of inner-city areas often subject of appalling overcrowding.[8] Developed between 1994 and 1995 by the Kaicheng Comprehensive Development, a subsidiary of the Municipal Construction Committee of Shanghai, Sanlinyuan occupies an 11.92-hectare single site of around 350 meters by 350 meters located, at the time, in the countryside. Framed on the outside by wide arterial roads, it is part of a regularized pattern of urban development intended for much of the Pudong New District. Internally, Sanlinyuan consists of six mid-rise housing clusters of seven-storey slab blocks, with elevator service and maisonette units on the top floors. Rows of units, roughly in a fishbone manner in plan, evoke some aspects of the *lilong* housing in Shanghai of the 1920s, and the mansard roofs, colored brickwork, and rich façade articulation also reflects old Shanghai and its *haipai* style. Community open space is located at the center of the scheme, together with a recreation center, meeting hall, kindergarten, and nursery. A 25-class primary school is also located inside the site on the north-eastern corner of the complex, minimizing disturbance of the residential environment, and a row of high-rise offices lines the northern edge of the mega-plot. The average size of dwelling units is 86 square meters, a step up from living conditions inside much of the city and some 2,092 dwelling units provide for a population of from 6,000 to 7,000 inhabitants and at a fairly high density of 590 people per hectare. Overall, the project was enabled by the successful

'three thirds' method of financing used during the early stages of China's efforts to monetize housing, with contributions from the state, a work unit, and individuals in more or less equal amounts.

Social programs of housing provision using superblocks and mega-plots were also developed and perpetuated in South Korea, beginning essentially in Seoul with the MAPO project by the Korean National Housing Corporation in 1962. From the outset of General Chung-Hee Park's aggressive program of modernization from the depths of economic depression in the wake of the Civil War and subsequent slow recovery, a dramatic change in housing was initiated towards high-rise modern apartment living on superblock sites. In fact, MAPO consisted of six-storey apartment blocks on an otherwise single open site created from the demolition of earlier substandard dwellings and housing up to 642 families.[9] With relatively small units ranging from 30 to 50 square meters, each apartment began to promote modern living with flushing toilets, kitchen facilities, and efficient layouts. As Seoul expanded very rapidly and crossed the Han River in the south, the new well-known Gangnam District began development in 1976 astride mega-plots of up to 850 meters by 700 meters bordered by major roads and again emphasizing construction efficiency. During the short span of some 12 years, the area became more or less fully developed in this manner, mainly by residential development spurred on by the 1972 Provisional Law on the Development of Special Regions.[10] Parallel rows of tower blocks ranging in height from 18 to 23 storeys were spread in the fashion of 'towers in a park' as the first application of this law in Gangnam. Moving ahead to a further response to a housing shortage in the Seoul Metropolitan Area, a program of new towns at some distance from the city proper was initiated during the late 1980s. Among these, Bundang rose as a well-appointed middle-income area linked back to central Seoul by subway and surrounded by and accessible to a verdant mountainous environment.[11] Housing was provided primarily on mega-plots of 550 meters by 350 meters, bordered yet again by major roads, and penetrated by well-landscaped pedestrian streets and pathways. Developed by the Korean Land Corporation, Bundang houses in excess of 40,000 inhabitants, primarily in high-rise apartment buildings within its mega-plots. The architecture of these buildings, although not as reduced in expression as earlier less well-endowed environments, is still relatively basic, functional, and sober-looking. The adjacent presence of community streets and vital non-residential areas, however, does allow residents to embrace a reasonably commodious and well-appointed urban lifestyle.[12]

In Japan, not renowned for superblock or mega-plot developments outside of the Shogunal era and, indeed, comprised of urban areas, like inner-city Tokyo, with relatively small property parcels, changes ensued in response to the bursting of the speculative real estate bubble during the early 1990s. The Nexus World Housing Project in Fukuoka, a city in southern Japan, was one example, developed by Fukuoka Jisho and planned by Arata Isozaki, to intro-

duce a new urban lifestyle to Japan.[13] Developed on a sizeable single superblock, bounded by major roadways, measuring 285 meters by 260 meters, the project featured what can be called 'demonstration projects' by one Japanese architect, in addition to Isozaki himself, and five non-Japanese architects primarily in the form of free-standing buildings on the block's perimeter. Among these, the project by OMA presented probably the most potentially tractable and interesting scheme for moving away from simply a perimeter building complex and into one that might be expected to cover substantial areas of a superblock condition. What OMA produced in 1997 was modest, at 24 dwelling units, each three storeys in height, but in the overall form of a mat building with light courts and direct access back into the site from the perimeter roadway. Interior and south-facing glass façades optimized solar insolation and a lower-level concourse led to individual front doors for each unit, beyond which was placed a patio. A continuous stairway led to individual rooms on the second floor and to living quarters on the third floor. The angled roofline also resonates with the mountainous profile bordering the Fukuoka Basin. Then, on Tokyo's waterfront at Koto-ku, also as alluded to earlier, large-block development was enabled, around 2000, through extensive areas of reclaimed land. In large part, this became the site of high-density, rental housing schemes, one of which, known as Shinonome Canal Court, was developed by an urban development corporation – CODAN – and designed primarily by Riken Yamamoto, with some participation by Toyo Ito and Kengo Kuma.[14] A first phase of 420 dwelling

Nexus World Housing Project © OMA Hiroyuki Kawano

Shinonome Canal Court

units out of an eventual 2,000 units was completed in 2003, covering a site area of over one hectare. Composition of buildings and landscape involved a double-decked ground plane with parking beneath and penetration by light courts in the manner of a 'field operation'. This thickened ground plane also included a curving pedestrian street among the bases of buildings distributed within the block, lined on both sides by stores, cafés, and community services. Located adjacent to a large shopping mall and accessible to Tokyo's subway, the project also proved popular with younger families looking for moderately expensive places to live in contemporary circumstances.

CONTEMPORARY CASES: CHINESE SUPERBLOCKS IN BEIJING

A city replete with superblocks that stand as physical legacies of gated neighborhoods from its imperial past and socialist work unit configurations from the last half of the twentieth century as alluded to earlier, Beijing has seen attempts to offer alternative approaches to the design of these mixed-use, urban-architectural typologies since the early 2000s. The emergence of these new spatial operations not only sought to break up the large block into smaller, more tractable plots, thereby improving the traffic circulation, but also to provide open communities with some degree of building variation as opposed to the enclosed, and somewhat repetitive, precincts that have defined much of the urban fabric in China's

cities. In Beijing, this move has coincided with the rising affluence of urban dwellers, concomitant responses by real estate developers to cater to changing lifestyles and the growing desire for quality and differentiated housing products, as well as efforts by the local government to redevelop particular districts and consequently commission master plans to address the unwieldy superblock configurations of the past. Two projects of note representing distinct approaches dealing with superblocks are Jian Wai SOHO, the first phase of which was completed in 2004, and the Linked Hybrid, completed later in 2009.[15] Located in the Chaoyang and Dongcheng districts of Beijing, they were developed by a younger generation of savvy entrepreneurs with an emphatic commitment to design, and in particular, to the significance of well-designed properties in offering compelling urban living environments for the New China.

This premium placed on design is evinced by the strategy adopted by Jian Wai SOHO, which thrives on the development of pure prime office space in collaboration with internationally-renowned architects. Established only in 1995 by the husband-and-wife team of Pan Shiyi and Zhang Xin, the company, which stands for Small Office Home Office – has carved out a niche for itself, catering to urban professionals and the affluent through the delivery of high-quality, innovative products that fulfill the needs of this demographic type. The Jian Wai SOHO project is one of more than a dozen that SOHO China has developed in Beijing alone, and is situated at the junction of the Third Ring Road and the Tonghui River in the Beijing

MAPO Apartment Complex

Central Business District. Nested in what was originally a 34-hectare superblock of old factories, the project itself was built out in seven phases, of which Phases I, II, III, and VI were completed in 2004, and Phases IV, V, and VII were finished later in 2007. The contiguous superblock was subdivided into nine smaller parcels in its redevelopment, in keeping with some of the principles put forward by Johnson Fain in their 2001 urban design and master plan for what was then slated to be Beijing's new CBD east of Tiananmen Square. In doing so, arterial roads and secondary streets were re-introduced into the super-block, together with the CBD park occupying one of the parcels along the river front. Within this expansive site, the entire Jian Wai SOHO development took up just 16.9 hectares spread across four and a half parcels.[16] As compared to the original block dimension of some 850 meters by 470 meters, the segmented parcels were much more amenable, and in the case of the two parcels comprising the first phase of Jian Wai SOHO completed in 2004, the dimension was on the order of 290 meters by 220 meters.

After an international design competition, Riken Yamamoto was engaged by SOHO China to design the master plan and the 20 apartment towers, together with Field Shop, while the four mid-rise office structures interspersed among the grid of nine towers, also known as "villas", were designed by C + A at Yamamoto's invitation. Jian Wai SOHO was Yamamoto's first venture in China, and he envisioned the mixed-use project combining collective housing and commercial facilities to be an open place with alleys running in between buildings and corridors bridging housing overhead, thereby offering moments of discovery and surprise within a multi-layered, maze-like condition. Drawing allegedly on the Moroccan city of Ceuta, Yamamoto imbues the site with similar spatial features, masterfully creating a constant change of scenery, where what seemed like an underground passage suddenly lays bare to the weather elements, or where an intimate alleyway opens up to a plaza and nexus of activity at the turn of a corner. Rather than working with an ultimate image in mind, he conceived of the elements of this urban microcosm as cells that are multiplied and interconnected both horizontally and vertically, giving rise to the eventual structure of activities that have the

inherent flexibility to adapt to the varying temporalities and subsequent evolution of the place.[17] While the project bears a resemblance to the Shinonome Canal Court project in Tokyo by Yamamoto, mentioned earlier and that served as a precursor to this development, here, the exploration of what might be termed a 'field operation' was pushed much further. In this first phase, the checkerboard layout of the nine slender towers and the four "villas" was offset by 25 degrees, maximizing the solar insolation on the site as well as providing views to the Tonghui River. Against this vertical 'forest' of small offices/home offices and commercial space with circulation access connecting the plinth of underground parking and common living spaces right through to the rooftop gardens, Yamamoto introduced a horizontal ground plane above the plinth and its lower-level arcade structures. This ground plane is articulated by the sinuous alleys criss-crossing the site along with landscape elements arranged in bands and gardens parallel to the 25-degree building displacement. It is also at this level where the pedestrianized public space is activated through the over 200 shops, restaurants, and cafés dispersed across the project, each with its own individual entrance. Finally, the three-dimensional character of the 'field operation' is enhanced by the array of sunken courtyards placed strategically within the interior, traversed by bridges on the ground plane above. These not only bring daylight to the lower levels in the plinth, but also serve as open spaces, some of which are used as recreational grounds. Collectively, these seemingly simple yet sophisticated maneuvers playing on perceptual depth and unfolding visual sequences endow a high degree of liveliness to the project, while heightening the overall spatial appreciation.

Intended to be priced for middle-income earners, the complex is popular as a trendy, desirable property and its prime location caused a rapid appreciation. The concrete and partially steel-framed square towers rising 100 meters in height are 27.3 meters wide, and are categorized into the L or 'pinwheel' type, the MS or 'grid' type, and the MSC type.[18] These three tower types contain a variety of unit layouts, with the L-type offering two different three-bedroom configurations, the MS-type housing one type of one-bedroom units and another three different types of two-bedroom units, and finally, the MSC-type containing a single configuration for the one-bedroom units and the maisonettes, along with two different two-bedroom unit types. The unit sizes range from 61.4 square meters for the smallest one-bedroom type up to 223.2 square meters for the largest three-bedroom unit type. Depth-wise, the units are as slim as 5.8 meters, reaching up to a maximum of only 11.7 meters, of which units with the latter depth are arranged in a pinwheel fashion along the corners of the L-type tower, ensuring that each unit has two adjacent façades allowing adequate light into the interiors. Each unit in essence becomes a work-live environment, and coupled with the proximity to other commercial and office space, less than a third of these SOHO units are in fact inhabited as residential spaces. In contrast to this diversity of dwelling units, the two office wings in the first phase of the project are more straightforward in their floor plans, with each floor containing six office units based on three configura-

tions, ranging from 279 to 329 square meters. Overall, the project has a total built area of around 700,000 square meters. Architecturally, Yamamoto endeavored to "avoid exclusionary and monumental" forms, thereby adopting an abstract expression of white columns and beams, juxtaposed against a fenestration of transparent and opaque glass panels, overlooking the ground level commercial facilities and sunken plazas where the urban action occurs. Jian Wai SOHO's success is attested by the increasing number of commercial and cultural activities that have chosen to locate there, and it has likewise become a favorite venue for live performances and cultural events that draw in the crowds during the vibrant summer months. More importantly, apart from suggesting an alternative to the making of attractive mixed-use superblock neighborhoods for China, the development has been an urban-architectural innovation that has promoted a new way of living for contemporary China.

JIAN WAI SOHO

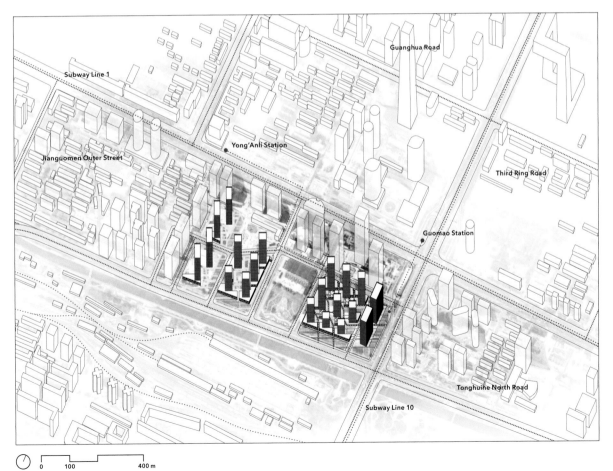

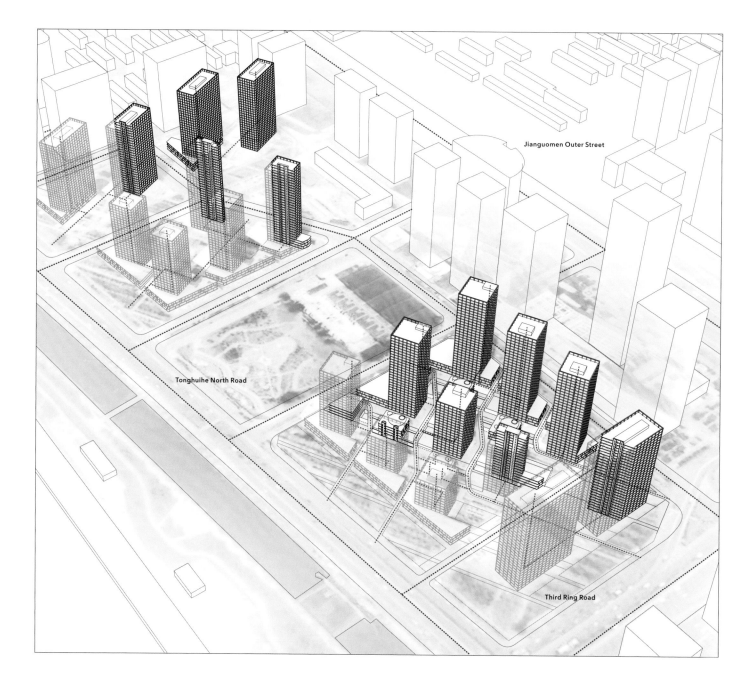

Jianguomen Outer Street

Tonghuihe North Road

Third Ring Road

SUPERBLOCK CONFIGURATIONS

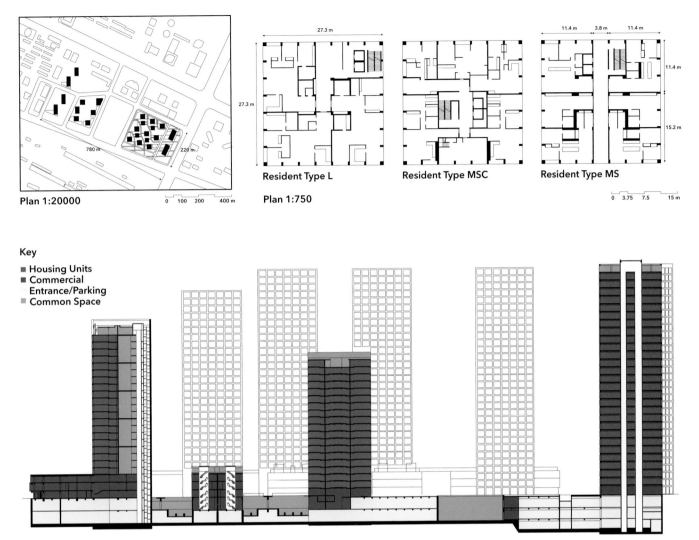

27.3 m

27.3 m

Resident Type L

Resident Type MSC

11.4 m   3.8 m   11.4 m

11.4 m

15.2 m

Resident Type MS

Plan 1:20000

780 m   220 m

0   100   200   400 m

Plan 1:750

0   3.75   7.5   15 m

Key
■ Housing Units
■ Commercial
  Entrance/Parking
■ Common Space

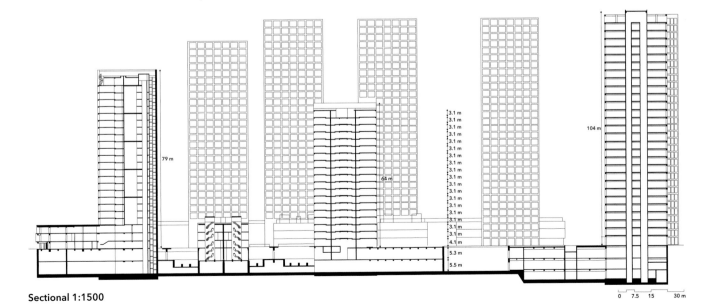

Sectional Variation (Other Uses)

79 m

64 m

3.1 m
3.1 m
3.1 m
3.1 m
3.1 m
3.1 m
3.1 m
3.1 m
3.1 m
3.1 m
3.1 m
3.1 m
3.1 m
3.1 m
3.1 m
4.1 m
5.3 m
5.5 m

104 m

Sectional 1:1500

0   7.5   15   30 m

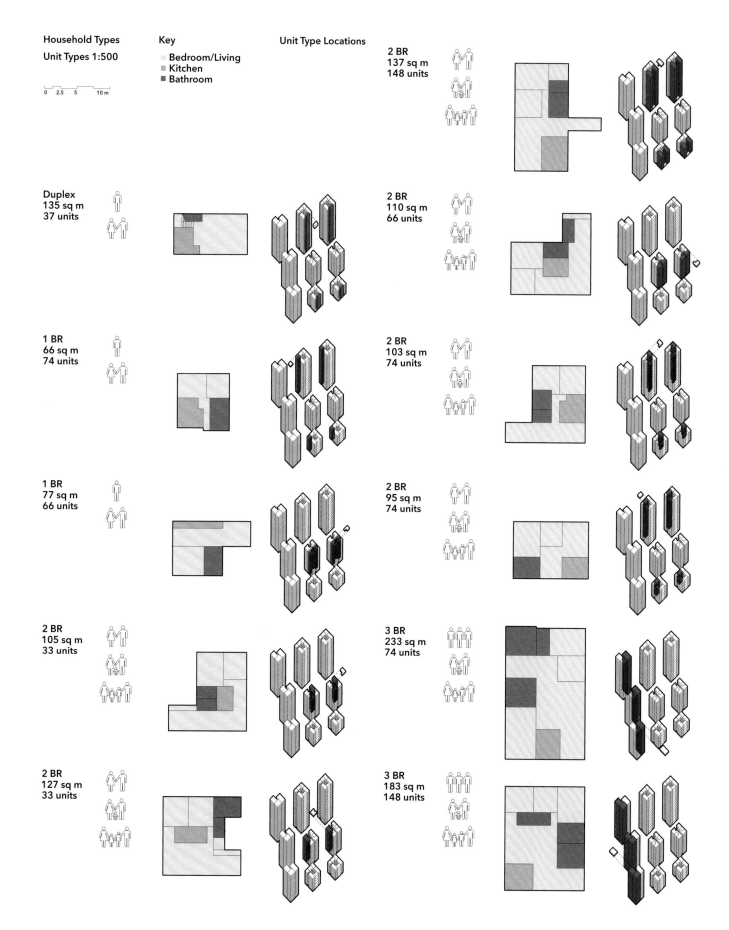

Household Types
Unit Types 1:500

0 2.5 5 10 m

Key
Bedroom/Living
Kitchen
Bathroom

Unit Type Locations

Duplex
135 sq m
37 units

1 BR
66 sq m
74 units

1 BR
77 sq m
66 units

2 BR
105 sq m
33 units

2 BR
127 sq m
33 units

2 BR
137 sq m
148 units

2 BR
110 sq m
66 units

2 BR
103 sq m
74 units

2 BR
95 sq m
74 units

3 BR
233 sq m
74 units

3 BR
183 sq m
148 units

SUPERBLOCK CONFIGURATIONS

Further north of the city, right at the junction of the Second Ring Road and the Airport Expressway sits the Linked Hybrid project by Steven Holl. Located on a smaller 6.18-hectare site that was part of the former Beijing First Paper Mill, one of the largest state-owned enterprises and work units from the socialist era, this development was undertaken by Modern Land (China), another real estate enterprise based in Beijing, established only in 2000 under Zhang Lei. To distinguish itself from its competitors, it marketed its properties using the "MOMA" concept, highlighting their aim and ability to provide high-quality living environments that are at once environmentally sustainable. According to the developer, with the high-technology energy-saving features built into their products, each MOMA project would only consume a third of the energy for an equivalent residential project at the same comfort level. Prior to the Linked Hybrid, which was marketed as "Modern MOMA", the company had undertaken similar projects where internationally acclaimed architects were commissioned to design sustainable, mixed-use residential complexes, such as "Mega Hall MOMA" and "Pop MOMA", also in the Dongcheng District of Beijing, by Dietmar Eberle. Both of these constituted Phases I to III of the MOMA development between 2000 and 2005, located on the southern blocks of the Beijing First Paper Mill, while "Modern MOMA" was Phase IV of the development, built on the northern block of the sprawling work unit after the Airport Expressway separating the two phases was completed in 2007.

When Holl was commissioned to design "Modern MOMA" in 2002, he set out to fulfill three personal aspirations at the urban scale through an architectural project. First, he sought to leverage on a large-scale, private development to shape public space. Second, drawing on a thesis he had begun in 1986 and published as *Pamphlet Architecture 11: Hybrid Buildings*, he wanted to realize this notion of hybrid buildings that would provide a programmatic diversity for residents to be able to live, work, and play on site. Finally, he aimed to introduce a three-dimensional approach, and in particular the 'Z' dimension, in shaping the urbanity.[19] The complex that resulted is composed of eight residential towers clad in Holl's signature steel-framed, grid-like façade, as well as a series of minor blocks. In his perspective, this exoskeletal frame would not only establish the exterior envelopes, it would also circumvent any individual articulation of the towers, endowing the project and the large public space it was intended to shape with an overall cohesiveness. On the ground floor, a mix of functions primarily commercial in nature, including stores, a hotel, restaurants, school, kindergarten, and a cinematheque was intended to provide a public realm accessible to both residents and visitors alike. To open up the programs to the public, the perimeter was to be lined with shops.[20] On the upper level, the complex is linked via a loop of suspension bridges intended to house a café, hotel bar, gallery, and swimming pool, constituting the so-called 'Z' dimension. Within this elevated passage, which Holl choreographed as a unique spatial experience, unparalleled views of the city are provided within a sequence of scenes that unfold and take on different characteristics as the light varies with the time of the day and the seasons. By introducing this bridge route, linking what would otherwise have been isolated, free-standing towers, Holl's aim was also to create a connected "city of spaces", and one with a "vertical horizontality".[21]

With a built area of 220,000 square meters, the complex contains 750 units in both the eight residential towers and the 11-storey cylindrically-shaped hotel. The eight residential towers are composed of four basic residential floor plans, with pairs of towers sharing the same unit layouts. In total, there are 20 different unit types in the eight residential towers alone, incorporating duplexes and lofts, ranging from 66 to 159 square meters in unit area. All the apartments utilize Holl's concept of a 'hinged space', first materialized in his Nexus World Fukuoka project, where folding panels incorporated into the units allowed spaces to be modified easily for use as living spaces or bedrooms, adapting to the changing life-cycle needs of a family. The rooms do not exceed 10 meters in depth, with Holl paying special attention to the sightlines and abundance of light within each unit. Environmentally sustainable features on the site include geothermal wells that reach 100 meters below ground, as well as a greywater recycling system that would allow 220,000 litres of water to be recycled on a daily basis to irrigate the gardens, roof gardens, and to offset evaporation from the central pond, producing a savings on the order of 41 percent of drinking water. These technologies were incorporated in the early stage of architectural design in collaboration with Transsolar, ensuring that these mechanical systems were well-integrated into the project to be able to attain a degree of impact on the architectural design, including the elimination of cooling towers. Within the courtyard, the central pond is traversed by bridges, some with multiple right-angled folds similar to those typically found in traditional Chinese gardens. In the middle of the pool, two inverted pyramid-shaped structures house the cinematheque. Beyond this centerpiece, the landscape continues atop, with roof gardens on the three-storey plinths that are connected to the ones above the cinematheque. Behind the building complex rise three mounds named the "Mound of Youth", "Mound of Middle Age", and the "Mound of Old Age", all of which are fitted with lifestyle amenities, including tennis courts, a Tai Chi platform, coffee and tea house, a wine tasting bar, and a meditation space.

The built outcomes at Linked Hybrid, however, present a stark divergence from Holl's original design intents. Contrary to his ambition to achieve "maximum urban porosity", the development was eventually closed off to the public with the erection of a wall around the perimeter, reverting yet again to the conventional gated community that Holl himself had set out to avoid. Unlike the Jian Wai SOHO project, which was privately developed but located within the CBD district overseen by the local government, the degree of openness and public accessibility here was determined by the private developers. The social condenser effect through the ground plane and the 'Z' dimension was never fully attained, with an active public realm contained largely on the ground floor. The popularity of the Linked Hybrid as a property investment rather than dwelling units that are fully occupied also accounted for the diminished residential population, adequate only to support just one and not both realms of programs. As such, while both projects had high population densities of around 57,140 people per square kilometer for Jian Wai SOHO and 31,262 people per square kilometer for the Linked Hybrid, and represent intense use of the sites, the different management strategies have led to vastly distinct results in the actual project performance.

LINKED HYBRID

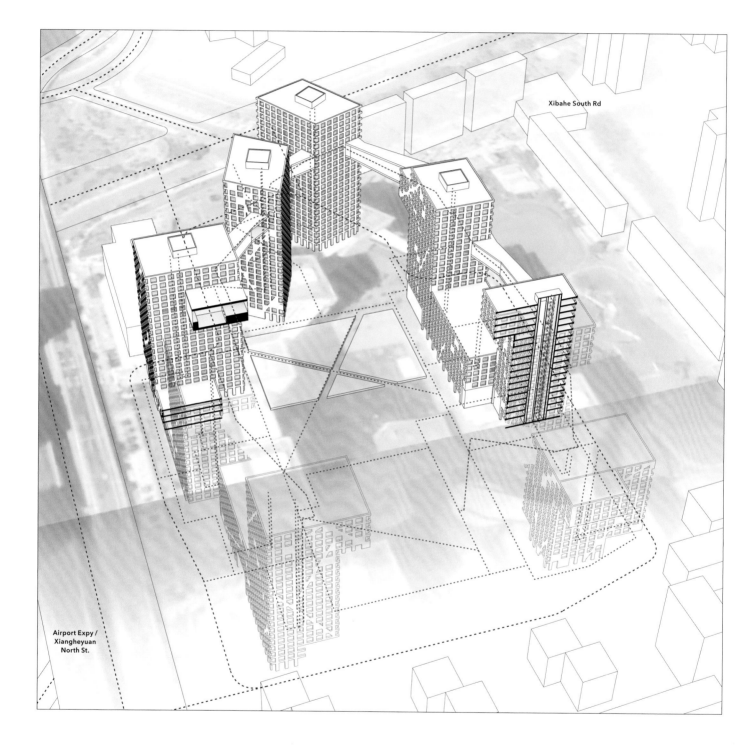

Xibahe South Rd

Airport Expy /
Xiangheyuan
North St.

SUPERBLOCK CONFIGURATIONS

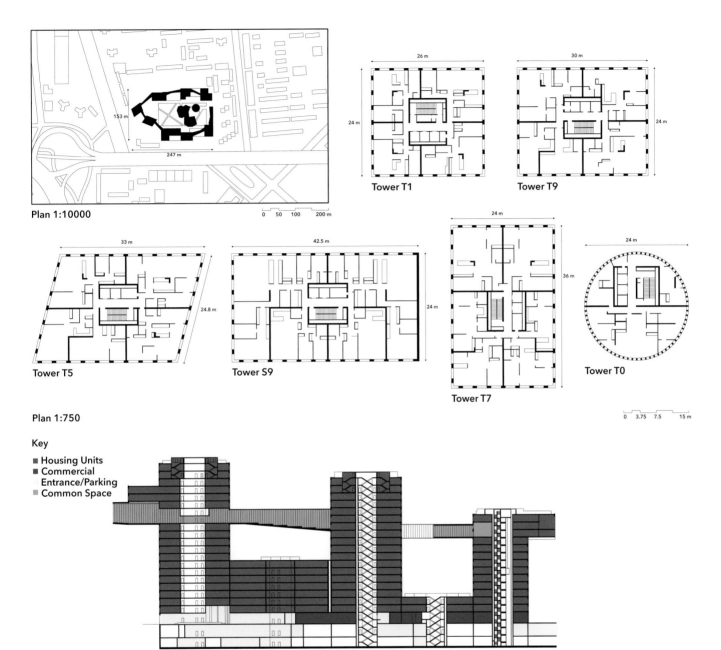

Plan 1:10000

153 m

247 m

0   50   100   200 m

26 m

24 m

Tower T1

30 m

24 m

Tower T9

33 m

24.8 m

Tower T5

42.5 m

24 m

Tower S9

24 m

36 m

Tower T7

24 m

Tower T0

Plan 1:750

0   3.75   7.5   15 m

Key

■ Housing Units
■ Commercial
■ Entrance/Parking
■ Common Space

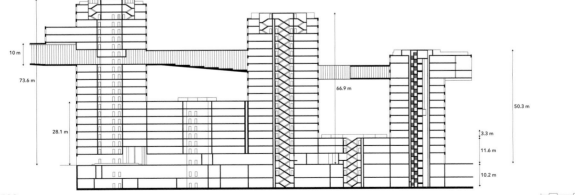

Sectional Variation (Other Uses)

10 m

73.6 m

28.1 m

66.9 m

50.3 m

3.3 m

11.6 m

10.2 m

Section 1:1500

0   7.5   15   30 m

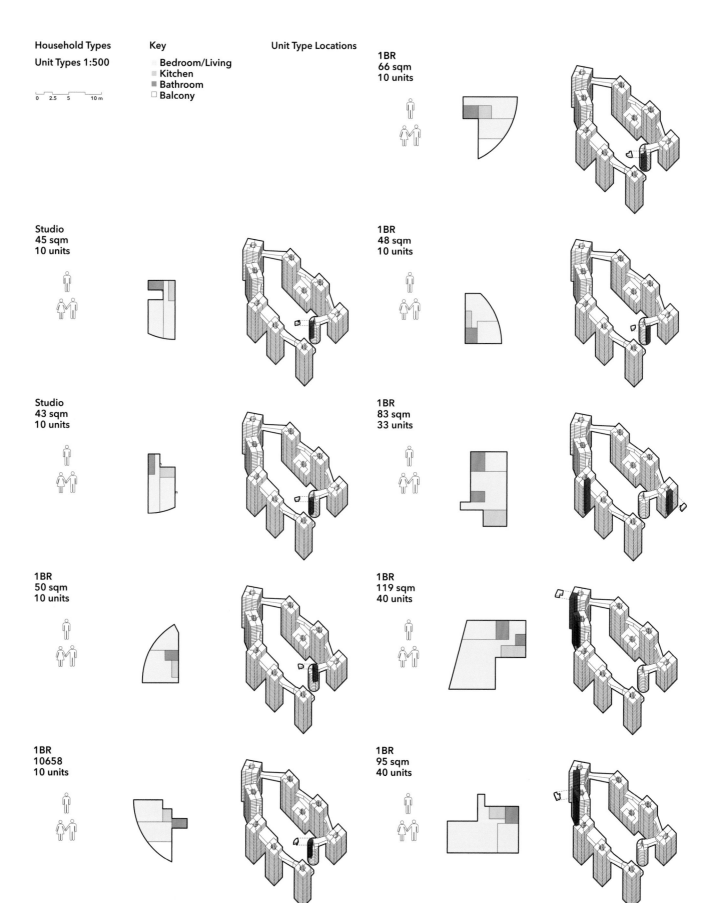

Household Types
Unit Types 1:500

Key
Bedroom/Living
Kitchen
Bathroom
Balcony

Unit Type Locations

0 2.5 5   10 m

1BR
66 sqm
10 units

Studio
45 sqm
10 units

1BR
48 sqm
10 units

Studio
43 sqm
10 units

1BR
83 sqm
33 units

1BR
50 sqm
10 units

1BR
119 sqm
40 units

1BR
10658
10 units

1BR
95 sqm
40 units

SUPERBLOCK CONFIGURATIONS

1BR
86 sqm
38 units

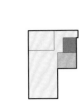

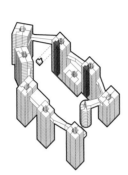

2BR
120 sqm
36 units

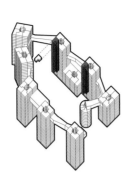
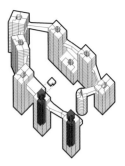

1BR
75 sqm
38 units

2BR
174 sqm
59 units

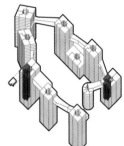
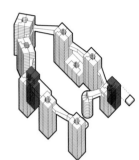

2BR
145 sqm
38 units

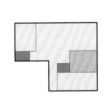

2BR
106 sqm
31 units

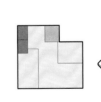
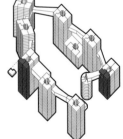

2BR
140 sqm
40 units

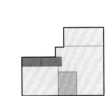
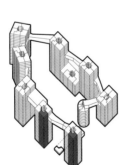

2BR
121 sqm
64 units

2BR
118 sqm
40 units

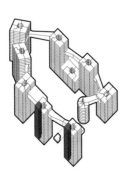

2BR
149 sqm
38 units

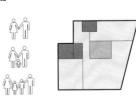
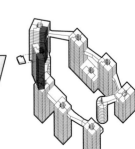

2BR
174 sqm
36 units

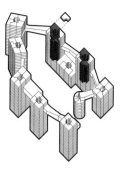

3BR
150 sqm
33 units

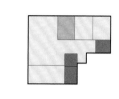
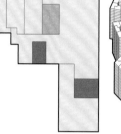

2BR
163 sqm
38 units

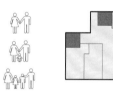
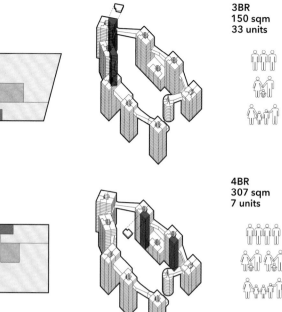

4BR
307 sqm
7 units

2BR
142 sqm
14 units

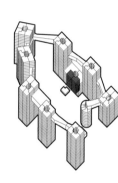

4BR
336 sqm
7 units

3BR
162 sqm
38 units

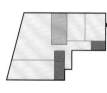
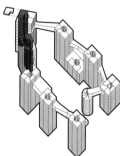
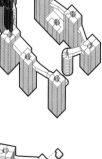

3BR
153 sqm
34 units

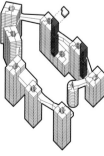

DIMENSIONAL ISSUES, STRATEGIES, AND DOMAIN DEFINITIONS

A convergence of features from this type of housing and territory includes the dimensional qualities of broad parcels of land, usually in excess of 200 meters on a side and often around 400 meters, bounded by major roads, either as superblocks derived from an aggregation and often demolition of smaller block structures in urban areas, or as mega-plots of land in other less-urbanized situations. Mostly, this appropriation of large land parcels is for economies of scale in the delivery of housing or other construction efficiencies. The relatively self-centered territory of large blocks can also provide for the safety and welfare of residential inhabitants, as well as serving to allow location of highly accessible, non-residential functions, along with demarcation of institutional or organizational processes. One problem with superblocks and their particular and often peculiar spatial development stems from difficulty in subsequent despecialization of uses and activities during times of substantial and persistent urban change. In these and other locations, the sheer lack of fine-grained roadway networks led to substantial susceptibility for traffic congestion and considerable social costs. Then too, there is the ease with which broad areas of a city became, unfortunately, somehow gated and fenced-off from public use, particularly in circumstances where active, project-centered community use is neither extensive nor space-demanding.

In coping with both the developmental and habitable opportunities and constraints proffered by superblocks and mega-plot configurations, a number of urban-architectural strategies have emerged. First and certainly foremost during early deployment, arrangements of buildings in the modernist manner of 'towers and/or slabs in a park' were commonplace. Depending upon the amount of repetition, which has been very high in places like China and South Korea, this strategy can produce high densities of occupation although rather monotonous and not particularly intense environments by way of interaction with other urban activities. Second, schemes that involved discrete, publicly-accessible subdivisions within a larger block, often using regular and reasonably closely-spaced, adjacent building footprints and common open spaces, represent another strategy. Here, borders between the complex in question and surrounding urban circumstances can be blurred together with the maintenance of an overall sense of a particular subdistrict like, for example, the Rockefeller Center in New York City or China Central in Beijing's Central Business District. A third organizational strategy involved interlinked or adjoining buildings and open courtyard spaces in the manner, say, of the Linked Hybrid in Beijing, discussed here, or the *höfe* of Berlin mentioned earlier. In these cases, limits in effectiveness and tractability seem to be dictated by the scale, or reach, of the architectural gestures required and the extent to which they are regarded as being somehow normal and not fantastic. Up to a point, the labyrinthine quality of the *höfe* can be comfortably engaged by most people, whereas technical paraphernalia of walkways among buildings may be less readily appreciated. Then too, a fourth strategy used what have been termed here as 'field operations', displaying highly articulated and multiple levels converging as a 'thick', single ground plane, as well as bringing diversity, intensity, and order to a large block configuration of buildings, as at Jian Wai SOHO.

Finally, arrangement of housing on large property parcels with space in between invariably raises issues of domain definition of perceptible public space, private space, and often semi-public and semi-private space. Furthermore, the two latter dimensions, unless they are well managed, can quickly become 'no person's land' or require upkeep that is incommensurate with direct use. Following on from this observation, schemes that produce clear distinctions between public and private realms at the most commonly-occupied ground level, would seem to fare best. This, in turn, places publicly-accessible block subdivisions and public courtyard schemes in advantageous positions, along with those deploying properly worked-out 'field operations'. As shown at Jian Wai SOHO, otherwise semi-public and semi-private spaces can be pushed upwards or downwards from the common pedestrian ground plane, rendering it either fully public or fully private. The same might also be said for the Rockefeller Center, at least with regard to its sunken plaza, and for New York University with its raised gardens out of the more truly public domain.

T A L L

Pinnacle@Duxton

T O W E R S

Modern high-rise residential buildings date from the middle 1920s in places like New York City and Chicago where many were built. Some were simply towers, rising up from city blocks, whereas others were shaped by building codes in operation at the time, stepping back in volume as they went up and rising from bases with indentations and courtyards in plan. On the demand side, high-rise dwelling responded to strong pressures for housing from both the well-to-do and less well-to-do, usually in well-serviced inner-city areas or locations with high transportation accessibility to employment that may be at a distance from city centers. It was also a form of dwelling with strong associations with modernity in many places during the early days, as well as more recently with luxury lifestyles and demands for higher diversity in living environments. On the supply side, high-rise dwelling responded to property scarcity and high property prices in areas of strong demand. It also required ready availability of an appropriate technical means of building and support such as frame construction, elevators, and mechanical services. While the ele-

vator dates back into the mid-nineteenth century, push-button or automatic elevators did not become available until around 1920, for instance. Steel-frame construction was also largely a twentieth-century phenomenon, even if first employed in a high-rise building of 10 storeys or above in 1885 in Chicago, with the Home Insurance Building.[1] Tall residential towers, on the other hand, could also be found in medieval Italy, for instance, where they were built for both defense and status. The Asinelli Tower of twelfth-century Bologna was a slender load-bearing structure rising to around 97 meters in height and some 75 or so towers of the *casati* or nobles of San Gimignano rose up to 50 meters in height.[2] Over time, modern high-rise housing began as a response to niche markets for well-appointed and fully-serviced living in residential hotels or similar accommodations. By the late 1930s and particularly into the post-Second World War period, mass provision of housing also assumed a high-rise profile including the production of affordable units. Recently, various forms of residences and hotels have re-appeared, alongside of other hybrids like home-offices, office-hotels, and micro- and macro-residential units. Finally, high-rise living altered or added to the spatial perception available to urban dwellers through panoramic vistas from high-rise apartments and usually with 'natural' circumstances held at a distance. This was very different from the middle-ground perspective of 'being immersed in a landscape' that was more generally prevalent at the time.

PRECEDENTS: EARLY BEGINNINGS, MASS PROVISION, AND DWELLING DIVERSITY

Precedents for fully residential tall buildings in New York City began occurring in the 1920s with hotels, including longer-term occupancy residential hotels. The Ritz Tower on Park Avenue at East 57th Street by Emery Roth and Carrère & Hastings of 1925 was a good example.[3] The 40-storey elegant Italianate-styled tower accomodated six-room residential apartments in its 17-storey base, with smaller suites in the narrower footprint of the tower. Also, duplex units with double-height spaces were provided along with a host of residentially-related functions and service amenities. Strictly speaking, residential units at the time in New York City were confined to the limits of the New Tenement Laws of 1901, which were largely lower walk-up configurations of units. The Pan-Hellenic Tower of 1928 by John Mead Howells

was another example of an apartment hotel, this time with a clubhouse and stately semi-public rooms for women college students coming to live in the city.[4] Apart from the Tenement Act, the other regulation shaping high-rise dwelling was the New York City Building Zoning Resolution of 1916 dealing with height restrictions, avoiding overshadowing and the so-called 'canyon effect' on adjacent streets, and in effect, setback rules required for gaining additional height. Studies by Roger Ferris in 1922, among others, led to the visualization of sculptured profiles under the zoning resolution while still maximizing the available building mass. Alfred Bossom's exhibition of skyscraper architecture between 1923 and 1925 also fueled the collective imagination about high-rise living.[5] Another outcome of this period was the 'bootleg hotel' disguising what was essentially high-rise residential development by getting around the Tenement Act although not the zoning resolution. One Fifth Avenue by Helme and Corbett of 1926 was an example of this. Its shapely 27-storey tower conformed to the 1916 setback regulations, although its residential status was disguised as an 'apartment hotel'.[6] Then, under increased demand for high-rise living during the boom period of the 1920s in New York, the Multiple Dwelling Law of 1929 was promulgated, making the residential skyscraper a legal reality. The law essentially mandated bulk and height restrictions for high-rise housing according to an envelope profile. This profile, in turn, on lots of at least 3,000 square meters, allowed a lower bulk

Asinelli Tower

The San Remo

of 1.75 times the adjacent street width, which was usually 17 storeys, capped by towers up to two in number rising a height equal to three times the street width, provided they were less than or equal to one fifth of the lot area.[7] Complicated though this formulation might seem, it gave rise to several elegant high-rise residential apartments, such as the San Remo of 1930 by Emery Roth on Central Park West, with its U-shaped base and two towers rising up to 29 storeys, crowned by Italianate towers. In a similar mould was the Eldorado of 1931, also by Emery Roth and again on Central Park West, not far from The Beresford of 1929 through 1930, yet again by Roth and the largest apartment house in the United States at the time.[8]

By the late 1930s, Shanghai had 35 or more high-rise buildings at or above 10 storeys, a number of which were residential apartments. The Park Hotel overlooking the racecourse by Ladislau Hudec from 1928 was the tallest, at around 28 storeys, and the tallest building in China until the contemporary period. Rising to 22 storeys, Broadway Mansions by Frazer, along with Palmer and Turner, commanded a prominent view of the Bund from its site beside Suzhou Creek, while the Picardie Apartments and Willow Court in the French Concession were only slightly lower at 16 and 13 storeys, respectively.[9] Like their American counterparts, all were constructed with masonry-clad steel-frame structures, taking advantage of the speed and efficiency of building and the relative lightness of the materials involved. Archi-

tecturally, most were rendered in an *art deco* or *art moderne* style, fashionable at the time and, again, similar to many structures in New York City. Occupying prime sites, these apartment buildings were also seen as a form of modern luxury living. Today, Shanghai has even moved ahead of New York City in the number of high-rise buildings above 20 storeys, with a total larger than 3,000 and fully 1,000 towers above the 100-meter mark of around 30 storeys.[10] A major driving force behind the profusion of high-rise buildings during the 1930s was the relatively confined area of the Foreign Concessions where almost all were built and the sheer primacy of many of these sites with regard to the central business areas around the Bund and Suzhou Creek. Another factor was the easy conduit provided through trade to American and other foreign technologies. The safety elevator, for instance, was introduced into Shanghai in 1911 and the automatic elevator almost immediately after its inception in the United States. In recent years, in places like South Korea, the conflation of modernity and high-rise living in East Asia has continued and flourished. As mentioned earlier, residential 'towers in a park' began during the modernizing era of Chung-Hee Park, when residential preferences moved dramatically away from low-rise courtyard houses and similar residential buildings towards high-rise apartments.

Away from both New York City and East Asia, an interesting and not uninfluential example of high-

Park Hotel

Les Gratte-ciel de Villeurbanne

rise living occurred with Les Gratte-ciel de Villeur-banne, or skyscrapers of Villeurbanne, on the east of Lyon in France between 1930 and 1934. A project mostly by Môrice Leroux, a relatively young architect, it was not without a precedent, given the presence of tall buildings in Francis Chollet's unbuilt proposal from the Pont Dieux plan of 1926.[11] Villeurbanne was an industrial area that was growing rapidly in Lyon, and a prime mover for the creation of a center to this area, as well as the provision of low- to moderate-income housing, was Lazare Goujon, the socialist mayor from 1924 to 1935.[12] The client for the project was a public-private corporation authorized under a national law for the purpose of improving sanitary and hygienic conditions in cities at the time. The project occupied a site area of 8.8 hectares and consisted of high-rise, stepped-back linear blocks of housing with two towers at one end. The two blocks lined both sides of the Avenue Henri Barbusse rising to between 10 and 12 storeys, with the towers reaching a height of 20 storeys. Provision was made for 1,500 dwelling units and a population of some 6,000 inhabitants. Non-residential buildings in the overall complex included the Hotel de Ville by Robert Giroud and the Palais du Travail, also by Môrice Leroux through a competition that brought the young architect to the attention of city officials in the first place. Construction largely emulated the American approach with steel-frame skeleton structures clad, in this case, with hollow bricks and a final stucco finish. Elevator service was incorporated throughout, as were ergonometric and carefully planned kitchens, alongside of roof decks on the building, set back for residents to relax from their daily industrial toil.

Units ranged in size from two to seven rooms, with 85 percent housing three rooms or less for reasons of affordability. All had heating provided by a central plant, and the density, though high at 680 plus people per hectare, was also amenable and well augmented in the scheme by capacious and well-appointed public plazas, as well as shops and restaurants on the lower floors adjacent to broad sidewalks.

During the post-Second World War period, as alluded to earlier, high-rise living also became associated with mass production of units and affordable housing. Two places where this took place on an overwhelming scale were Hong Kong and Singapore during both their attempts to house large numbers of immigrants in public housing estates and to rid the cities of squatter settlements and other inadequate housing. Poor conditions in refugee camps came to a head in Hong Kong on Christmas Day of 1953 with the Shek Kip Mei fire, when many people were killed and public action to do something about it became aroused. Over the next 50 years or so, a program of public housing provision was mobilized, materially affecting around 70 percent of Hong Kong's population, starting with the Mark I, eight-storey emergency housing, with little more than two square meters of livable space per person and shared bathroom and kitchen facilities. From then on, public housing rose in height and stature to the 40-floor Concord and Harmony series of towers of the 1980s and '90s.[13] Over time, differences between market-rate high-rise housing, more the norm than the exception, and publicly-provided housing shrank, enabling Hong Kong to avoid the

Hong Kong public housing estates

Singapore public housing estates

Illa de la Llum © Lluis Casals

Absolute Towers © Tom Arban

stigmatization associated with lower-income dwelling that befell places like the United States. Tall and in pinwheel plan formations, spot densities on the order of 2,000 people per hectare were not uncommon. Commercial and community services in podia at the base or nearby to these towers provided for many day-to-day needs of inhabitants. The New Town Programme, initiated in 1973, also deployed large amounts of publicly-provided housing, usually in close conjunction with the well-serviced Mass Transit Railway system, enabling relatively convenient commutes to places of employment.[14]

From the founding of Singapore in 1965 onwards, the city state pursued a policy of collective consumption, whereby publicly-provided housing, married to publicly-run mass transit, allowed labor costs to be written down in a manner that became attractive to industry and other direct foreign investment. Over time, the Ring Concept Plan for the city was solidified through construction of large-scale, high-rise housing estates interlocked with employment and commercial centers through convenient mass transit.[15] During this time, fully 85 percent of Singaporeans were accommodated in publicly-sponsored housing, the highest percentage among industrialized countries in the world. Contemporary projects, along with market-rate housing, also joined into Singapore's aggressive program to 'green' the island state. Furthermore, public housing, through projects like the Pinnacle@Duxton completed in 2009, has been pushed to the leading edge of architecture in the service of a livable and lively Singapore.[16] Designed by ARC Studio Architecture + Urbanism for the Housing and Development Board, the project rises 50 sto-

reys across seven slab-like towers, interlinked at the 26th and 50th floors by skybridges accommodating community facilities at the lower level and a publicly accessible roofscape at the top. Some 1,848 units, in three different basic configurations, although with variations within them, provide for some 7,400 residents. Commercial, cultural, and community spaces are also located at the base of the apartment towers, along with 1,274 parking spaces. Like elsewhere in Singapore, the project is located close to mass transit. A certain emphasis on diversity of habitation in the project also extends to a variety of different types of balconies and terraces that can be selected by residents for attachment to their units.

Elsewhere, contemporary high-rise housing seems to come in one of two types. The first are what might be termed 'shapely towers', with an emphasis on the overall form in the rise of the tower itself, epitomized, for instance, by the circular and outward spiraling form of the Absolute Towers, by MAD in Toronto of 2012.[17] A second general category of residential tower can be characterized by assemblages of units often giving rise to irregular shapes and/or punctuation of a more or less even rise to a building with open spaces and protrusions. The Illa de la Llum in Barcelona of 2005, by Clotet and Paricio, conforms well to this category, with several towers comprising 230 units in a stacked arrangement of different floor plates and dwelling unit types irregularly introduced into the overall trapezoidal form of the complex. An articulate façade full of movable parts, like screens and windows, further animates the visual quality of the buildings.[18] The Mirador Apartments in Madrid of 2004, by MVRDV and Blanco Léo,

Boutique Monaco

incorporates a spacious 'sky plaza' at the 18th floor of its 21-storey structure, housing 157 units in what amounts to a slab block comprised of three sections: one in the middle with separate vertical access and duplex and triplex units, flanked on both sides by what are effectively towers of units.[19] Then, the Boutique Monaco "Missing Matrix" apartment tower with commercial, cultural, and community spaces on the lower levels in the Gangnam District of Seoul provides multi-storeyed cutouts and garden terraces within the rise of the otherwise rectilinear building with its U-shaped plan.[20] Designed by Minsuk Cho of Mass Studies, the building rises 27 floors with five basement levels primarily for parking, and provides for a variety of 49 different unit types aimed at rental in a hotel-office market. The cutouts were not predetermined or otherwise arbitrary, but came about in order to deal with the allowable floor area ratio for the building. The exposed, criss-crossed structure at the lower levels was also introduced as a means for load transferal from the units above, through the relatively open lower floors to the basement level below. This was already being constructed when the architects took over the project. The overall result is an unusual and elegant assemblage of parts including the garden void spaces within the building.

CONTEMPORARY CASES: EXPRESSIONS OF SUSTAINABILITY AND VARIATION

Tall towers, as mentioned earlier, are typically deployed to accommodate a larger number of dwelling units and population within sites of relatively limited space. Often, such a housing operation is not only expedient in terms of the amount of production based on the aggregation of several basic unit types comprising the floor plan, but also a means of maximizing the returns as well as land value of a particular property development. The cases of interest here are emblematic of how tall towers are utilized in contemporary urban conditions of both high densities and intensities and, at the same time, stand as well-designed projects that have sought to engage with sustainable building and architectural variation. The first is Moulmein Rise, another example from Singapore, completed in 2003, by WOHA Architects, as a private, high-rise condominium for United Overseas Land (UOL) Group Limited. Prior to this project, the local real estate developer had specialized largely in hospitality, before its forays into the commercial and residential sectors. While most of UOL's initial residential developments were located in the suburban estates in Singapore, Moulmein Rise was its first residential investment in the prime area of Novena, right at the fringe of downtown Singapore, including the core retail district of Orchard Road. In fact, UOL had already begun to establish its presence in Novena, rejuvenating this neighborhood then dominated by offices and both low- and high-rise residences with two mixed-use developments combining office and retail – Novena Square and United Square – that have since become the commercial core of the area. As the local property market took a beating from the Asian Financial Crisis of 1997, UOL acquired a small 0.23-hectare site in the vicinity to be developed into mid- or high-rise housing.

Besides the proximity to both the commercial core at Novena and Orchard Road, the site for Moulmein Rise is just north of a wedge of green area surrounded by low-rise single-family attached dwellings, beyond which lie the presidential grounds. Given this uninterrupted view of the downtown to the south, along with the developer's desire for a striking high-rise project that would maximize the returns on their investment, a closed competition was held among four architectural firms to obtain the optimal design solution. While the original intention by UOL was for a larger building footprint and a structure that would be lower in height, WOHA's principals, having won the competition, convinced their clients otherwise. This resulted in a slender, modern, elegant design rising 28 storeys in height that fully leveraged on the views of the surroundings, but also the southern exposure and enhanced cross-ventilation through the smaller footprint and increases in height. With a floor area ratio or plot ratio of 2.8, the project reflects a high intensity of use on the site – a condition commonly found in land-scarce Singapore where at least 79 percent of the city-state's residential building stock is in the form of high-rises with plot ratios of at least 2.1.[21] Housing a total of 48 apartments units and two penthouses, with two units per floor, the design paid considerable attention to ensuring a high degree of privacy in this relatively upscale residential project. As such, two private elevators were installed to provide direct access to each apartment, with access for visitors limited to a separate public elevator. Other on-site amenities include an underground carpark, a small gymnasium, and a 50-meter lap pool set within a tropical garden that cascades down three tiers along the slope of the site towards the street front.

The most outstanding features of Moulmein Rise, it must be said, was its innovative incorporation of vernacular climate control strategies and expression of architectural variation through a recombination system of simple, standard elements. Located in the hot and humid equatorial region, Singapore is subjected to heavy convectional rains and seasonal monsoons. Therefore, as much as high-rise residences could have benefited from the cooler air higher up, the frequent rains often resulted in closed windows. Having lived in a high-rise public housing unit, Wong Mun Summ, one of WOHA's principals, was eager to address this untapped ventilation and the entry of precipitation into the buildings by the force of winds from different directions. Moulmein Rise, which was their first large-scale residential project, presented

a welcome opportunity to tackle these construction issues. A primary outcome of WOHA's research was what they called a 'tropical' approach to high-rises, including the adoption of monsoon windows framed under the sills of the more conventional bay windows running continuously along the façade. Made of a perforated aluminum screen that sits perpendicular to the glass windows, this sliding panel is operated by a winder, affording natural ventilation into each of the units while also serving as a shelf, even when the glass windows are closed. Due to this inflow of air, particularly at the higher levels, many occupants found that it was no longer necessary to cool their apartments with the energy-consumptive air-conditioners in the evenings.[22] Besides the monsoon windows to improve the cross-ventilation, the apartments have a depth of no more than 12.2 meters, further enhancing this purpose. To optimize solar performance, the building is oriented in a north-south direction, and each unit is open on three sides. All the windows are well-shaded with deep overhangs on the south and north façades, thereby reducing direct heat gains and protecting the windows from the driving rains.

In terms of the architectural design, WOHA's other aspiration was to avoid a simple extrusion of the units upwards, and the creation of what merely would be an urban object. To this end, they strove to endow the façade with some 'personality', injecting a degree of variation and complexity such that each apartment would have its own identity. Indeed, from afar, Moulmein Rise stands out for its rhythmic façades. On the south, the two units on each floor are distinguished and expressed materially on the exterior, whereas the units on the west are defined by alternating bands of glass and overhangs, while the units on the east are fenestrated by a seemingly random array of bay windows and planters. On the north, the building is clad in bands of perforated aluminum screens concealing the air-conditioner ledges and drying racks but also serving as sunshading devices. These are displaced marginally on each floor, thereby revealing parts of the circling stairway and monsoon windows while generating a lively, environmental façade. By mixing these three basic elements – the monsoon windows, screens, and planters – in a repetitive, haphazard fashion, and then stacked up vertically in a random order, the architects successfully created visually complex yet engaging façades that doubled up as environmentally sensible curtain walls. Moreover, the extra space taken up by these elements is exempt from development tax but still counts as saleable area, a fact that contributes to the commercial interests of UOL, for the special façade features simultaneously enhance the amenity and value of the apartments. This notion of variation is taken up further and applied to the interiors with the creation of a modular system based on multiples of 0.30 meters that regulate a range of architectural dimensioning, such as floor-to-floor heights.

Within the typical units, the circulation spine bisects the apartments into two halves, with the master bedroom and open living and dining area located to the north for greater privacy, while the two smaller bedrooms and service areas such as the kitchen and bathrooms are located to the south.

Flexibility in layout is achieved by the open living area, as well as the potential to combine the two smaller bedrooms as needed. The two penthouses each have a unique layout but generally adhere to the same spatial logic, albeit with larger master bedrooms and double-height open living and dining areas. Space-wise, the two typical units are 120 and 122 square meters, while the penthouses cover an area of 220 and 235 square meters, both of which are relatively commodious. Upon entering the units, there is a continuous flow in the interior, created largely through the circulation spine opening up to views on both the eastern and western ends, as well as across with the open space concept of the living and dining area. With a density of nearly 215 dwelling units per hectare, Moulmein Rise stands as an instance of an innovative, low-energy approach towards tropical, high-rise living, establishing its presence in a high-density urban setting that at the same time expresses a high degree of individuality through the plan and façade variations.

MOULMEIN RISE

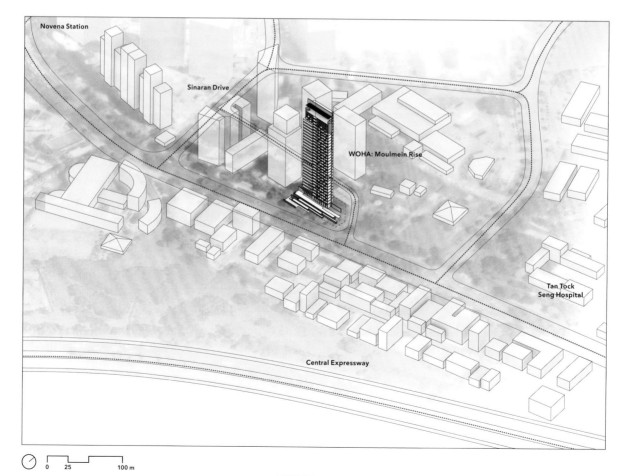

Novena Station

Sinaran Drive

WOHA: Moulmein Rise

Tan Tock Seng Hospital

Central Expressway

0   25   100 m

TALL TOWERS

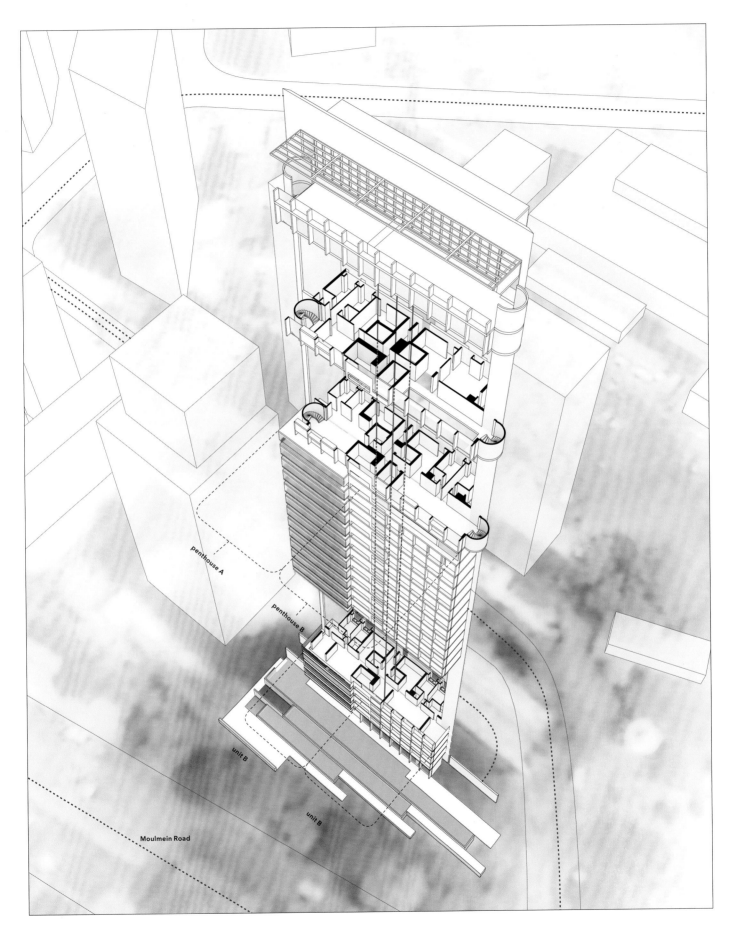

penthouse A

penthouse B

unit B

unit B

Moulmein Road

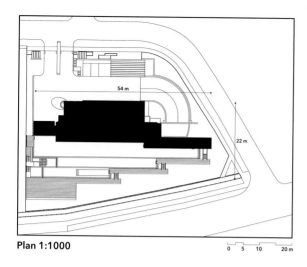

Plan 1:1000

0   5   10   20 m

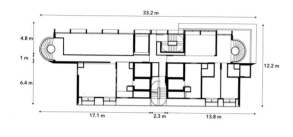

Plan 1:500

0   2.5   5   10 m

Key
■ Housing Units
■ Entrance/Parking
■ Common Space

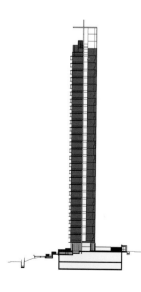

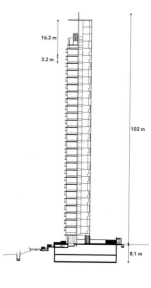

Sectional Variation (Other Uses)   Sectional 1:1500

0   7.5   15   30 m

Household Types
Unit Types 1:750

0   2.5   5   10 m

Key
■ Bedroom/Living
■ Kitchen
■ Bathroom
□ Balcony

Unit Type Locations

3 BR
120 sq m
24 units

3 BR
120 sq m
24 units

Penthouse / 3 BR
235 sq m
1 unit

Penthouse / 3 BR
220 sq m
1 unit

In the North American context, a high-rise project completed recently in 2011 and launched with much fanfare is 8 Spruce Street in New York City, also known as the Beekman Tower or New York by Gehry. Soaring to an impressive height of 267 meters and thus earning the accolade of being the 'tallest residential tower in the western hemisphere' at the time of its completion, this iconic addition to the Manhattan skyline was designed by Frank Gehry & Partners.[23] Developed by Forest City Ratner, the 0.40-hectare site was one of the largest undeveloped parcels in Manhattan at the time, and was owned and used by the New York Downtown Hospital as an open-air parking lot.[24] Acknowledging the parcel's development potential in the city's Financial District, particularly since the site was not subjected to any design ordinances or neighborhood development jurisdictions, the Hospital issued a request for proposal, before selecting Forest City Ratner as the winner. Originally, a third of the mixed-use project was slated to accommodate classrooms, offices, and dormitories for Pace University but the partnership fell through due to dramatic increases in the projected costs.[25] This opened up the possibility of incorporating other programs as part of the redesign, resulting in the kindergarten-to-8th-grade public elementary school occupying the first to fourth floors of the building's podium. As an initiative put forward by the city, this offer would in return provide Forest City Ratner a pro-rata share of the property's air rights, as well as US$190 million worth of Liberty Bonds and US$476.1 million in taxable bonds from the New York City Housing Development Corporation.[26] Apart from increasing the height limits on the project, the taxable bonds exempted the development from the 80/20 affordable housing program in New York City, where 20 percent of the apartment units would have had to be reserved for low-income tenants, although Forest City Ratner was obliged to constrain its annual rent increases until the bonds are retired.

Besides the 9,290-square-meter public school, later named the Spruce Street School, the final design for the skyscraper also housed below-grade hospital parking, ground floor retail, a 2,323-square-meter ambulatory care center operated by the Hospital, residential amenities like a grilling terrace, swimming pool, fitness center, library, and children's playroom on parts of the sixth to eighth floors, and a total of 903 rental units. These programs are stacked vertically on a T-shaped pedestal, creating a gradual zone of transition between the first and ninth floors from public to semi-private, and finally private space. This public/private differentiation is also expressed architecturally, with the five-storey podium of public programs clad in nondescript red bricks with at least double-height floors, beyond which the elaborate stainless-steel form of the residential tower and its communal amenities rises up to dizzying heights on the 76th floor. The industrial warehouse-styled masonry base deftly integrates the building with the Beaux-Arts structures in the vicinity, while the rippling curtain wall design cloaking seven sides of the eight-sided structure, the only exception being the flat southern façade, is a progressive statement heralding a new chapter in the city's rich architectural history. Broken down into four volumes sitting above the podium, the residential tower conforms to the century-old building regulations and setback requirements, with each volume receding further back from the building envelope, much like the classic Woolworth Building and other skyscrapers emblematic of Lower Manhattan.

The soaring tower accommodating an impressive density of approximately 2,258 dwelling units per hectare asserts a remarkable presence among the bevy of high-rise beauties with its arresting, silky finish. Supposedly inspired by the 'hard folds' of Bernini and the 'soft folds' of Michelangelo, Gehry and his office designed an eye-catching façade that draped delicately over the angular T-shaped volumes, generating a masterful illusion of movement activated by the play of light and shadows upon the gentle ripples across the surface. To realize this unique, undulating form, Permasteelisa North America, a long-time collaborator of Gehry's since 1992 when they created the Barcelona Fish sculpture, was brought into the design-assist phase. The façade was installed using a unitized curtain wall system, where rain screen panels of varying radii were fabricated to be attached to corresponding flat unitized curtain wall panels through interlocking male-female mullions and a mating horizontal stack. These rain screen panels producing the folds can curve out between six inches to six feet, and with a steel angel hair finish to diffuse light and reduce glare from the surface, the façade attains a visual softness and exuberance.[27] This system effectively reduced the costs for this unorthodox façade, keeping it to no more than what it would have been for a basic equivalent of the same material and scope, while still attaining an aesthetically exceptional outcome. More importantly, it was the plethora of bay windows shaped by the multiple folds and ripples in this curtain wall that determined the unit 'variation' in the project. Apart from the desirability of panoramic views afforded by this architectural element from all the major rooms in each apartment, particularly for a high-rise residential project, the shifting bay windows that differed from floor to floor resulted in irregular floor plans for each floor. As a result, the project had purportedly hundreds of 'unique' unit plan types, spread across the studios, one-bedroom units, two-bedroom units, three-bedroom units, terrace residences, and penthouses. With the exception of the three distinct penthouses individually designed by Gehry, the actual variation of the unit plans though is perhaps open to question since it was driven by subtle modifications to the façade from floor to floor, whereas each one of the residential volumes was derived by a basic floor plate: one from the ninth to the 22nd floor, another from the 23rd to the 37th floor, a third from the 38th to the 50th floor, and the final one from the 51st to the 75th floor.[28] Nonetheless, together with the project's coveted address, and its high-quality interior finishes and fixtures selected by the architect himself, this diversity in unit plans has become a successful selling point for the luxury residences.

8 SPRUCE STREET

Broadway

Spruce street

0   50   200 m

Broadway

Park Row

Spruce Street

TALL TOWERS

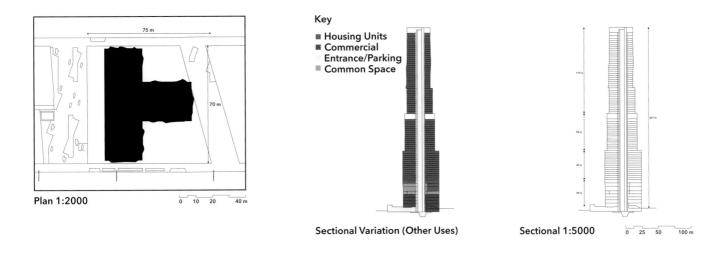

Plan 1:2000

Key
■ Housing Units
■ Commercial
■ Entrance/Parking
■ Common Space

0 10 20 40 m

Sectional Variation (Other Uses)

Sectional 1:5000

0 25 50 100 m

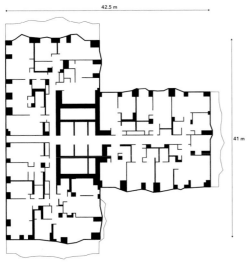

42.5 m

41 m

F 51-75

11.5 m   10 m   25 m

14 m

16.5 m

13.5 m

F 39-49

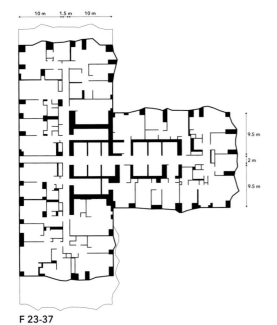

10 m   1.5 m   10 m

9.5 m

2 m

9.5 m

F 23-37

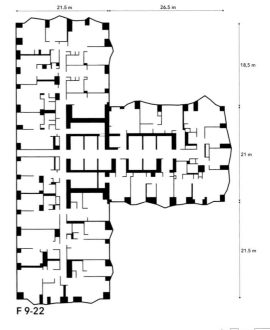

21.5 m   26.5 m

18,5 m

21 m

21.5 m

F 9-22

Plan 1:750

0 3.75 7.5 15 m

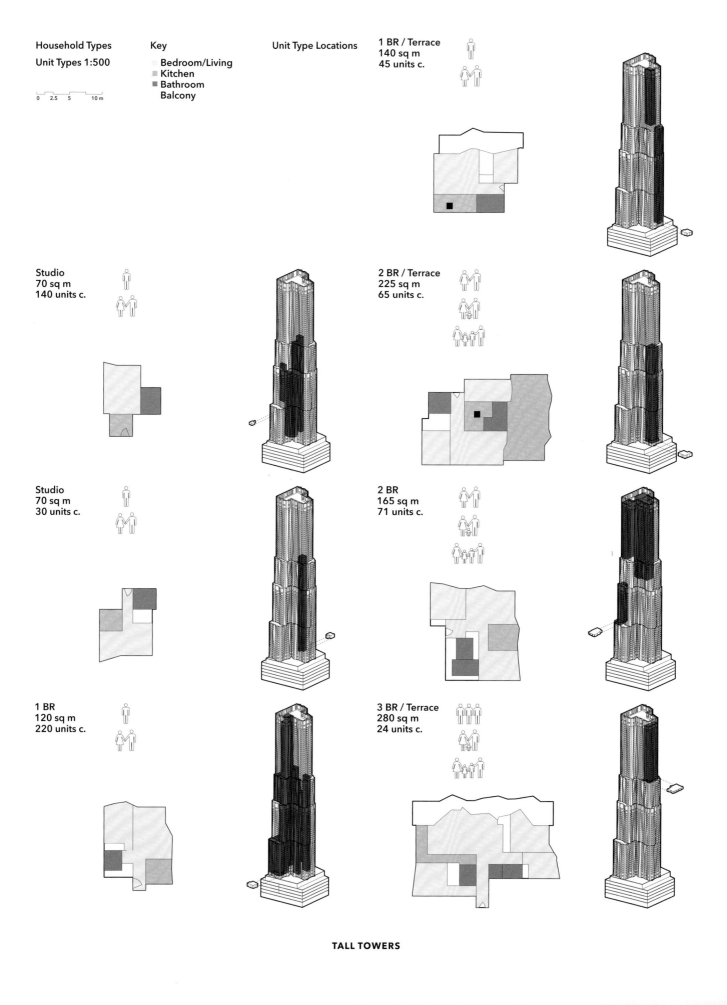

Household Types
Unit Types 1:500

Key
Bedroom/Living
Kitchen
Bathroom
Balcony

0   2.5   5   10 m

Unit Type Locations

1 BR / Terrace
140 sq m
45 units c.

Studio
70 sq m
140 units c.

2 BR / Terrace
225 sq m
65 units c.

Studio
70 sq m
30 units c.

2 BR
165 sq m
71 units c.

1 BR
120 sq m
220 units c.

3 BR / Terrace
280 sq m
24 units c.

Another recent project of note from North America is The Contemporaine by Perkins+Will, located in the River North area of Chicago on a modest 0.08-hectare site. Completed earlier in 2004, the 15-storey-tall building is situated in a neighborhood with an eclectic mix of redundant and converted warehouses, water towers, low-rise commercial and new high-rise dwellings that were developed in response to then Mayor Richard M. Daley's interest in the rapid development of the city's downtown core. The Contemporaine is composed of a level of retail on the ground floor along with the entry lobby, three floors of parking stacked above, and 11 floors of apartments and penthouses floating on top of this podium. Constructed with cast-concrete floors supported by slender columns, the building is clad in glass from floor to ceiling, thereby affording a high degree of transparency to the structural and material elements in this contemporary, poetic composition that clearly pays tribute to Le Corbusier and the modernist movement. Variation on the façade was cleverly achieved by reversing the orientation of every other window frame, creating a "Mondrian-esque mullion pattern".[29] The building mass is broken down not only by the lightness of the glazed façades, but also the use of deep slots, the narrow, cantilevered balconies on all four sides of the building, as well as the emphasis on the vertical four-storey-tall columns visible along the podium and a solitary one on the rooftop supporting the exposed-concrete portico-like structure. Inside, the apartments are served by a central core of elevators and stairs alongside a central corridor that opens up to each unit. Within the units, the service functions such as the bathrooms and storage rooms are located closer to the core, thereby freeing up the façade and the views beyond to the habitable rooms. Ensuring a degree of flexibility in openness within the units was also of importance to the architects, and thus they opted for open plan kitchens in the living rooms, which are placed close to other service areas and away from the windows. Designed originally for 52 units, many were later combined by owners who purchased multiples, yielding a final tally of 28 units, ranging from 86 square meters to 341 square meters in size.[30] Even then, the overall residential density is high at 650 dwelling units per hectare. At night, the building glows from within, endowed with a captivating theatricality that plays on its modernist architectural elements.

THE CONTEMPORAINE

TALL TOWERS

Full Floor Penthouse 1

Full Floor Penthouse 2

Half Floor Penthouse 1

Half Floor Penthouse 2

Standard Floor

Parking Podium

North Wells Street

West Grand Ave.

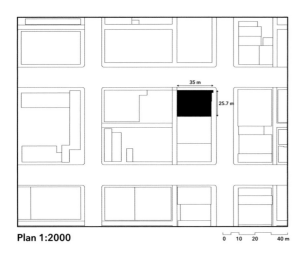

35 m

25.7 m

Plan 1:2000

0   10   20   40 m

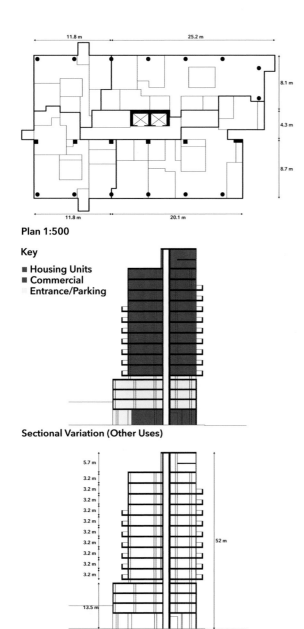

11.8 m   25.2 m

8.1 m

4.3 m

8.7 m

11.8 m   20.1 m

Plan 1:500

Key
■ Housing Units
■ Commercial
□ Entrance/Parking

Sectional Variation (Other Uses)

5.7 m
3.2 m
3.2 m
3.2 m
3.2 m
3.2 m
3.2 m
3.2 m
3.2 m
3.2 m
3.2 m

52 m

13.5 m

Sectional 1:2500

0   12.5   25   50 m

Household Types

Unit Types 1:750

Key
□ Bedroom/Living
□ Kitchen
■ Bathroom
□ Balcony

Unit Type Locations

0   2.5   5   10 m

1BR
100 sq m
8 units

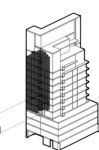

2BR
140 sq m
8 units

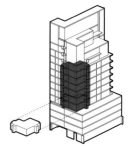

2BR
185 sq m
8 units

3BR
215 sq m
8 units

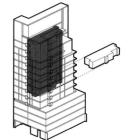

Penthouse
4 units

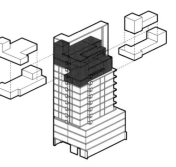

BALANCING DWELLING AND CONDITIONS OF VARIATION, SEPARATION, AND RESILIENCE

High-rise provision of housing, particularly in contemporary times, often involves the balancing of particular requirements and general trends. For instance, in many if not most cultural and social settings, entry and elevator services for residents are separated from those serving other functions that may be in a high-rise building, including office commercial and retail commercial. This is done for the purposes of security, maintenance, and even the exclusivity of a particular address. Nevertheless, recent and not so recent trends towards integration of a variety of different uses in residential and other building complexes have also been influential, raising questions about degrees and kinds of proximity between strictly residential uses and other functions, especially those on the 'community service' side of non-residential use. Of course, solutions can and have been found allowing for reasonable and creative parsing of exclusivity with integration, although it often involves at least a separation of residential from office commercial functions, except when home-offices and hotel-offices are predominant functions. Even then, either the domicile or office aspect tends to dominate in any particular complex.

Another aspect that requires balance involves effective and reasonable discrimination of variance among unit types, unless some form of unbridled variation is provided in a cost-effective manner that is endemic to a systematic property of building construction, as in the case at 8 Spruce Street, or the cutouts in Boutique Monaco. Even then, there needs to be something more on offer than simply difference for difference's sake. One potential aspect and advantage of high-rise housing is a capacity to vary units in both plan and section throughout the rise of the building. Several examples discussed here do just that and provide for different household formations, economic means, and lifestyle requirements.

Yet another aspect of high-rise housing that requires consideration and balancing towards potentially productive outcomes concerns obsolescence and the maintenance of resilience to changes in markets and lifestyle conditions. Towers, unlike smaller and more singular dwelling units and types, tend to lock-in units in manners that often prove difficult and expensive to retrofit. Broadly applicable decisions in some settings, like in China and elsewhere now and in the past to limit sizes and varieties of units, particularly to the lower end of usable space standards, can induce rapid obsolescence when market and related circumstances change for the better, with substantial associated social costs. In effect, buildings quickly become moribund and can only be replaced. By contrast, contemporary trends towards keeping building façades free for habitable spaces and concentrating necessary structure in compact cores and external structure, together with space-saving mechanical systems, can provide for more fully-flexible layouts of dwelling units. Although these units may not change rapidly, depending upon the tenancy and ownership involved, they can technically be altered well inside the life span of the overall building structure and services. Finally, manners of appreciating the verticality of high-rise living, including the views on offer, appear to have broadened into the contemporary era, including multiple choices of balconies, roof garden orientations, community sky decks, and variations in façade treatments according to insolation and visual prospects. In most cases, these are net positive outcomes helping to rebalance tall housing against the prevalent uniformity of some former eras.

B I G

Climat de France, Henri Delleuse,
from *Fernand Pouillon* (1986), p.77

Gallaratese

B U I L
D I N G S

The housing category of 'big buildings' broadly conforms to a type of extensive residential complex that is generally mid-rise or mid-to-high-rise and where dwelling units and other functions are accommodated in a single structure or a few interlocked structures. The type also broadly conforms to the idea of the 'submultiple' providing for integrated dwelling environments at levels below that of a district but comparable to that of a neighborhood. More pointedly, they are complexes where housing and community services are no longer seen as separate facilities or spatially-separated functions, but are contained together in a single structure. The term 'submultiple' was coined by Leonardo Benevolo in 1984, among others, and was usually applied to single building complexes of 1,000 plus units and at densities of around 400 to 550 people per hectare. This is roughly equivalent to the idea of a neighborhood in a single building. Spatially, submultiples were at least partially supported by models of social interaction, which stressed the priority and centrality of certain functions over others. And while the quest for an appropriate submultiple was not unique to the modern era, its importance was certainly magnified by prevailing technocratic preoccupations with control, management, and functional interdependence of the modern era. In most cases, submultiples as big buildings were built in the post-Second World War period towards and on the periphery of cities in the cause of mass-produced housing. More recently, submultiples as big buildings have continued in this vein on greenfield sites, as well as on brownfield sites slated for large-scale redevelopment.

PRECEDENTS: FROM *UNITÉS* TO SPRAWLING COMPLEXES AND GREEN BUILDINGS

Although not exactly conceived of as a vertical neighborhood, the Unité d'habitation de grandeur conforme by Le Corbusier was of sufficient size and did conform within a single building all the local shops, services, and recreational opportunities for a community of some 1,200 to 1,600 people. Comparable to Fourier's Phalanstère, with which Le Corbusier was quite familiar, the Unité was to be the basic cell of the

Corviale

Unité d'habitation © José Baltanás Ramírez

Via Verde © David Sundberg/ESTO

new city. Furthermore, as a single building and plastic entity, the Unité promised to make the formation of subdistricts within a city architecturally tractable.[1] Le Corbusier commenced work on the Unité concept in 1944, with proposals for the Unité d'habitation de transitoires, or emerging housing, although many of the ideas embodied draw on his earlier work including the 1922 Immeubles-villas. This was also when Le Corbusier transformed this thinking from the individual house to the context of collective living. Then, in 1946, the newly created Ministry of Reconstruction and Urban Planning in France provided an opportunity of a trial application of the Unité d'habitation de Marseille. Completed in 1952, the project drew considerable attention and others were built at Nantes in 1955, Berlin in 1957, Briey in 1961, and Firminy in 1968.[2] Raised off the ground *en pilotis,* allowing landscape to flow underneath it, the *Unité* at Marseilles rose to a height of 17 storeys or 56 meters and was 165 meters in length and 24 meters in width, sufficient to allow cross-ventilation into units. Fully 337 apartments were composed as double-height units juxtaposed in section and interlocked together with internal streets centrally placed within the building every three floors. A 'street' lined with some 26 commercial and community service spaces was placed at an intermediate level between the seventh and eighth floors. The interlocking 'maisonette units' also had terraces open to the outside along with *brise soleil,* or sunscreens, to both the east and west. The longitudinal façade was asymmetrical in composition, with one end given over to elevators and internal stairs for vertical circulation. Considerable

variety was introduced into the various apartment units, with 23 distinct unit types adaptable to specific requirements of habitation. These ranged from student apartments, through dwellings for sizeable families, to hotel-type rooms. Interior moving screen walls also added to spatial flexibility. The roofscape consisted of sculptural forms housing a gymnasium, a running track, a pool, a kindergarten, an outdoor theater and vent stacks, as well as utility rooms. Several other Unités were also designed and built by others in France, including the Unité de voisinage at Bron-Parilly, by Bourdeix, Gagès, and Grimal. Later, the so-called 'collective units' of housing, rising as much as 15 floors at Toulouse Le Mirail, also in France, by Candilis-Josic-Woods of 1960 through 1966, share many of the hallmarks of the Unité.[3]

At much the same time as the Unités at Marseilles and Nantes, Fernand Pouillon designed and built his version in the new town of Climat de France at Oued Koriche in Algeria, completing it just before the War of Independence between 1958 and 1962. In the form of an enclosed perimeter block with a monumental peristyle surrounding the Place Bar el Aghab, also known as the Place of the 200 Columns, the entire edifice is large, at 260 meters in length and 65 meters in width. A clear precedent was the Maydan-i Shah at Isfahan in Iran, which Pouillon visited in 1955.[4] Comprised of some 360 dwelling units, at around 120 per floor, on top of 200 or so shops at plaza level, the columns framed a three-storey-tall colonnade. Located laterally across a sloping hillside to the west of the Casbah in Algiers, the complex affords splendid views to the Mediterranean and is part of the larger community of 4,000 or so dwellings on a 30-hectare site, built for the City of Algiers under France's then ZUP, or Zone à urbaniser en priorité program. In fact, Pouillon was named by the mayor of Algiers as Chief Architect for the city. Dwelling unit plans throughout were standardized and relatively large, spanning across the entire building from the interior courtyard to the exterior walls facing outside streets. With a resulting overall building thickness of some 12.5 meters, similar to the earlier 'block shapers', the totally paved monumental court was very ample at 235 meters by 40 meters forming a major center and day-to-day activity space for the entire community. All told, the building rises some seven storeys above the street, with the interior peristyle of rectangular columns forming the majority of the interior façades. Indeed, the peristyle fulfills its traditional role of mediation between the very public court on the outside and the private precincts on the inside of the complex. It also forms something of a street and a climatic relief from the hot Algerian sun. Finally the peristyle helps the complex pay homage to the idea of a 'palace for the people'. Roof spaces above are gendered and appropriated by women as their spaces for laundry and other activities.

The submultiples of Rome in Italy got underway in the wake of the migratory influxes to the city during the 1950s and 1960s. The 1962 plan prepared the city for further peripheral development, incorporating the circumferential Grande Raccordo-Anulare (GRA) and the national Law 167 of the same year, and forced local administrations to expropriate land, at reasonable prices, proportional to local populations and assign it to the construction of public housing. Subsequently, Plans for Economic and Popular Housing (PEEPs) were designated within the areas zoned under Law 167 and construction commenced in 1964.[5] A number of urban districts, or *quartieri*, were produced, beginning with the Quartiere di Spinaceto of 1964 or 1965 in south-west Rome just beyond the GRA and about four kilometers from the major employment site at the EUR (Esposizione Universale Roma). Overall, the project was large, housing over 26,000 people on a 187-hectare greenfield site of rolling countryside. The plan was by Piero Moroni with Lucio Barbera and Nicola Di Cagno as architects, among

others. The disposition of dwelling units took the form of linear slab buildings, ranging from four and five storeys to 10 storeys, running roughly parallel with main roads winding through the site with its topography, and containing housing, shops, and community facilities within them. Of the 8,000 or so dwelling units constructed, larger buildings accommodate upwards of 400 units.[6] Later, during a second version of the PEEP encouraging individual architectural experimentation, the Quartiere Laurentino 38 by Petro Barucci began construction in 1976 and was also located in the south of Rome near the EUR, although inside the GRA. Consisting of well-composed, eight-storey slab blocks and some towers running perpendicular on podia of community services and facilities, again next to a curving roadway, each submultiple contained on the order of 400 dwelling units.[7] Among the submultiples in the form of big buildings during this period, Corviale by Mario Fiorentino of 1972 through 1974 is among the most striking and controversial. Extending as a single building for one kilometer on a 60-hectare relatively isolated site inside the GRA, Corviale is reminiscent of the *unité* in sectional development, although much larger. Housing on the order of 8,500 inhabitants, Corviale featured community services and commercial facilities, along with parking, at the lower entry levels and in an intermediate space five floors up. The first five floors of dwellings were served by a double-loaded corridor, whereas those above the non-residential intermediate level were split into two separated building volumes, with an open space in between for a further four levels and a rooftop area.[8] The tragedy of this and some other big building schemes from the era derived, at least in large part, from poor attempts to micro-manage living environments in the face of overwhelming complexities, exacerbated when the projects became dumping grounds for the poor, indigent, and drug abusers. Later projects, like the Quartiere di Torrevecchia, completed in 1984 and housing around 3,600 people, by Pietro Barucci again, were more modest and fared better.[9]

Remaining in Italy but moving away from Rome, probably the most notable big building submultiple was the Gallaratese on the outskirts of Milan by Carlo Aymonino, Aldo Rossi, and Studio Ayde. The property was owned and developed by the Monte Amiata

Fusuijing Commune

Quartiere Laurentino 38

Edificio Copan, from Casabella (No. 810, 2012), p. 15

Association, which commissioned the plan in 1967 and conveyed the finished project in 1974 to the City of Milan.[10] A complex of five buildings interconnected on a 6.5-hectare irregular site was construed to create a sense of community, with shops, offices, community facilities, and an amphitheater, in addition to dwellings for some 2,500 people. Most of the project was designed by Aymonino in the form of an eight-storey double-loaded slab, splayed in plan at around 120 degrees; a six-storey slab block; and a two-storey bridge block, linking the other slabs, with a raised piazza and amphitheater. Housing five basic kinds of dwelling units, from studios to larger duplexes, the architecture of the slab blocks was strongly animated by elevator shafts, stairways, and a complex building section of interlocking units, with courtyard units at the base as well as maisonettes on top. Allegedly, Aymonino was influenced in the repetitive cellular arrangement of the stepped section by Trajan's Market in Rome. Rossi's 'galleria' building, rising four storeys, was accessed via a two- and three-storey public arcade at the base, running the full length of the complex. Here, the reference was apparently to the *ballatoio* of Milan from the 1920s as well as to rationalist architecture from much of the same period. The crisp geometry of the housing block, together with the monumental arcade, was also reminiscent of Pouillon's earlier work at Climat de France. Apparently, the number of visitors to the project swelled in the 1970s to a point where an entry fee into the complex was charged. Elsewhere entirely, big buildings were also constructed, including the Fusuijing Commune in Beijing of the 1950s, Edificio Copan in São Paulo, Brazil, by Oscar Niemeyer of 1951, and Sewoon Sangga in central Seoul of 1967 by Soo-Guen Kim.

Moving into the contemporary era, in addition to the three cases defined in more detail in the next section of this chapter, other projects come to mind, including Via Verde in the Melrose neighborhood of the Bronx in New York City. This was a product of a competition organized in 2006 by Shaun Donovan, now the U.S. Secretary of the Department of Housing and Urban Development and then the Commissioner of New York City's Department of Housing Preservation and Development.[11] The aim was to combine green building concepts with good architecture for public housing and to produce an exemplary project in an area of the Bronx that had been ravaged by blight, neglect, and physical desolation. The vacant site located at 156th Street and Brook Avenue was long and tapered, formerly occupied by mid-rise buildings that had since been torn down. The competition was won by a consortium of Grimshaw Architects from the United Kingdom, Dattner Architects as a local firm, and Lee Weintraub, a local landscape architect. The developers for the project arose from a partnership between Phipps Housing and the Jonathan Rose company, both long in the business as affordable housing providers, with the Phipps family's involvement dating back to at least 1905.[12] Completed in 2012, Via Verde consists of a single, stepped building complex that rises from three- to four-storey townhouses at one end, through mid-rise duplex units up to a 20-storey tower. The whole complex also encloses a ground level open-air court and an abundance of green roofs forming a cascading garden landscape and range of community gardens that also provide for a promenade for residents up and over the building components. The 220 dwelling units of various types are broadly divided among lower-income rental units, accounting for roughly 60 percent, and middle-income owner units in a cooperative arrangement. A fitness center is prominently located on the top of the building, which also includes a health and wellness center in a ground floor retail-like space, as well as some other community facilities. Indeed, the production of fresh produce in the community garden venture; the mix of public and private open space to encourage residents to spend time outside in the fresh air, including the garden terraces; and the massing of the building to allow for plenty of natural light; all aim to produce an affordable, green, and healthy building environment.[13] So also do the myriad of roof-mounted solar panels, the prolific amount of material recycling both during and after construction, and the prefabricated façade treatment for efficient and cost-saving construction.

CONTEMPORARY CASES: BIG BUILDINGS IN URBAN CIRCUMSTANCES

Much like the tall tower typology that is used to provide a larger number of units, big buildings and submultiples also serve the same ends, although without the same site limitations but with a clear intent to incorporate other amenities and programs within a singular structure. The period of the 1990s and the turn of the twenty-first century saw a resurgence of this particular typology, including three remarkable projects completed in Amsterdam and Copenhagen. The two Dutch examples of interest are the Piraeus block and The Whale, designed by Hans Kollhoff and Christian Rapp, and de Architekten Cie respectively. Located in the Eastern Harbor District (Oostelijk Havengebied) of Amsterdam, the two projects are also representative of how former infrastructural sites, and in this case commercial docklands, could be transformed into new uses. Before Rotterdam emerged as the largest Dutch shipping port in 1962, Amsterdam's development was in fact shaped profoundly by its harbors. The docklands in the Eastern Harbor were the first deep-water harbor in the city, and were created as landfill islands during Amsterdam's 'Second Golden Age' in the latter half of the nineteenth century. The advent of railroads and steamships necessitated docks of much longer

lengths to allow goods to be efficiently transferred to and from the sea-faring vessels.[14] By 1915, the entire Eastern Harbor District was fully developed and equipped with all the infrastructural support, comprising six major sections including KNSM-eiland, Sporenburg, Borneo-eiland, Java-eiland, Oostelijke Handelskade, and Rietlanden. Of these, the Piraeus block and The Whale were developed on the KNSM-eiland and Sporenburg island respectively.

After the Second World War, the Eastern Harbor District began to lose its competitiveness, so the city authorities decided to acquire the district and revealed in their 1978-1982 program that the islands would be redeveloped as a residential area. This initiative was further fleshed out in the Policy Document on Basic Principles on the Amsterdam Eastern Harbor District issued by the City Council in 1985, which coincided with a period of depopulation from the city center and an intense demand for housing. Subsequent urban renewal efforts focused on housing, due in large part to the considerable involvement of the Steering Group for Supplementary Housing.[15] After several iterations, a second policy document was issued and adopted in 1990. Specifically, the basic principles called for the island structure to be the foundation for metropolitan housing and employment, with further specifications demanding the incorporation of parking within the apartment buildings, construction of as many dwelling units as possible that have a clear division between a 'busy' or public side as opposed to a 'quiet' or private side, variation in building heights with most to range between 15 and 25 meters and some high-rise exceptions of up to 60 or even 100 meters, and the recasting of water as a 'recreational element' with the housing. More notably, Amsterdam signed an agreement with the Dutch government where the city would receive 79.6 million Dutch guilders if it managed to construct 5,767 units before 1995, or the equivalent of 100 dwelling units per hectare, half of which was to be market-rate non-subsidized or lightly-subsidized housing as opposed to the conventional social housing provision.[16]

The KNSM-eiland was the first of the docklands in the district to be redeveloped. Two structural layouts were proposed: the first was by Arne van

Herk and Sabine de Kleijn where building strips in an open parcel were to be positioned in relation to the dock; the second was by the Spatial Planning Department (DRO) which promulgated for large, enclosed residential buildings of six to eight storeys in height, opening to views of the water on one side, and to an avenue, plaza, or courtyard on the other.[17] With the City Council in favor of the DRO's proposal, Jo Coenen was commissioned by the Eastern Harbor District project group to elaborate on the structural sketch and to design the master plan in 1989. Drawing upon the monumental character of the KNSM dockland, Coenen bisected the long dockland with a central avenue, the KNSM-laan. Large residential buildings alongside old harbor facilities were located on either side of this axis which terminates on Coenen's own project, the circular residential 'Emerald Empire'.[18]

Coenen's master plan had prescribed the two monumental buildings to be composed of large perimeter blocks with circular courtyards, complete with commercial space, shops, and restaurants along their ground levels. In the case of what was later renamed the Piraeus block, there was also a stipulation by the city to preserve the old KNSM administration building located right at the center of the southern façade. Rather than translating Coenen's vision directly into built form, Kollhoff and Rapp took his plan as a starting point, transforming the monolithic volume submultiples measuring 170 meters long by 60 meters wide into what later became one of the most outstanding and influential buildings in the Eastern Harbor District. Kollhoff and Rapp first did away with the circular courtyard, moulding the limbs instead into folded wings wrapped around the conservation landmark before enjoining the northern length of the block. In making these folds, asymmetrical wedges were cut out from the block, especially along the eastern half of the volume, thereby offering some visual relief from what would have been a monotonous front along the southern edge, while also serving as a spatial funnel guiding pedestrians through a passageway connecting this new block back to KNSM-laan. To preserve the links to the former dockland park to the west, the architects opened up the western edge of the block on the first five storeys, allowing the remaining floors of housing above to float on an arcade of slender columns, thereby maintaining the visual and physical continuity between the park and the open garden within this western half of the volume. Finally, to maximize views on this waterfront site, the architects played with the overall elevations, retaining the maximum height on the northern edge while reducing the height gradually along the western and eastern edges of the block to approximately six storeys on the southern elevation, before dropping down eventually to four storeys at the tail end of the wings tucked back under the opening on the northern edge. In addition, the roofs of the sculptural block were sloped downwards back into the block punctuated by skylights, so as to let sunlight from the south into the courtyard and the units on the top floors, apart from opening up views to the waterfront for the residents in the northern edge.

Constructed primarily with bricks in keeping with the materiality of the small, historic building it wraps around, the massive building is topped with an uninterrupted aluminum roof that further accentuates the coherence of the mega-form but also acts as a reflective surface increasing the diffusion of light within the courtyards. Apart from harkening back to the expressionism embodied by the Amsterdam School of Architecture with their playful use of bricks to create an integrated architectural sculpture, the choice of brick further underscores Kollhoff's belief that "the architecture of the city center needs to look solid".[19] Much as the Piraeus block appears imposing, the introduction of the open courtyard connected to the park on the west, the central passageway, as well as the enclosed courtyard on the east effectively break the scale of the large block, generating instead more intimate spaces within. Further, the dark brick façade is broken up by a rhythmic pattern of light-colored wooden entryways at the street level, constituting the internal system of point-loading that provides access to two apartments per floor. From the fifth storey and above, the building envelope manifests yet another kind of circulation logic within the building: here, access is made possible by elevators that are connected to corridors which are either projected in glazed volumes from the façade, or contained within recessed galleries.

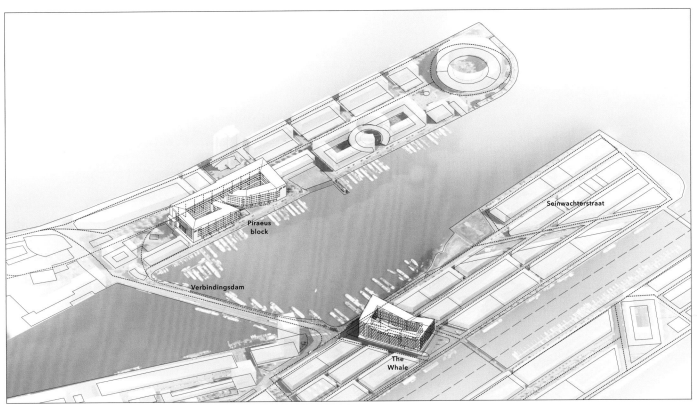

Piraeus
block

Seinwachterstraat

Verbindingsdam

The
Whale

0   25   100 m

PIRAEUS

Java-eiland

KNSM-laan

Levantkade

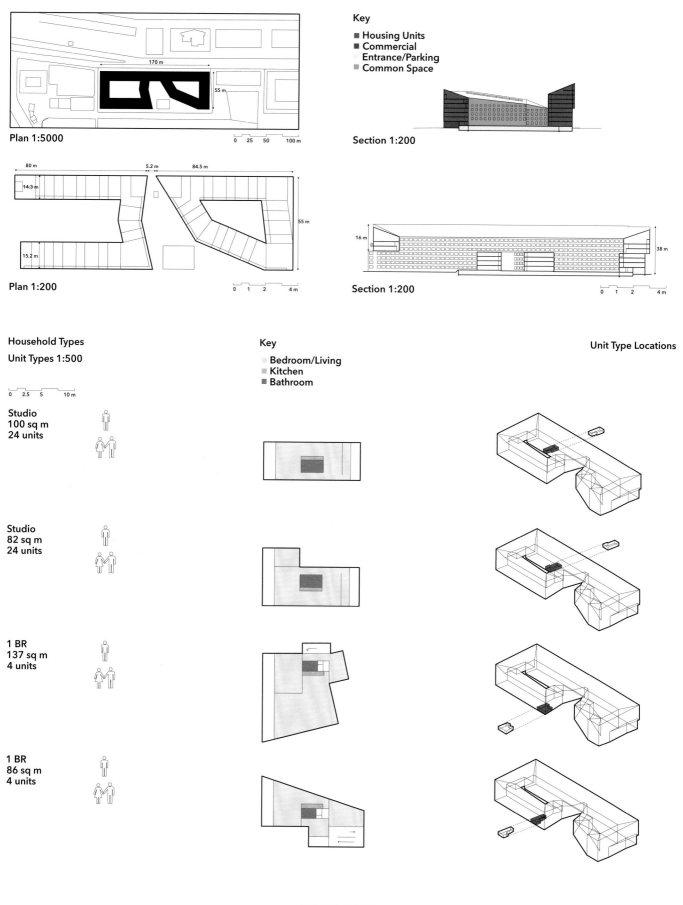

Plan 1:5000

170 m

55 m

0   25   50   100 m

Key

■ Housing Units
■ Commercial
□ Entrance/Parking
▨ Common Space

Section 1:200

80 m   5.2 m   84.5 m

14.3 m

15.2 m

55 m

Plan 1:200

0   1   2   4 m

16 m

38 m

Section 1:200

0   1   2   4 m

Household Types

Unit Types 1:500

0   2.5   5   10 m

Studio
100 sq m
24 units

Studio
82 sq m
24 units

1 BR
137 sq m
4 units

1 BR
86 sq m
4 units

Key

■ Bedroom/Living
■ Kitchen
■ Bathroom

Unit Type Locations

Household Types
Unit Types 1:500

0   2.5   5   10 m

2 BR
118 sq m
16 units

2 BR
149 sq m
4 units

2 BR
115 sq m
4 units

2 BR
98 sq m
12 units

3 BR
135 sq m
3 units

3 BR
174 sq m
4 units

3 BR
159 sq m
5 units

3 BR
120 sq m
16 units

Key
▢ Bedroom/Living
▢ Kitchen
■ Bathroom

Unit Type Locations

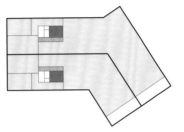
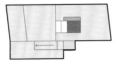
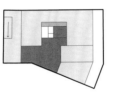
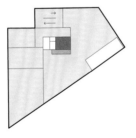

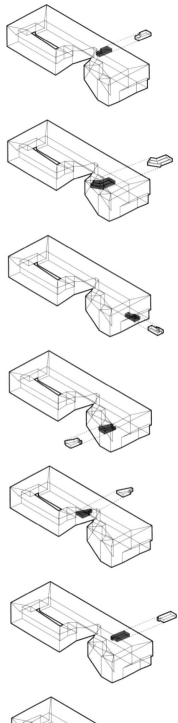

The overall coherence of the Piraeus block and its classical style of straight continuous lines and regularly spaced windows that seem to suggest an internal repetition belies the fact that the building contains an impressive diversity of living units. In total, it houses more than 50 different unit types within 304 rental apartments, varying from studios to three-bedroom apartments, and between 82 to 174 square meters, with a mix of live-work and non-live-work units. The residential density too, not surprisingly, is high at 298 dwelling units per hectare. Within the assortment of unit types, there appears to be a general convergence on a basic type that is rectangular in shape, containing a centralized core of service elements flanked by a living axis and a smaller, secondary service axis, as well as a thickened boundary and a glazed winter garden along the exposed façade. The more unique layouts though arise largely from conditions where the building envelope deviates from the orthogonal, such as the unusual folds in the building, as well as where the sloping roof defines the upper limits of an apartment unit. As the first building to be constructed on KNSM-eiland and completed in 1994, the Piraeus attained a tectonic expression central to Kollhoff's works, and stands as a timeless, civic tribute that also recalls the warehouses of its infrastructural heritage.

Situated directly across the water from the Piraeus block is yet another striking landmark in this Eastern Harbor District – The Whale. Finished in 2000, this housing complex by de Architekten Cie is part of the Borneo-Sporenburg redevelopment that began in 1996, after the completion of KNSM-eiland. The plan called for a low-rise, high-density residential district, on the order of 100 dwelling units per hectare. The Whale is one of three large sculptural blocks or 'meteorites' as they were dubbed by Adriaan Geuze from West 8, that were interdicted within this low-rise milieu in the firm's urban planning vision for the two islands. Together, they were positioned strategically to relate visually to other significant points in the surroundings, including the waterfront and the assertive presence of the Piraeus block. Of the three, only The Whale and the Pacman, located on Borneo island by Koen van Velsen, were materialized; the Fountainhead, designed by Kees Christiaanse, remains un-built. Comprising 150 social housing units and another 64 private apartments for rent, the silver-grey, zinc-clad project rises above a sea of brown brick row houses when viewed from afar.[20] Up close, the block appears to float above the ground. Beginning with the traditional Berlage perimeter block measuring 100 meters by 50 meters and orienting it length-wise in line with the bridge connecting KNSM-eiland and Sporenburg island, Frits van Dongen then played with the design by lifting the shorter widths, giving emphasis to the two opposite corners. This allowed light to enter into the courtyard from these openings, as well as from above, while permitting views out to the water from both ends as well as into the garden within. Moreover, by elevating the two roof corners, a sloping roof was generated, corresponding to the sun angles at their highest and lowest points.

Designed by West 8, the small courtyard garden continues the silver-grey piscine theme through the placement of four free-standing 18-foot-tall zinc vases along a path laid with Norwegian slate, set within a manicured lawn interspersed with several geometrically-shaped hedges and Gingko trees. Unlike the open courtyards of the Piraeus, this enclosure at The Whale is only visually accessible, meant clearly for viewing and contemplation rather than for occupation and interaction. The ground floor of the project is lined with commercial premises, distinguished from the residential apartments above with their floor-to-ceiling glazed façades. Access to the apartments is limited to the two glass stairways at the base of the building's lifted corners, connected by L-shaped,

or straight, horizontal galleries that alternate between the even- and the odd-numbered floors, and every other floor is linked by a secondary system of stairs grafted to the exterior of the building within the courtyard. These galleries and railings are covered in warm larch wood, contrasting with the cool, metallic finish of the external fenestration with its uniform bands of windows that alternate every other floor. In terms of unit variation, The Whale has a smaller range compared to the Piraeus block, with several standard plans that line the center of each side, and the corners as well as the top levels under the sloped roof and soffit planes occupied by deviations from the norm, including larger units and duplexes. The units are generally divided length-wise in their spatial organization into a living axis as well as a secondary service axis; the bathrooms are typically located in the center of the units, with the kitchen adjacent or right across an internal corridor. Each unit is dual aspect and no more than 14 meters deep, offering views to both the courtyard and the surroundings but also returning again to the fundamental design principle of bringing plenty of light into dwellings. While it does not share the same degree of unit diversity as the Piraeus block, The Whale does accommodate an even higher residential density of 428 dwelling units per hectare.

THE WHALE

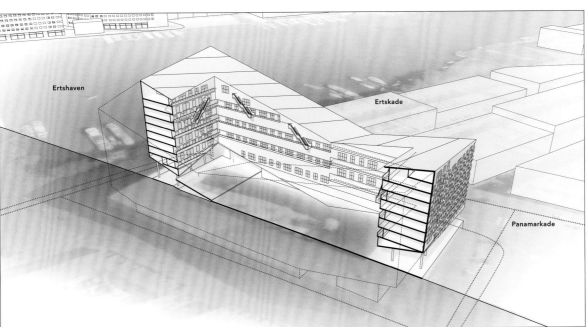

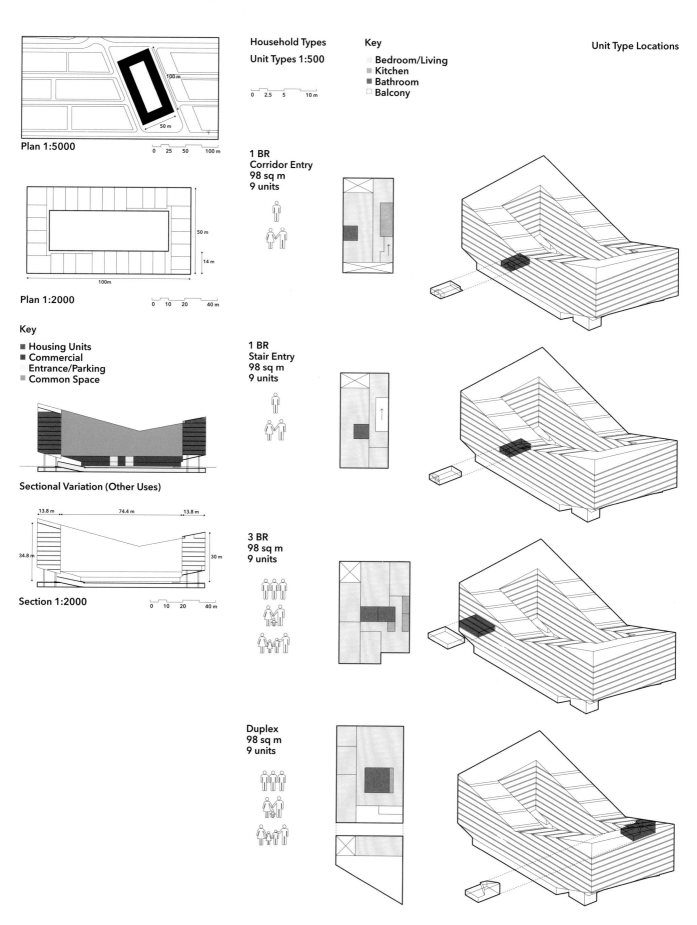

Household Types
Unit Types 1:500

Key
▢ Bedroom/Living
▪ Kitchen
■ Bathroom
▢ Balcony

Unit Type Locations

Plan 1:5000

0   25   50   100 m

Plan 1:2000

0   10   20   40 m

Key
■ Housing Units
■ Commercial
▢ Entrance/Parking
▨ Common Space

Sectional Variation (Other Uses)

Section 1:2000

0   10   20   40 m

1 BR
Corridor Entry
98 sq m
9 units

1 BR
Stair Entry
98 sq m
9 units

3 BR
98 sq m
9 units

Duplex
98 sq m
9 units

An iconic submultiple that represents an experiment in generating diversity of unit types taken to a whole other level is the 8 Tallet project by Bjarke Ingels Group (BIG) completed in 2010. Unlike the brownfield redevelopments undertaken in the two examples above, this project was constructed on a greenfield site in Ørestad, a new five-kilometer strip of development in southern Copenhagen between the historic city and the Kalvebod Fælled (Common) nature reserve. Just 10 minutes to the city center by metro, Ørestad was planned as Copenhagen's 'sixth finger' of urban growth in 1994, and is expected to accommodate 20,000 residents and 60,000 to 80,000 employees by the time it is completely built out.[21] Intended to support a highly diverse population as reflected by the range of large and small dwellings in apartment complexes alongside of student dormitories, residence halls, and housing for the elderly, Ørestad was envisioned as a dense,

mixed-use, live-work urban quarter with adequate public infrastructure and transit services, and easy access to nature. The master plan for the district was won by a Danish-Finnish studio named ARKKI which subdivided the long strip into four smaller districts, threaded together by a system of canals and waterways as well as the Vestamager metro line that opened early on in 2002 when the districts were under construction. From the outset, the competition brief stipulated "full artistic freedom concerning architectural form, so that the new city quarter… will boast state-of-the-art within architecture and art".[22] Considerable attention was thus paid to design and constructing buildings of outstanding architectural quality through the engagement of both Danish and international architects who were commissioned to undertake projects in a district conceived to be a contemporary, lively, and attractive neighborhood.

In 2006, St. Frederikslund Holding and Høpfner Projects Ltd commissioned the BIG team to design what was then Denmark's largest private residential development at the very edge of the nature reserve. In particular, this was a collaboration initiated by Per Høpfner who had already formed a working partnership with Bjarke Ingels dating back to two earlier projects also in the Ørestad – the V & M Houses, and the Mountain House – which were designed by PLOT before Ingels and Julien De Smedt parted ways. As at The Whale, the BIG team started with a 10-storey, 230 meters by 110 meters perimeter block. Rather than adhering to the conventional Danish treatment where the variation on the façade is produced as a serial permutation of different waterfront row houses, the team decided instead to stack the functions: they began with a commercial base, followed by a layer of row houses as a modern interpretation of the traditional *kartoffelrækkerne* or 'potato rows' of townhouses with private gardens, another layer of apartments, and finally a tier of penthouses topped by a complete green roof meant to reduce the urban heat-island effect while blending the massive development with its natural environs. This stacking of programs is expressed on the building's eastern façade, where the glazed commercial layer is topped by three aluminum bands in different shades of grey. A pedestrian pathway connects the Richard Mortensens Vej road west of the complex across a canal to the Hein Heinsens Square on the east, and at the point where this pathway intersects with the block, the team introduced a knot, resulting in the figure of '8' that became a defining feature of the project. Next, several push-and-pull operations were conducted to merge the ground floor commercial units with the street, maximize solar insolation into the two internal courtyards, as well as to create a slope on the south-western edges of the block to maximize views to the water body and the nature reserve beyond. Anchoring the south-western corner of the complex is a popular café servicing the residents and visitors, while the rest of the commercial space is given over to offices, a small grocery store, as well as a childcare center, creating a submultiple with integration of housing and community services.

From Ingels' perspective, 8 Tallet was designed to be a "three-dimensional neighborhood rather than an architectural object… [w]here social life, the spontaneous encounter, and neighbor interaction traditionally… restricted to the ground level" is allowed to "expand all the way to the top".[23] This 'three-dimensional' character of the project takes its form in two key spatial operations: first, the strata of some 150 *kartoffelrækkerne* townhouses that stretched continuously in a loop from the street level up to four or five storeys above ground and back down again; and second, a public path wide enough to accommodate pedestrians and cyclists that winds alongside this townhouse configuration, simulating the sense of an elevated street and sidewalk section that concomitantly maximizes views of the lush reserve and the interior courtyards. The project was similarly very intentional in its landscaping design, creating two contrasting gardens. The smaller, northern courtyard is composed of circular mounds and several trees surrounded by gravel, intimating the topographical elevations generated by the building structure itself. In comparison, the southern courtyard is more expansive, framed by the two green slopes converging upon the café at the south-western corner; the circulation access is demarcated by a black-tiled foot and bicycle path winding around the irregularly-shaped geometrical lawns that are gently terraced for a variety of outdoor activities. Housing a total of 476 dwelling units, ranging from studios to two- to six-room configurations, this submultiple offers a variety of residences with amenities for people in different life stages. Each of these room configurations is no more than 12 meters deep with dual aspect, and they have their own assortment of unit types, amounting to more than 45 different unit variations cleverly disguised in a seemingly straightforward envelope. This extremely high degree of unit diversity stems from the architect's desire to "offer not one, but many possibilities" of living.[24] Area-wise, these units range from 58 square meters to 175 square meters, all of which are relatively commodious in their space provisions. Besides this exceptional degree of diversity, 8 Tallet was also successful in creating a dense live-work environment, attaining a residential density of 188 dwelling units per hectare.

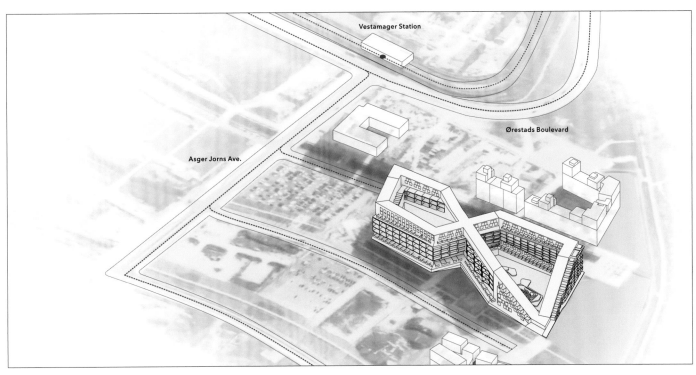

Vestamager Station

Ørestads Boulevard

Asger Jorns Ave.

0   25   100 m

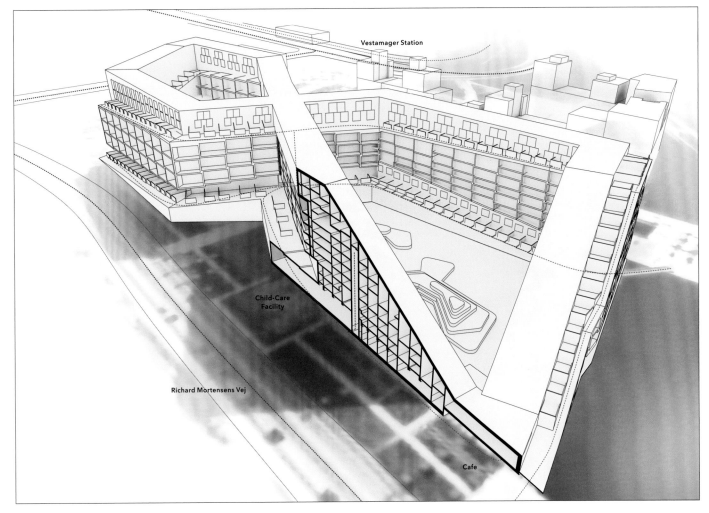

Vestamager Station

Child-Care
Facility

Richard Mortensens Vej

Cafe

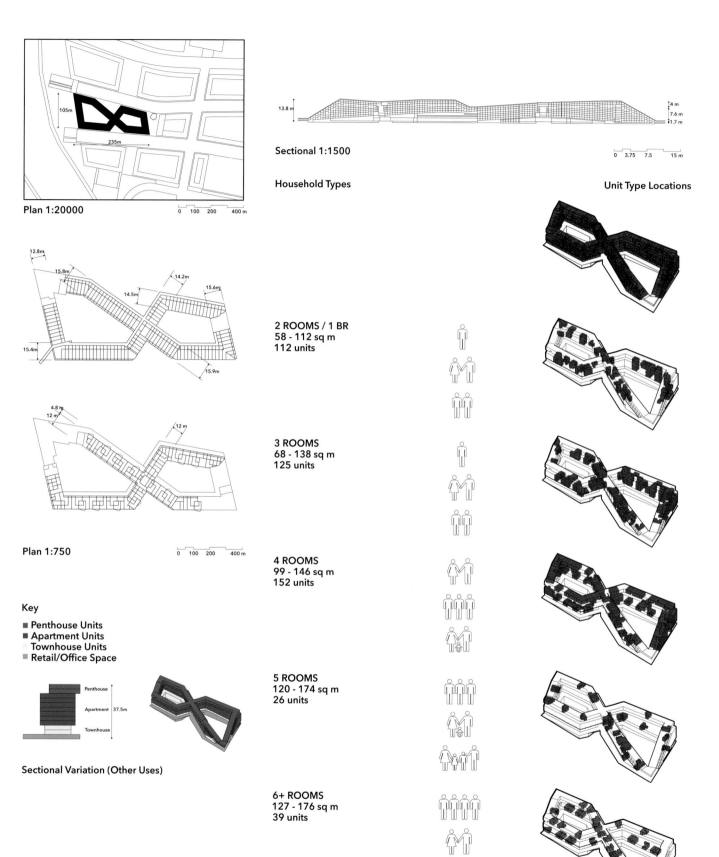

Plan 1:20000

0   100   200   400 m

Sectional 1:1500

0   3.75   7.5   15 m

Household Types

Unit Type Locations

Plan 1:750

0   100   200   400 m

Key

■ Penthouse Units
■ Apartment Units
□ Townhouse Units
■ Retail/Office Space

Penthouse
Apartment   37.5m
Townhouse

Sectional Variation (Other Uses)

2 ROOMS / 1 BR
58 - 112 sq m
112 units

3 ROOMS
68 - 138 sq m
125 units

4 ROOMS
99 - 146 sq m
152 units

5 ROOMS
120 - 174 sq m
26 units

6+ ROOMS
127 - 176 sq m
39 units

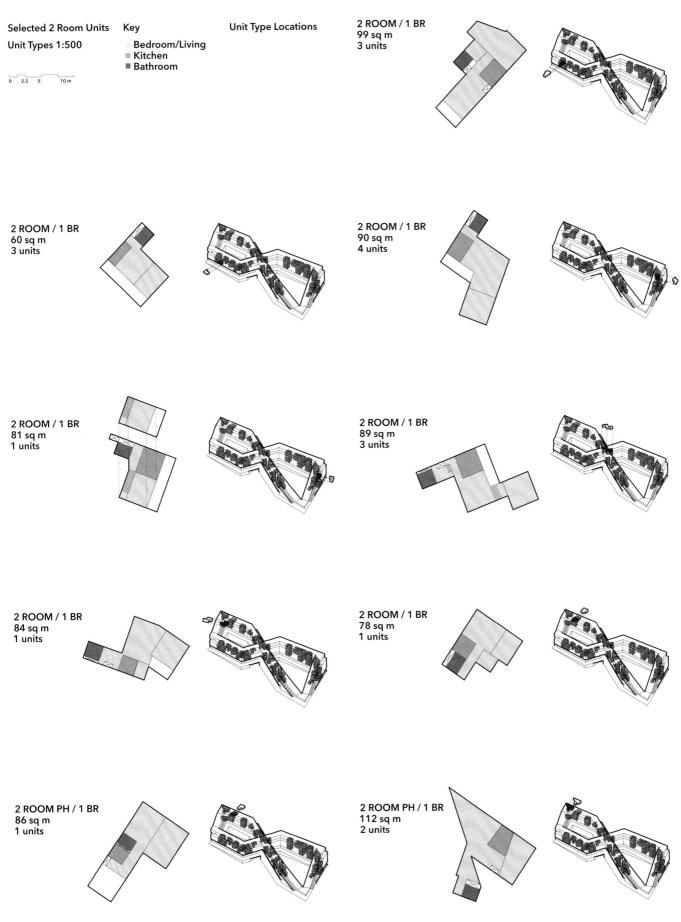

Selected 2 Room Units
Unit Types 1:500

Key
　Bedroom/Living
■ Kitchen
■ Bathroom

Unit Type Locations

2 ROOM / 1 BR
99 sq m
3 units

2 ROOM / 1 BR
60 sq m
3 units

2 ROOM / 1 BR
90 sq m
4 units

2 ROOM / 1 BR
81 sq m
1 units

2 ROOM / 1 BR
89 sq m
3 units

2 ROOM / 1 BR
84 sq m
1 units

2 ROOM / 1 BR
78 sq m
1 units

2 ROOM PH / 1 BR
86 sq m
1 units

2 ROOM PH / 1 BR
112 sq m
2 units

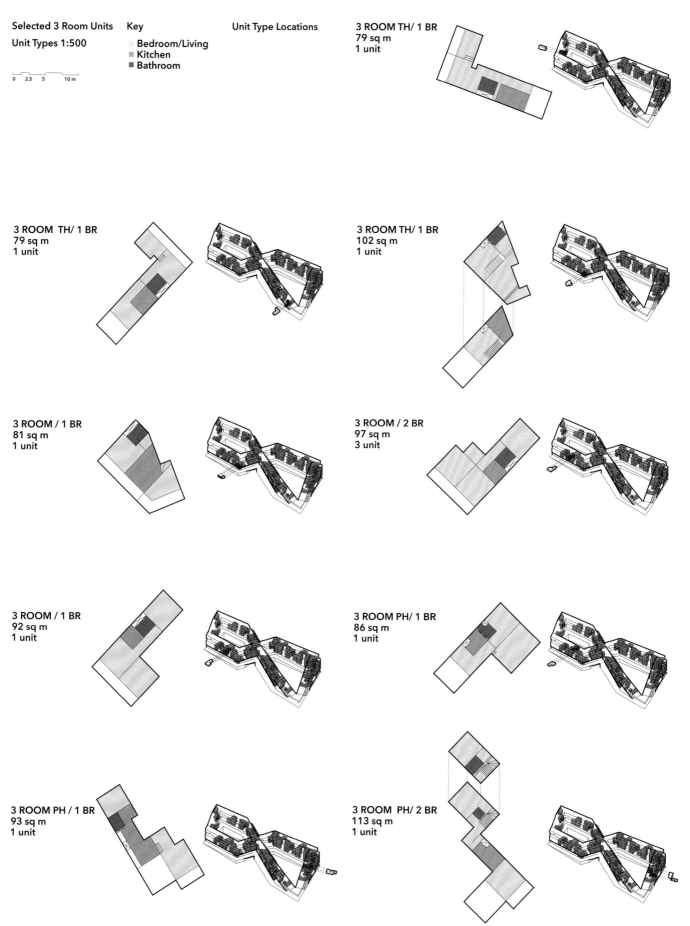

Selected 3 Room Units
Unit Types 1:500

Key
□ Bedroom/Living
■ Kitchen
■ Bathroom

Unit Type Locations

0 2.5 5   10 m

3 ROOM TH/ 1 BR
79 sq m
1 unit

3 ROOM TH/ 1 BR
79 sq m
1 unit

3 ROOM TH/ 1 BR
102 sq m
1 unit

3 ROOM / 1 BR
81 sq m
1 unit

3 ROOM / 2 BR
97 sq m
3 unit

3 ROOM / 1 BR
92 sq m
1 unit

3 ROOM PH/ 1 BR
86 sq m
1 unit

3 ROOM PH / 1 BR
93 sq m
1 unit

3 ROOM PH/ 2 BR
113 sq m
1 unit

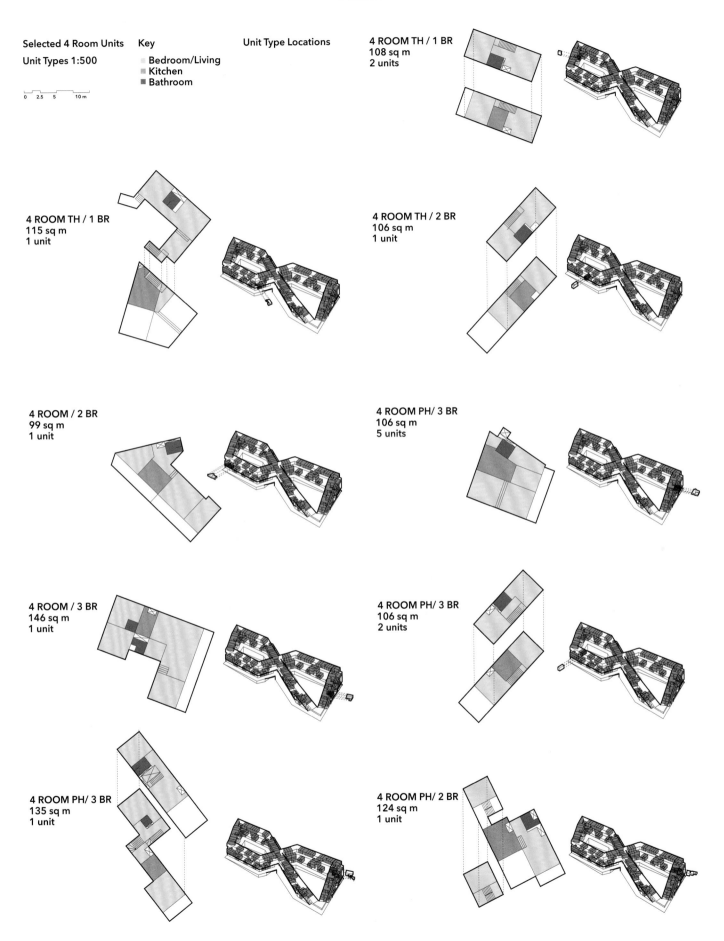

Selected 4 Room Units
Unit Types 1:500

Key
- Bedroom/Living
- Kitchen
- Bathroom

Unit Type Locations

0   2.5   5   10 m

4 ROOM TH / 1 BR
108 sq m
2 units

4 ROOM TH / 1 BR
115 sq m
1 unit

4 ROOM TH / 2 BR
106 sq m
1 unit

4 ROOM / 2 BR
99 sq m
1 unit

4 ROOM PH/ 3 BR
106 sq m
5 units

4 ROOM / 3 BR
146 sq m
1 unit

4 ROOM PH/ 3 BR
106 sq m
2 units

4 ROOM PH/ 3 BR
135 sq m
1 unit

4 ROOM PH/ 2 BR
124 sq m
1 unit

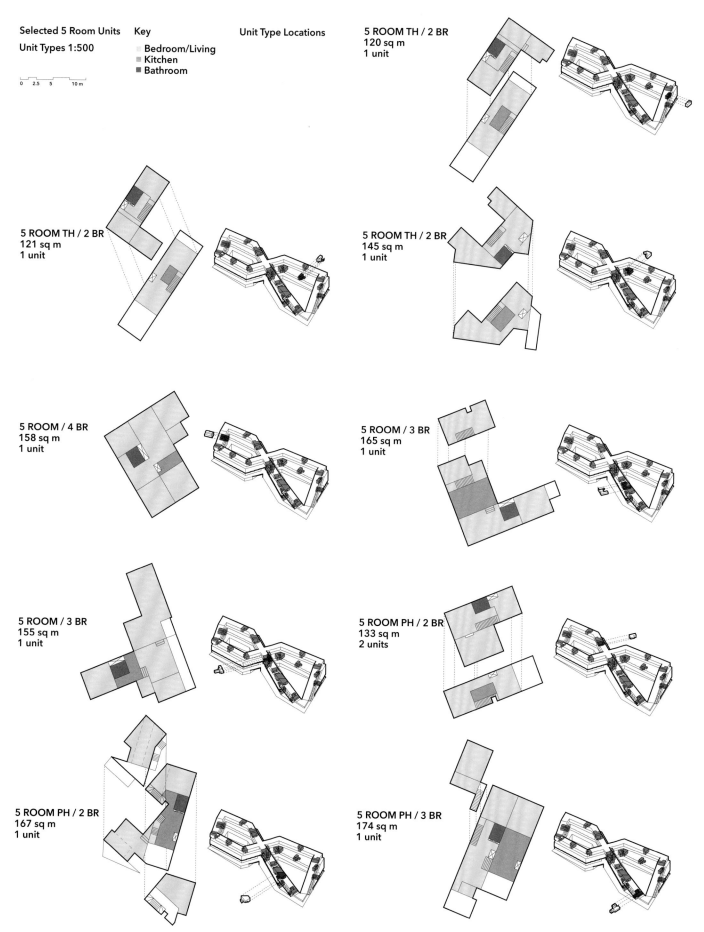

Selected 5 Room Units
Unit Types 1:500

Key
Bedroom/Living
Kitchen
Bathroom

Unit Type Locations

0 2.5 5   10 m

5 ROOM TH / 2 BR
120 sq m
1 unit

5 ROOM TH / 2 BR
121 sq m
1 unit

5 ROOM TH / 2 BR
145 sq m
1 unit

5 ROOM / 4 BR
158 sq m
1 unit

5 ROOM / 3 BR
165 sq m
1 unit

5 ROOM / 3 BR
155 sq m
1 unit

5 ROOM PH / 2 BR
133 sq m
2 units

5 ROOM PH / 2 BR
167 sq m
1 unit

5 ROOM PH / 3 BR
174 sq m
1 unit

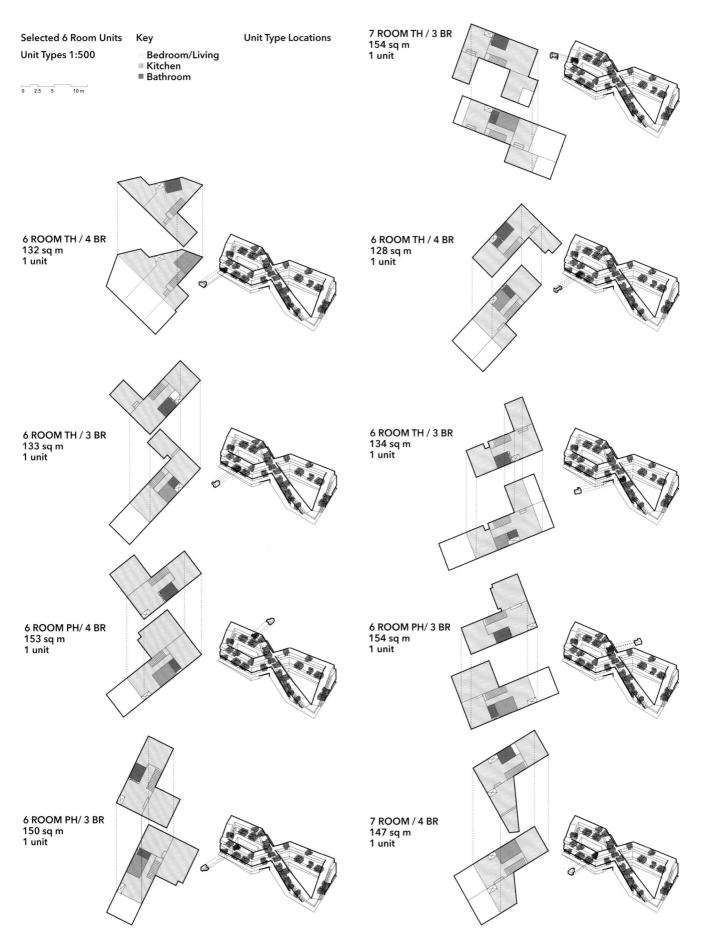

Selected 6 Room Units
Unit Types 1:500

Key
- Bedroom/Living
- Kitchen
- Bathroom

Unit Type Locations

0   2.5   5   10 m

7 ROOM TH / 3 BR
154 sq m
1 unit

6 ROOM TH / 4 BR
132 sq m
1 unit

6 ROOM TH / 4 BR
128 sq m
1 unit

6 ROOM TH / 3 BR
133 sq m
1 unit

6 ROOM TH / 3 BR
134 sq m
1 unit

6 ROOM PH/ 4 BR
153 sq m
1 unit

6 ROOM PH/ 3 BR
154 sq m
1 unit

6 ROOM PH/ 3 BR
150 sq m
1 unit

7 ROOM / 4 BR
147 sq m
1 unit

8 TALLET

COMMUNITY AND BALANCES AMONG RESIDENTIAL AND OTHER FACTORS

Looking across this material depicting big buildings as submultiples in the pursuit of housing communities, several common issues are present. The first involves striking an appropriate balance among residential and related functions. A core idea of the submultiple typology is an alignment between dwelling and its necessary and desirable non-residential services and suppliers at convenient scales and eases of access. One advantage, in these regards, of big buildings is that they can readily allow for physical proximity and connection within a single facility. A disadvantage is that the scale and number of supporting non-residential facilities can be limited in physical terms to the geometry and scale of the residential aspect of big buildings. In short, footprints, modes of access, and orientations often do not readily match. Also, the inherently deterministic approach used in the development of many big building submultiples can be roundly criticized by simple observations: just because a certain number of dwelling units is sufficient to support a particular facility does not mean that all people in the building will use the facility. On the contrary, the more isolated the facility is from other similar facilities, the less likely it is to survive. Nevertheless, in the relative absence of this determinism in today's housing environments, it is an open question what is in a big building serving as a submultiple of a non-strictly residential nature. Or to put it the other way around, especially in relatively undeveloped sites either inside or on the edge of urban areas, it is what is *not* in the big building at the public street level that can present problems of convenience and real neighborly community use.

A second issue involves big buildings and the accommodation of different dwelling unit types. This concerns circumstances of assemblage and how to achieve a certain sense of wholeness alongside of diversity in accommodation. Here, at least four different strategies can be observed. First, and especially in the case of the Unités, relatively generous provision of interlocking and double-height dwelling spaces subject to internal subdivision was combined with insertion of non-residential uses at lower, interlocking, and upper building levels. A result was an ensemble of units and service functions that had a distinct and rather straightforward unity. A second approach involved segmentation of housing into slabs and towers, interlocked and conjoined with other and non-residential facilities. This was particularly apparent in many of the Italian big buildings and submultiples. A third strategy involved differentiation and then integration of units and other functions such that distinct housing types were assembled next to or above and below one another and then tied into relatively unitary schemes, with non-residential functions planned at upper, intermediate, and lower levels. Both 8 Tallet and Via Verde have these characteristics about them. Then finally, there are the more fully inter-mixed deployments of dwelling unit types with variations occurring at relatively close and sometimes regular intervals, all within an otherwise strongly defined building envelope. Throughout, the quality of results seems to depend strongly on the sectional development of the big building, particularly with regard to unit locations, access, intermediary non-residential space inclusions, and the use of residual conditions of stacking and sideways assemblage for particular purposes like terraces, arcades, rooftop gardens, and the like.

A third issue is the making of a distinctly recognizable civic and public space and even one that stands in its representational significance above or outside of its immediate residential environment. As with Rossi and Pouillon and their uses of loggias, galleries, and arcades, this can be accomplished in a monumental manner, or at least in a form that is clearly civic-minded in appearance. It can also be accomplished via well-shaped and developed community and public courtyard spaces as in the Piraeus and The Whale in Holland. In addition, the magnification of a common feature related to dwelling, like its ancillary landscape, can be accomplished to register a community and even civic presence. This is clearly on display at Via Verde in the Bronx of New York City and at 8 Tallet in Copenhagen with cascading gardens and earthworks. Especially at the scale of more or less the equivalent of a neighborhood in a single building, some sense of a collective civic identity seems to be warranted, sometimes if not often complicating the search for an architectural solution for something that has become more than simply a building.

INFRA STRUCTURAL ENGAGE MENTS

As used here, 'infrastructural engagements' are rather more territorial than they are about housing and building types *per se*, even though they involve housing and some presence of infrastructure in a manner that has a shaping influence on the housing. The term 'infrastructure' has a multitude of uses but generally refers to installations that are necessary for the functioning of some undertaking, even if they are subordinate to that undertaking and, etymologically, 'below' that undertaking. Apparently, the term first entered the English language in 1927 although in a direct connection with prior French usage that had been around since the latter part of the nineteenth century, referring to rails, bridges, and tunnels or the subgrade of French railroads.[1] In the context of this book, 'infrastructural engagements' refer to at least three kinds of housing conditions. The first is where housing comes to occupy the sites of infrastructure from a former time, such as abandoned railroad yards, disused shipyards and port facilities and, potentially, moribund airports. Aspects of these engagements shaping housing are sometimes dimensional and concerned, for instance, with widths of wharves and dimensional characteristics of rail sidings, along with the manner in which these aspects are reflected in housing form. Also at stake can be the relative prominence of a former infrastructural site in a city, such as along a waterfront, and issues of public access and use together with the priority and position of housing in that cause. Technical concerns with remediation of brownfield sites and related foundational capacities may also bear on what can be housed appropriately. The second kind of infrastructural engagement is when a local element of infrastructure, such as a road or utility improvement, is manifest in an overt expressive fashion within the housing complex. This immediately raises the issue of how and why this was done, especially returning to the earlier definitions of infrastructure as being somehow less visible. Finally, the third kind of infrastructural engagement concerns housing alongside of particular infrastructure in a manner of mutual dependency. This can involve both infrastructure in support of undertakings involving housing and *vice versa*, housing taking advantage of particular infrastructural alignments and other related circumstances. Often in each instance, the impetus shaping housing derives from the precise point and style of contextual engagement.

PRECEDENTS: DIRECT ENGAGEMENTS AND REIFICATIONS

Relatively early on in Japan's and Tokyo's process of modernization direct engagement between railroad infrastructure and housing was a significant component of urban expansion. The circumferential Yamanote line that roughly circumscribed the 23 inner-city wards of Tokyo was completed by Japan Rail – the national rail company – by 1919. Urban expansion beyond was accelerated in the wake of the disastrous Kantō earthquake of 1923 and often took the unusual form of real estate companies and promoters going into the railroad business in order to make their suburban sites more accessible and, therefore, more attractive. This applied to both residential as well as to retail commercial markets still visible today with the naming of subway lines according to retail chains like Tōkyū. Amid these developments, Shibusawa Eiichi founded his Garden City Corporation in 1918 with the aim of demonstrating the efficacy of Garden City principles in the urbanization of Tokyo.[2] This non-profit corporation purchased 405 hectares of land near the Tama River to the south and west of central Tokyo for which a plan for Denenchōfu, as the development was called, emerged in 1924. The project was targeted towards middle-class homebuyers and consisted of sites mainly for single-family dwellings on relatively large lots and within a street pattern that radiated out from the more or less central location of a railroad station on the Meguro-kamata line. Overall, accommodation was to be provided for 30,000 inhabitants, consistent with Garden City principles of founders like Ebenezer Howard and Raymond Unwin. Adjacent to the station, non-residential functions were conveniently located around a village-like semi-circular plaza. Incorporation of the project had to await completion of the railway link, which in turn was slowed by the calamitous aftermath of the Kantō earthquake. Guidelines for the residences, constructed mainly at the behest of individual homeowners, included stipulations about minimizing disturbance to neighbors, building to land cover ratios of less than 50 percent, constructing structures of no more than three storeys in height, accommodating street to building setbacks of around half the width of the street, and conforming to minimum cost requirements in order to further maintain a high quality of development. Styles of houses ranged from Taishō period hybrids, to teahouse style, and even to overtly western pre-modern references. Today, Denenchōfu has become denser by way of building occupation, as smaller houses have been added to or demolished and replaced by larger dwellings. Nevertheless, much of the earlier vegetated character and quiet neighborhood feel has been preserved.

Housing responding in the opposite direction, namely to the opportunities presented by infrastructure investments, like railroads, are far more common and generally follow, in the density and type of configuration, relationships corresponding roughly to 'highest and best use' of land based on accessibility. One such project is housing associated with Euralille, France,[3] under a plan prepared by OMA around 1994 in association with Lille becoming the pivot point for high-speed trains (TGV) from the north-east of the

Denenchōfu

Euralille, from *El Croquis* (No. 88-89 1998) p.109

Byker Redevelopment

continent and from across the Channel in England. Essentially Euralille was a specially-chartered company as a public-private enterprise and the project site was located on the western side of the city among an *ad hoc* arrangement of buildings around the *périphérique* of Lille. The basic components of the project were accommodations for the TVG station, 45,000 square meters of office space, 31,000 square meters of shopping, a 10-hectare park, three hotels, and 700 apartments. The housing component is located adjacent to the Euralille Center, a complex that combines most of the other programmatic elements of the overall project into a more or less singular project of tower blocks interlocked with the sprawling mass of shopping and entertainment venues. In fact, it is directly next to and otherwise extends existing housing into the Euralille site. The first phase of the housing is by Xaveer de Geyter and covers 13 hectares in the form of low- to mid-rise slab blocks that respect the location of existing vegetation and other building envelope constraints. The parallel linear arrays of housing also incorporate a variety of courtyard and other community open spaces across the ground plane. A second phase of housing has been proposed to the south-east of the station by Leclercq and Dusapin, rounding out the dwelling unit total. Again, it is being built in response to the opportunity presented by the infrastructure and other improvements, rather than the other way around as in Japan.

Manifestation of the literal presence of an infrastructural element in conjunction with housing occurred with the so-called 'wall' component of the Byker Redevelopment in Newcastle-upon-Tyne of 1969 through 1982, mentioned earlier. As described, the issue at hand was audial and visual screening

of a motorway that was planned to pass along the northern edge of the project. It also provided spatial enclosure to the Byker community and evoked a certain recall of a Roman wall that allegedly had been built in the general area during antiquity. As it turned out, the motorway was never built, but its anticipation in the Kendall neighborhood of the community led to the architectural reification of the line of the roadway improvement.[4] Designed by Ralph Erskine with Roger Tillotson and Vernon Gracie, the Byker Wall also housed the existing Shipley Baths and a church from the prior era. In common with other non-residential facilities of the old neighborhood, these functions were preserved, improved, and incorporated into the overall scheme of the Byker. Rising some eight storeys in height, the 'wall' component functioned as a big building submultiple on a 1.82-hectare site, incorporating 212 dwelling units and a density of close to 400 people per hectare. Although relatively blank on the outside 'motorway' aspect of the project, open balconies, terraces, and walkways across the façade facing out towards the Tyne River offered superb views and a sunlit dwelling environment. Bridges extending from the wall to adjacent so-called 'link units' also extended the infrastructural aspect of the project into other parts of the scheme, running downhill towards the river. Open space next to and nearby the 'wall' also offered a variety of private and community-oriented garden conditions.

Another example of the overt manifestation of infrastructures occurred at the Malagueira Quarter housing project by Álvaro Siza, dating from 1977, in Évora in central Portugal. Built on the site of the Quinta da Malagueira, a former *latifundia* estate, the quarter was a part of the municipal government's

Malagueira Quarter

Battery Park City

low-cost housing program, including accommodation for a local gypsy population. It also coincided with efforts to better integrate peripheral zones of cities in Portugal with surrounding areas. Covering some 27 hectares, the project was comprised of around 1,200 dwelling units in total, divided into blocks of about 100 units, with parallel linear arrangements of attached courtyard houses and also including a modest array of community facilities and public open space.[5] The reified infrastructural element of the project took the form of large rectilinear utility ducts constructed from concrete blocks and spanning between one-storey-high supports. These elements, in turn, linked various blocks of houses together, as well as providing a palpable backbone to the courtyard houses themselves, set on small lots of around 96 square meters each. In the context of this kind of evolutionary housing, which could be added on to over time, the infrastructural ducts provided both a sense of completion to the project along with a sense of community identity as well as formal order in the surrounding landscape. Far from being unusual in the setting of Évora and its countryside, they also referenced the aqueducts in the former Roman town itself, as well as the later eighteenth-century versions that criss-cross the agricultural estates outside. Housing ranged from single- to double-storey units with courts to the front or rear, constructed of concrete block, poured-in-place slabs and white stucco finish. Relatively narrow yet well-scaled streets also provided a sense of familiarity with nearby earlier informal settlements. Also, with a residential density of 75 units per hectare, or 300 people per hectare, the project was relatively dense for low-rise construction.

With regard to infrastructural engagements, concerned with occupation of sites of former infra-structural improvements, there are, of course, many precedents in various parts of the world. These could include the Charlestown Navy Yard housing in Boston, Massachusetts, parts of the Docklands in East London, and even Battery Park City in New York. In addition to replacing the finger wharves that extended into the Hudson River on Lower Manhattan's west side, the last project also involved landfill to fully create the site, taken largely from the excavations of the World Trade Center Towers built in 1973. The plan that was implemented was by Cooper & Eckstut in 1979 and extended the roadway infrastructure of the city into the landfilled site, culminating in a well-amenitized pedestrian promenade along the riverfront of the project.[6] High-rise in character, the built fabric, consisting mainly of housing, conforms to the street pattern and offers extraordinary views towards New Jersey in a manner reminiscent of New York's earlier tall buildings discussed in a prior chapter.

CONTEMPORARY CASES: RE-OCCUPATION OF URBAN SITES

The docklands of Amsterdam also offered an opportunity for the city to reclaim the prime waterfront site, for the importance of the local shipping industry had been declining for years. Besides the Borneo Sporenburg project, which was briefly discussed as part of the Eastern Harbor District redevelopment in the previous chapter, an earlier example that later became influential was the IJ-Plein by OMA, designed between 1980 and 1982, and completed in 1988. Located across the Het IJ from Amsterdam's historic center and the Eastern Harbor District (Oostelijk

127

Havengebied), the site was a former shipyard right at the tip of the industrial district known as Amsterdam-Noord. Prior to the 1900s, Amsterdam-Noord was not considered an official part of Amsterdam city; its administrative recognition and emergence at the turn of the twentieth century was associated with the concentration of industries, particularly those related to shipping, resulting in its growth as a working-class, industrial area. The area's fortunes changed, however, after the Second World War and during the latter half of the twentieth century with the beginnings of de-industrialization and the city's diminishing role as a major shipping port.

With the closure of the west harbor division of the Amsterdam Dry Dock Company that had occupied the site right at the tip of Amsterdam-Noord bordering the IJ, a window of opportunity presented itself for the construction of the IJ-Plein, the first housing project in the district to recover the waterfront, a significant change of orientation for a city that had essentially turned its back to the harbor for most of the nineteenth and twentieth centuries. In fact, as early as 1974, the city had revealed its plans to convert the shipyard and the IJ-Plein and its environs into a new residential sub-centre for the city, under the direction of the Stuurgroep Aanvullende Woningbouw or Steering Group for Supplementary Housing which played a central role in urban renewal.[7] The land itself was acquired by the city government, which thus maintained the powers to strategically determine the use, quality, and amount of land available for development. Thereafter, the city's Department of Town and Country Planning (DRO) designed a plan in 1980 for the redevelopment of the IJ-Plein, composed primarily of five-storey closed perimeter residential blocks arrayed across the site. Unfortunately, the scheme was not well received by the Amsterdam-Noord inhabitants who demanded unobstructed views of the IJ and the historic city. It was at this juncture that Rem Koolhaas and OMA were appointed by the Public Housing Department to serve as a 'conditioning architect', mediating between the DRO and the various architects who would be involved in different sections of the plan, but more significantly, to devise an improved plan.[8] Koolhaas and OMA first assumed a brainstorming session where 25 different housing typologies, ranging from Le Corbusier's *Ville*

contemporaine and *Unité d'habitation* to Cerdà's Plan for the Extension of Barcelona, were tested out on the site, on the assumption that there were no limiting constraints, so as to figure out how the same number of dwelling units could be accommodated within the various models.[9] Initial design sketches that followed revealed the team's preoccupation to extend the visual axis from the Meeuwenlaan road meandering along the edge to the water, effectively dividing the site into two. In addition, the team proposed for land reclamation to be undertaken in filling the shape of the dock to increase the available land area for development. In this preliminary plan, the eastern, triangular-shaped section was to be composed of low-rise buildings in open blocks, whereas the western section was intended to be a dense cluster of high-rises, separated from the eastern half by a park that served as a visual corridor. The park was to be situated above the newly-reclaimed land, thereby preserving part of the original form of the site. Spanning across the three sections was an east-west axis to link them together.

The neighboring residents, however, vetoed the high-rise element of OMA's initial proposal, prompting the team to revise the western section based on the model by the Luckhardt brothers in Berlin during the 1920s for a '*Stadt ohne Höfe*' or 'City without Courtyards'; such a model consists of low- to mid-rise bars flanked by urban villas. Further, with the IJ-tunnel running under the western section, the team had to ensure that construction above grade along this infrastructural right-of-way was minimized.[10] The final master plan was composed in the form of a montage, setting out parallel bars of housing in the eastern section, with a triangular open space in the center, while the western section was a mixture of urban villas arranged in bands alongside the two longer bars. Diverging from these vertical striations were horizontal slabs raised on *pilotis* straddling across at the southern edge of the triangular park on the eastern half, oriented towards central Amsterdam. To attain a certain degree of formal coherence for the district, OMA established a set of urban design guidelines that intervened using a zoning envelope, stipulating the circulatory access to the residents, down to details like establishing the color of the façades and the materials.[11] In total, 1,375 units of social housing were accommodated on the 17-hectare site, equivalent to a relatively low density of 81 units per hectare, supported by shops, a school, community center, and a variety of public green spaces. Apart from the two slender bars defining the eastern edge of the site and the public school along the waterfront that were designed by OMA, the rest of the buildings were commissioned to a cast of different architects, including Bureau Hein van Meer which designed three of the urban villas, Architectengroep 69 which designed the horizontal slab, and Bureau Budding en Wilken that designed the Youth Center adjacent to Meeuwenlaan and the bright-orange pavilion by the water's edge.

Of the pair of parallel blocks by OMA, the longer slab with a built area of 11,860 square meters is raised on *pilotis*, underneath which is tucked an assortment of programs, including a market and a community center, each of which is housed in a triangular structure, shops which are accommodated in two glazed oval structures, bicycle parking, and lobby entrances to the apartments above. Moreover, by opening up the ground level of the slab, the street is allowed to pass underneath the building, creating more open space at this level, rather than acting like a wall-like barrier enclosing the perimeter. Vehicular parking is provided for by the space in front of the slab, running alongside the marina where boats are docked. Although the building bears a formal vocabulary similar to the rest of the blocks with its flat roof, strip windows, and stuccoed treatment, the interior circulation showcases an ingenious way of producing unit variation through the deployment of different stair systems. Besides the apparent use of metal-clad switch-back stairs that grace the structure where the ground level is free, providing access to units with balconies supported by perforated steel columns rising four-storeys above the ground, OMA also incorporated two other systems. One is the conventional galleries accessed by two stairway cores, used for the single-loaded narrow 'HAT units', as they were dubbed, along the northernmost third of the bar. The other is a transverse system of cascading stairs used for accessing the one- and two-bedroom units at the southernmost third of the bar, where the unusual section cuts generated a layout that shifts at every level. On the top floor where the stairs merge, the gallery is encased within a translucent glass enclosure to ensure a degree of privacy for the apartment terraces sandwiched between them.

Separated by a pedestrian court is the shorter of the two blocks, with a built area of 4,560 square meters. Here, unlike the switch-back stairs that are spaced regularly along the longer block, the façade of this shorter block is lined with a multitude of glass-covered stoops providing direct access to three- or four-bedroom apartments on the first three floors, creating a rhythmic interplay and contrast between the two bars. Inside the seemingly straightforward block, OMA introduced a system of lateral cascading stairs running through the spine of the block, resulting in an ingenious stacking of apartment units, and communal living arrangements on the top floor. In total, 202 units ranging from dormitories to five-room configurations are accommodated in this pair of buildings. Within the dwelling units, which are no more than 15 meters deep in the longer block and 11 meters deep in the shorter one, glass walls are copiously deployed, such as between the living and dining areas, lending a sense of spaciousness as well as transparency. In addition to the lengths of these buildings that reify the original dimensions of the shipyard site, the intentional choice of materials, in particular the metal-clad staircases and elevator shaft, and the perforated steel columns, pay homage to the industrial heritage of the place, albeit in modern, subtle gestures.

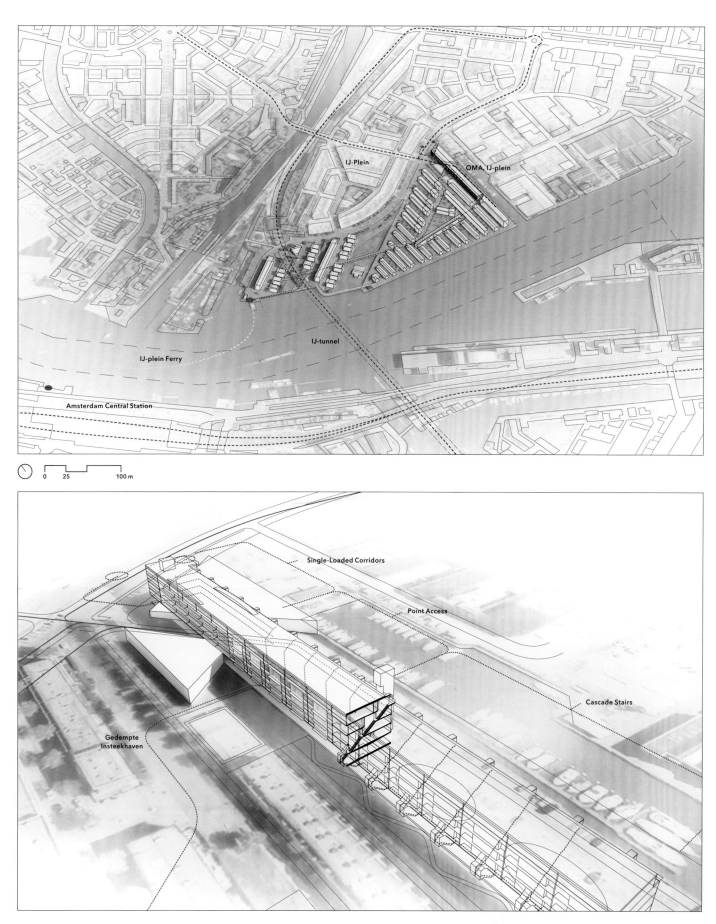

INFRASTRUCTURAL ENGAGEMENTS

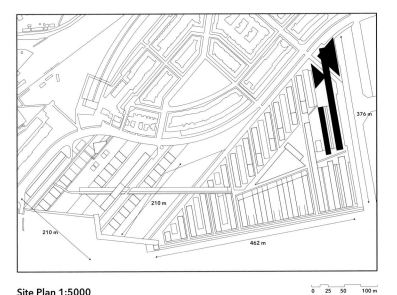

Site Plan 1:5000

376 m

210 m

210 m

462 m

0 25 50 100 m

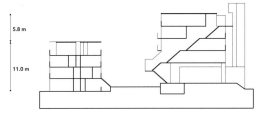

5.8 m

11.0 m

Section 1:500

0 2.5 5 10 m

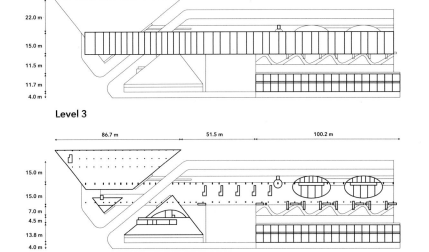

20.5 m   117.7 m   95.8 m   5.2 m

22.0 m
15.0 m
11.5 m
11.7 m
4.0 m

Level 3

86.7 m   51.5 m   100.2 m

15.0 m
15.0 m
7.0 m
4.5 m
13.8 m
4.0 m

Level 1

Plan 1:1500

0 7.5 15 30 m

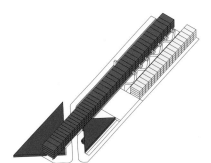

Key

■ Apartment Type
□ Terrace Type
■ Commerical
■ Parking/Entrance

Household Types

Unit Types 1:500

0 2.5 5 10 m

202 units

Key

□ Bedroom/Living
■ Kitchen
■ Bathroom

Unit Type Locations

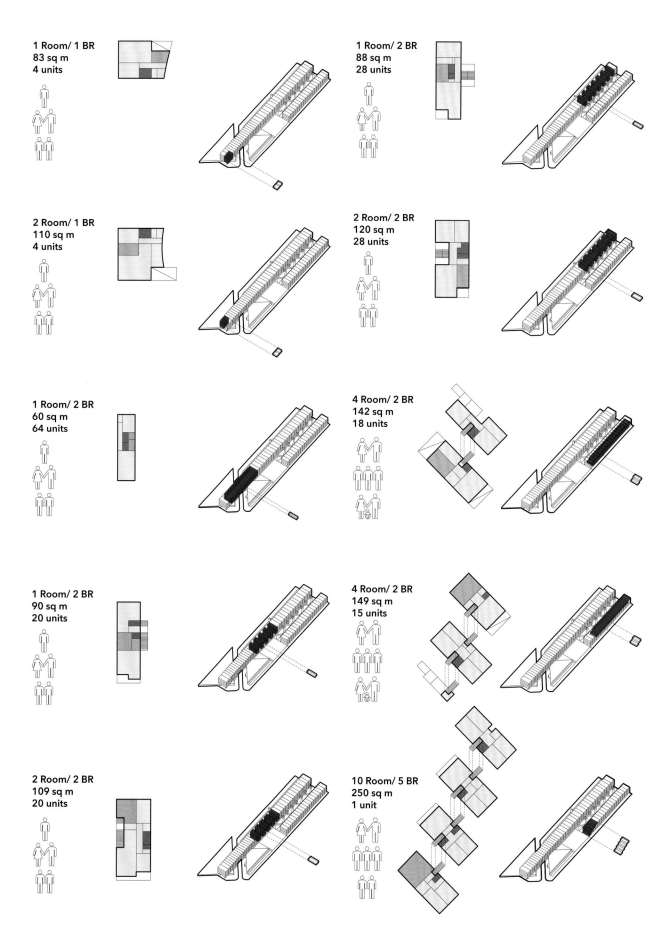

1 Room/ 1 BR
83 sq m
4 units

1 Room/ 2 BR
88 sq m
28 units

2 Room/ 1 BR
110 sq m
4 units

2 Room/ 2 BR
120 sq m
28 units

1 Room/ 2 BR
60 sq m
64 units

4 Room/ 2 BR
142 sq m
18 units

1 Room/ 2 BR
90 sq m
20 units

4 Room/ 2 BR
149 sq m
15 units

2 Room/ 2 BR
109 sq m
20 units

10 Room/ 5 BR
250 sq m
1 unit

INFRASTRUCTURAL ENGAGEMENTS

If the IJ-Plein had set the precedence for subsequent redevelopment of the abandoned docklands in Amsterdam, the Eastern Harbor District, of which Borneo Sporenburg was a part, arguably showcases the evolution and array of spatial strategies in revitalizing former infrastructural sites in a key area of the urban center. Identified as early as 1974 to be a sub-centre, the Eastern Harbor District took another 13 years of much planning and revision before the first pylons were driven into the ground for the new residences that would later occupy the site. Up until the mid-1980s, land reclamation and filling-in of the docklands was the *modus operandi* for the harbor basins, yielding larger plots of land that would presumably lend themselves easier to carrying out the redevelopment while providing room for green space and recreational amenities. Residents who had occupied the district as well as squatters who had lived there illegally after it was abandoned, lobbied against this notion and called for the retention of the original docklands character of the place. Their emphasis was on the water and the intrinsic value of the canals or as a type of blue open space, encapsulated in their legendary slogan, 'blue is green' which later profoundly shaped the approach in which the district was redeveloped.[12] A key design principle arising from this was the use of the "island structure as the foundation" upon which the residential areas would be constructed as articulated in the memorandum issued by the city planning department.[13] In contrast to the IJ-Plein which filled in parts of the harbor, the original form and dimensions of the Eastern Harbor District docklands thus had to be preserved, with development to occur alongside the elongated nature of the quays as a means of response to the inherent structure of the site.

To overcome the problem of north-south connection across the site, and together with a policy on improving the competitiveness of public transport beginning in the 1980s, bus routes were introduced as the islands were transformed in phases, running in a radial fashion primarily along the western edges of the islands and the length of Java-eiland, with occasional stops extending into the middle of the islands, as was the case of Sporenburg. The bus services were supplemented by the extension of tram lines to Java-eiland and the opening of the IJ-tram that traversed the district in an east-west manner terminating at the IJ-burg further out to the east. Development on Borneo Sporenburg was initiated in 1992, and at that time, a survey of the recently completed KNSM-eiland revealed that there were only singles or couples residing in the owner-occupied apartments with hardly any children.[14] Moreover, the housing on Borneo Sporenburg would be ready for sale around the same time as the new apartments on Java-eiland.[15] The main objective thus was to provide distinctive housing types that would appeal to families with children, and primarily in the form of low-rise, single-family dwellings without shared or semi-public stairwells, lifts, galleries, or corridors in a manner that would still be able to meet the density requirement of 100 dwellings per hectare. In concert with the deregulation of the Dutch housing market in the early 1990s moving away from state-subsidized social rental housing, housing associations and private developers had to work creatively in catering to a freer market economy. In the case of Borneo Sporenburg, only 30 percent of the 2,150 units were reserved for social rental housing, while the remaining 70 percent would be owner-occupied. The development was undertaken by New Deal, a consortium of three housing corporations, which had the permission from the city to develop an urban plan and construct most of the residences.

After two rounds of commissioned studies by nine different architectural firms, the scheme by West 8 was selected for its incorporation of the basic design principles set out by the Spatial Planning Department. Refined later by Rudy Uytenhaak, who had devised the Java-eiland plan, the scheme was composed of low-rise, high-density housing bands that combined street-front and walk-up units, terminating in 'end block' typologies that responded to the idiosyncratic parcels at the ends, as well as the 'meteorites' inspired by the large blocks such as the Piraeus located across on the KNSM-eiland. By combining this sea of single-family dwellings with the apartment complexes, Adriaan Geuze and his team were able to attain the density stipulated by the city and the developer. Within this primarily residential order were other programs including two schools, a sports center, a medical institution, shops, offices, restaurants, and a yacht club. The most unusual and arguably most documented feature of this project built between 1996 and 2000 was the 60 freehold parcels that were sold to individual owners through a lottery system by the municipality in which the owners had the autonomy to work with their preferred architects in designing their canal houses.

To maintain the formal and figural cohesiveness of the two islands while still producing an impressive assortment of architectural expressiveness, the owners and architects had to work within the design parameters established by West 8 in their re-interpretation of the traditional Dutch canal house. First and foremost, a 30 to 50 percent void was dictated within each of the free parcels, resulting in creative internal configurations through the rhythmic interplay of voids and solids. In doing so, the typical outdoor gardens and spaces in the Dutch row house were interiorized, complete with private courtyards, roof gardens, and patios. A second specification was for individual access to each of the single-family dwellings, such that each unit had a front door to the street, as opposed to the shared access in the sculptural blocks or the mid-rise complexes on the other islands. A major deviation from the conventional floor-to-floor height of 2.4 meters in the Dutch context was a push towards a higher standard of 3.5 meters.[16] Since the parcels ranged from 15 to 19 meters in depth, and just 4.2 to six meters in width, increasing the floor-to-floor height was vital to allowing more daylight penetration, and potentially for the future commercial rezoning of the ground floor. Finally, the building materials were limited to a palette of dark-red mixed brick, Oregon Pine and Western Red Cedar, and steel lattice gates.[17]

For the 60 free parcels in particular, these guidelines generated an architectonic diversity, both in the floor plans and the façades, within a uniform urban envelope. Apart from local Dutch architects who were commissioned to design these free parcels, internationally-renowned architects like Herzog & de Meuron, Xaveer de Geyter, and MVRDV were also involved. In Borneo 12 and Borneo 18, for instance, which were designed by MVRDV, two distinct elevations on the street front were deployed: Borneo 12 as a seemingly enclosed solid mass with a void in the form of a private alleyway occupying half the width as compared to the transparent glass-box-like façade of Borneo 18. Spatially, Borneo 12 played on the notion of 'bands' in the two islands, dividing the mass into two narrow 'strips'. One of the strips runs through the entire depth of the parcel at the full height of 9.5 meters, while the other is broken down into two volumes grafted onto the main 'stem'; the displacement of these two volumes allows the continuation of the void into the house, creating an air well that brings in more light into the house. The lower of the two volumes contains a double-height work space, while the other which extends across the upper two floors of the house serves as a bedroom/bathroom suite. In Borneo 18, MVRDV began with a four-storey section measuring 12 meters deep that was cleverly accommodated within the height confines of the envelope. Here, a void was left at the back of the house fronting the canal, creating a four by five meter garden plot on the basement level right by the water. However, by sliding the second floor out towards the back, this resulted in the capacious, light-filled living room extending three storeys in height on the front, and an outdoor balcony on the third floor resting atop the enclosed block, housing the bedroom and bathroom, with a view above the canal on the second floor.[18]

The rest of the end blocks and low-rise dwellings were subjected to the same design provisions, and given over to a cast of international and local architects, including OMA, Josep Lluís Mateo, UNStudio, Kees Christiaanse, and Claus en Kaan. In Mateo's rectilinear housing block at the head of the Borneo island, a total of 11 different floor plans ranging from 110 to 180 square meters were accommodated in the 26 narrow terraced houses arranged back to back. While the project comes across as a massive, tight scheme on the exterior, clad in red cedar timber paneling on the southern façades and brickwork on the northern facades, relief is provided by the cutouts on the upper two floors yielding small private courtyards, gardens, and roof terraces, as well as internalized green spaces.[19] This clear separation of the inside/outside, private/public is a trope that manifests similarly in the projects undertaken by Claus en Kaan in Borneo Sporenburg, spanning seven sites including an end block on Sporenburg. All the narrow dwellings are again laid out in a back-to-back fashion with two basic forms that are then articulated to attain a variety of configurations by combining the living rooms, voids, patios, and roof terraces differently.[20] Overall, by adopting the same strategy as OMA for the IJ-Plein where an assortment of architects was assembled to respond to established design codes specific to the two districts, a diversity of forms and unit types were produced, resulting in two lively yet architecturally cohesive neighborhoods on pre-viously derelict infrastructural sites. Located in the same city yet completed close to two decades apart, they reflect not only a continued desire to reclaim the waterfront, but also shifting approaches in working with and (in the case of Borneo Sporenburg and the greater Eastern Harbor District) amplifying the con-ditions and dimensions endowed by the shipyards and docklands of the past.

BORNEO SPORENBURG

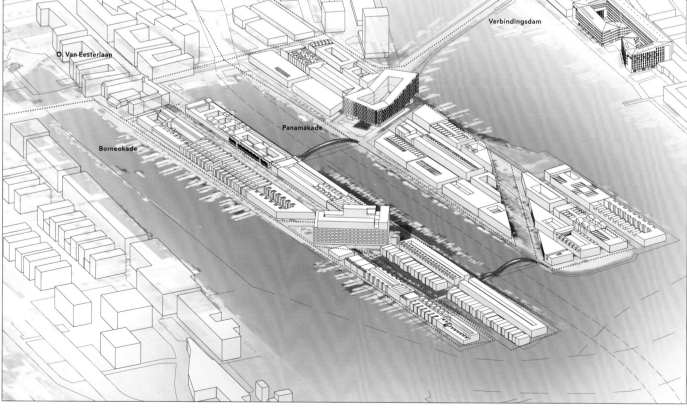

INFRASTRUCTURAL ENGAGEMENTS

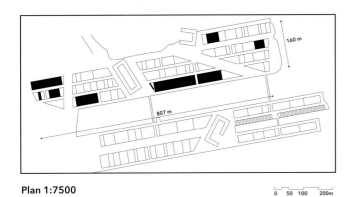

Plan 1:7500

0   50 100   200m

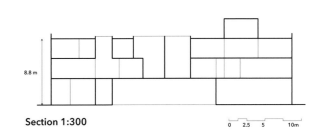

Section 1:300

0   2.5   5   10m

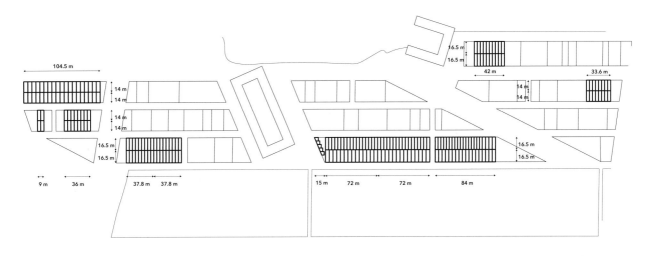

Plan 1:3000

0   25   50   100m

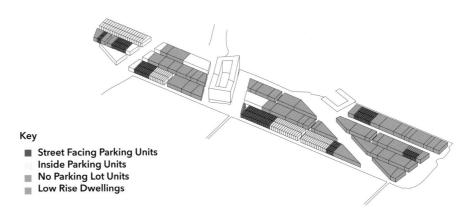

Key

■ Street Facing Parking Units
□ Inside Parking Units
▨ No Parking Lot Units
▨ Low Rise Dwellings

BORNEO SPORENBURG

Unit Types 1:500
Household Types

- ☐ Bedroom/Living
- ▨ Kitchen
- ■ Bathroom

236 units

Unit Type Locations

Unit Type Sections

2 Room/ 2 BR
148 sq m
105 units

4 Room/ 2 BR
167 sq m
118 units

3 Room/ 1 BR
69 sq m
13 units

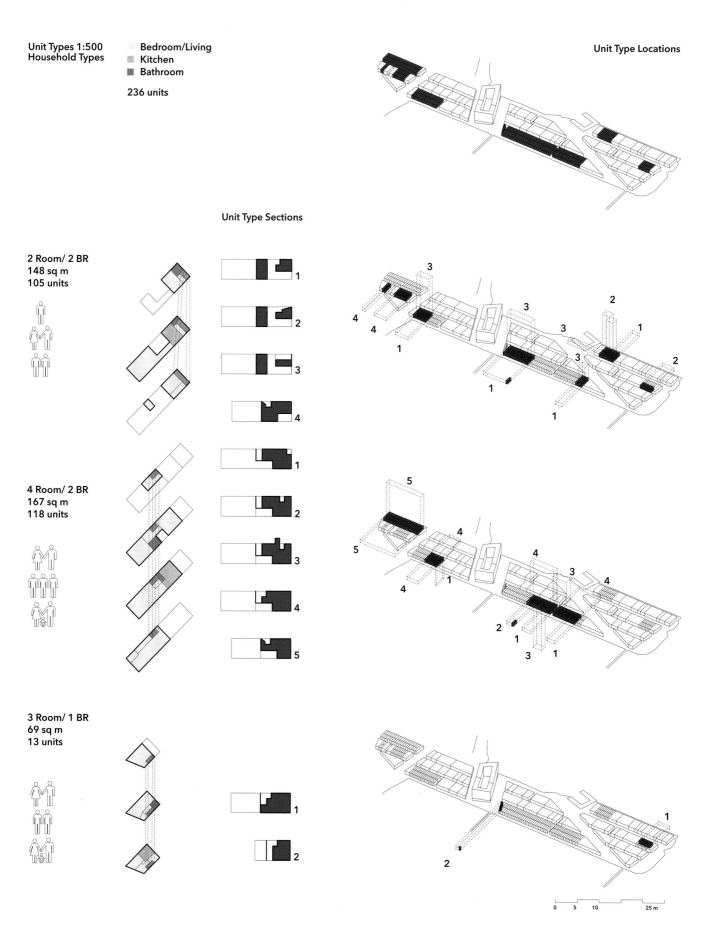

0 5 10   25 m

INFRASTRUCTURAL ENGAGEMENTS

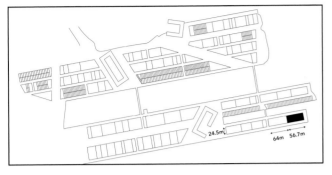

Site Plan 1:7500

0 50 100   200m

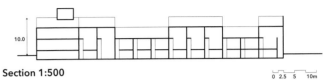

Section 1:500

0 2.5 5   10m

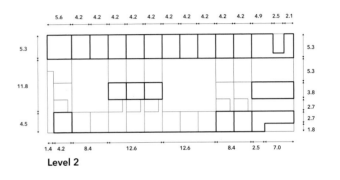

Level 2

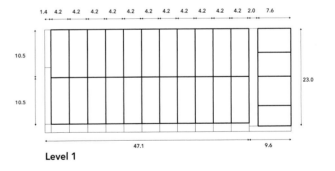

Level 1

Plan 1:500

0 2.5 5   10m

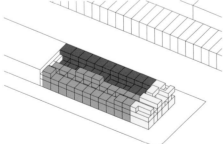

Key

■ Apartment Type
□ Terrace Type
▨ Courtyard Type
▨ Storage

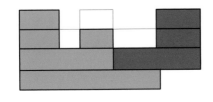

Unit Types 1:500
Household Types

▫ Bedroom/Living
▨ Kitchen
■ Bathroom

26 units

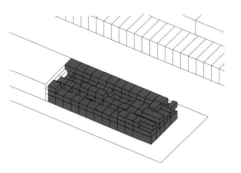

BORNEO SPORENBURG

Unit Type Locations

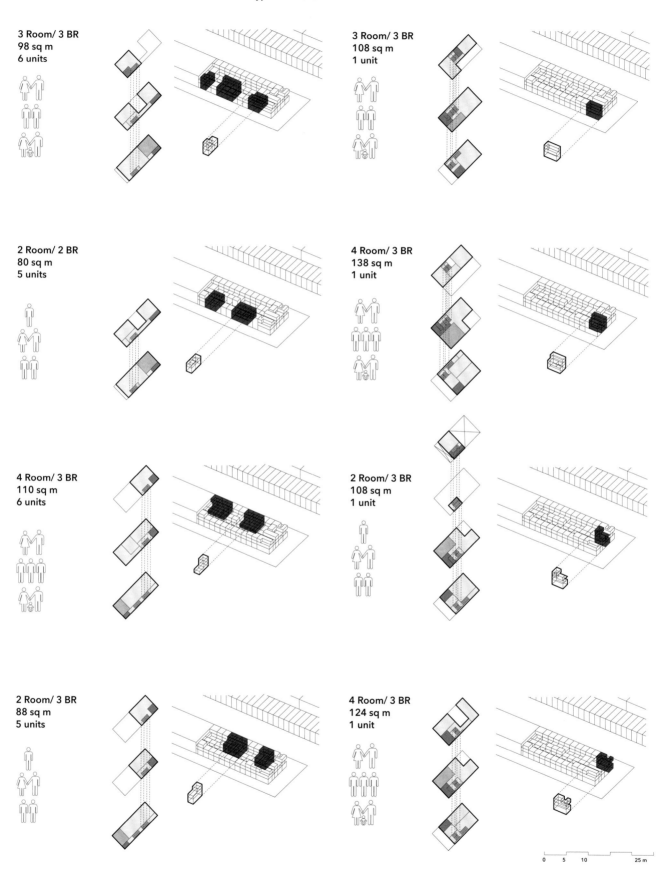

3 Room/ 3 BR
98 sq m
6 units

3 Room/ 3 BR
108 sq m
1 unit

2 Room/ 2 BR
80 sq m
5 units

4 Room/ 3 BR
138 sq m
1 unit

4 Room/ 3 BR
110 sq m
6 units

2 Room/ 3 BR
108 sq m
1 unit

2 Room/ 3 BR
88 sq m
5 units

4 Room/ 3 BR
124 sq m
1 unit

0   5   10   25 m

INFRASTRUCTURAL ENGAGEMENTS

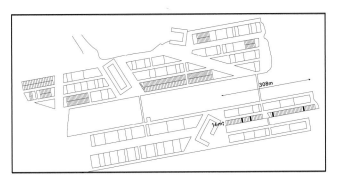

Plan 1:7500

308m

16mt

0 50 100 200m

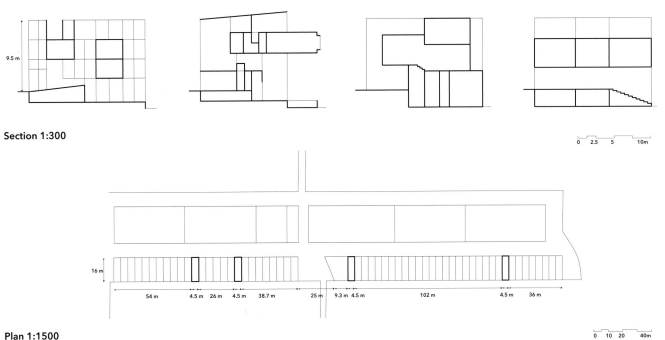

Section 1:300

9.5 m

0   2.5   5   10m

16 m

54 m   4.5 m   26 m   4.5 m   38.7 m   25 m   9.3 m 4.5 m   102 m   4.5 m   36 m

Plan 1:1500

0   10   20   40m

Unit Types 1:500
Household Types

□ Bedroom/Living
▨ Kitchen
■ Bathroom

4 units

Unit Type Locations

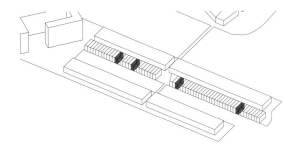

2 Room/ 3 BR
245 sq m
1 unit

3 Room/ 2 BR
169 sq m
1 unit

2 Room/ 3 BR
201 sq m
1 unit

8 Room/ 9 BR
382 sq m
1 unit

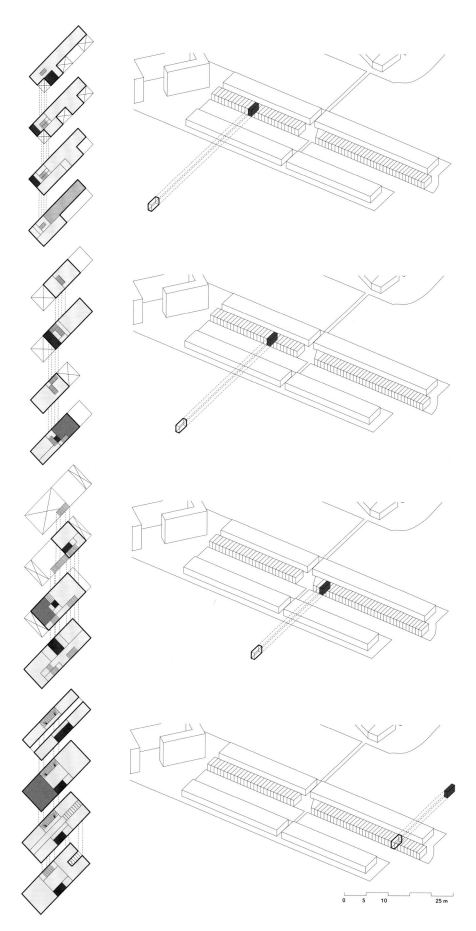

0   5   10   25 m

INFRASTRUCTURAL ENGAGEMENTS

BORNEO SPORENBURG

TYPAL INDEPENDENCE, RECIPROCITY, AND CONTEXTUAL INFLUENCE

Looking across this material, several general observations can be made. First, there is a relative independence, in this largely territorial type, of housing types *per se*. The cases presented show a wide range from single-family dwellings up to tall buildings, as well as big buildings as submultiples. It all depends on the particular territory involved, its infrastructural conditions, and the suitability of one housing type over others. Second, there is reciprocity in the infrastructural engagements. As alluded to in the introduction, infrastructure brings housing and housing brings infrastructure. Clearly, in the case of Denenchōfu and many other Japanese residential developments, the infrastructure, in the form of a railroad, was used to bring value to the resultant site and to facilitate its development. In short, real estate companies were in the railway business. At Euralille, by contrast, site circumstances, along with the massive high-speed rail installations and ancillary commercial interests, created a fertile ground for housing development. In the cases where infrastructure was expressively reified within housing complexes, as at Malagueira and the Byker Wall, reciprocity also applied. The planned motorway, for instance, occasioned the Byker Wall housing complex and not the other way around, whereas the linear grouping of housing also in need of basic utilities occasioned the viaduct-like installation at Malagueira.

Then too, the presence of former or existing infrastructure can present both opportunities and constraints for housing and suggest contextual manners of shaping housing. The wharves at Borneo Sporenburg, for instance, suggested a historical landscape of attached row house-like dwellings, so typical of Amsterdam waterfronts, which was partially emulated in the contemporary proposal. The focal point of the station at the center of the Denenchōfu estate clearly suggested the radiating pattern of streets emanating from the small plaza in front of the station. Also, the Byker Wall had really no other alternative but to follow and parallel the alignment of the planned motorway. Further, in a closely related manner, the introduction of housing in place of infrastructure rather immediately offers a different reading and ambience to a section of a city. Suddenly it is habitable and approachable rather than being only serviceable and often off-limits. It is also a domestic landscape in lieu of one that is commercial or industrial. Finally, in those cases where some aspect of infrastructure is reified, such as the viaduct of utilities at Malagueira, a question arises as to whether the strong formal manifestation of infrastructure is justified. In other words, in what terms should this aspect of the project really be assessed? Of course, in this particular case, the reification of the infrastructure is largely symbolic, even if it is functional and offers a certain ease of longer-term maintenance. Moreover, it is symbolic in at least two senses. First, it connotes a kind of community solidarity among residents who are typically often footloose. Second, it is also in line with a long-standing chronicle of the manner in which water and other utility resources are brought to the landscape of Évora in Portugal, namely via viaducts and aqueducts.

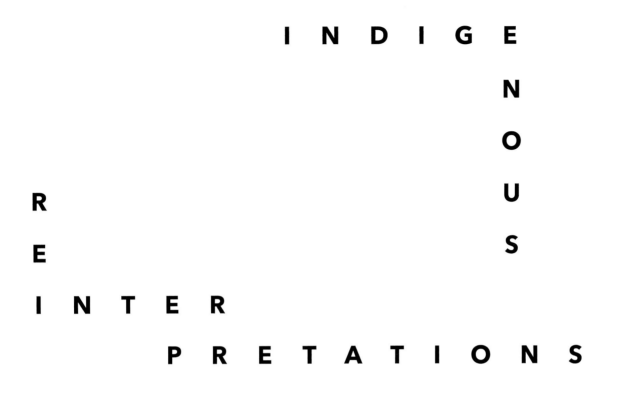

INDIGENOUS REINTERPRETATIONS

First and foremost, 'indigenous reinterpretation' is self-consciously concerned with the architectural tradition and past practice, or constructed context of a place. It has waxed and waned from early concerns with historical conservation and preservation, at least as far back as the eighteenth century in Europe, up through periods of modernity and more recent concerns with existing building contexts.[1] For many, it is a means of conforming housing to local conditions in a manner that is somehow familiar, comfortable, and well-fitted with what is already in place. In lower-income housing circumstances, for instance, it has been pursued as a means of avoiding any stigma that may arise from too obvious a material difference. In housing immigrant populations in urban areas, it can also serve to reference the building practices from where they are from, as was clear in the case of Tiburtino, discussed in Chapter Two. In the realm of historic conservation, it is a means of maintaining and even renewing housing in a manner that is consistent with aims of perpetuating an overall environmental integrity. In this regard, it is different from preservation, *per se*, which implies literal maintenance of structures in place and, in some instances, reconstruction and replication. Nevertheless, always at work is a backward turn, which in the case of housing may also be bound up with expressions of social status, some-thing clearly on display in the neo-colonial McMansion estates in suburban United States. Alternatively, pursuit of older indigenous building techniques can arise in conjunction with local material use and the interests of using local skills and lowering costs. At root here, however, is not something that is exactly the same as an original in all respects, but where certain elements or qualities are adhered to fully or very closely. This, in turn, raises the question of what it is that is being reinterpreted: If we conceive of housing as a bundle of parts, properties, and qualities, when we speak of indigenous reinterpretation, along which of them might it be usefully pursued? Moreover, the choices made, although often lasting, are also subject to change as indigenous conditions are reconsidered and the necessity of conforming, or not, to what is there in place became either relaxed or reinforced.

PRECEDENTS: CODES, ASSOCIATIONS, AND REPRODUCTIONS

Almost invariably, different cultural contexts involve different manners of housing, often in line with their indigenous architectural traditions. Arab environments of the Middle East are not exceptions, even when experiencing the levelling effects of Western-oriented modernization. Indeed, in some places within the Kingdom of Saudi Arabia and the Emirates, people still live in traditional housing. This is particularly true in coastal areas like parts of Jeddah and on the Red Sea, and smaller towns in the Arabian Gulf of Saudi Arabia and in some of the preserved areas of Dubai and Abu Dhabi where the prominent wind towers are a conspicuous local architectural expression. Typically, traditional Arab houses are courtyard houses with interior courts open to the sky surrounded by the rooms and domestic quarters of the house. Gender separation is *de rigueur* with the *haram* set aside for women and the family in general and the *majlis* set aside for reception, entertainment, and meeting on the part of male members of the household. Usually this involves two entries, with access to the *haram* more private than that to the *majlis*. Location of houses along the narrow lanes of larger residential blocks, or *hara*, especially in former times, secured the same privacy and protection for women, whereas bustling commercial streets on the outside, framed by commercial and other mixed uses, provided the public spaces and places of market transactions for the men. Visual seclusion of one house from others was achieved through a variety of screening devices, including the elaborate and ornate wooden *mashrabiya* that hang on the sides of houses, creating semi-enclosed and discretely screened terraces. Passage for community residents through their environments was also secured by usufructural requirements in addition to more normal public, semi-public, and private rights of way. Material composition of housing, ranging from one to three or more storeys in height, was usually of masonry or mud brick covered in stucco, forming walls with good solar insolation qualities. Roofs tended to be flat, often with tall parapets forming roof terraces, occupiable during evenings and nights, in contrast to the folly of high-rise European-style residential towers and so-called 'crash housing' in Saudi Arabia.[2] Several successful attempts have been made to entrain this kind of cultural rule structure of traditional patterns of housing in formal layouts that are also expressive of, if materially dissimilar from, traditional enclaves. The 650-hectare Diplomatic Quarter next to the Wadi Hanifa in southeast Riyadh, for instance, with urban design by Ali Shuaibi and others, is a prominent example, as is the housing scheme by the same architect closer into the center of Riyadh, the Saudi capital.[3]

One case in which several cultural contexts framed the reference for recent housing is Villa Victoria in the South End of Boston, dating from the late 1960s into the early 1980s and designed by John Sharratt. There, engagement with a population primarily from somewhere else and reinterpretation both in terms of where they were from and where they appeared to be going can be readily discerned. In 1965, under the South End Urban Renewal Area designated by the Federal Department of Housing and Urban Development, wholesale demolition was to be visited on the area, clearing it of many substandard and vacant properties. At much the same time, substantial numbers of low-income Puerto Rican immigrants had moved into the area in search of cheap rents, welfare benefits, low-skilled jobs, and proximity to others like themselves. Their plight was then taken up by the Episcopalian Church, among others, and by Sharratt as an advocacy planner

Traditional Arab houses

Villa Victoria

INDIGENOUS REINTERPRETATIONS

alongside the Emergency Tenants' Association and Inquilinos Boricuas en Acción. A plan for an area of the South End was approved in 1970 and with aid from available tax incentives for low-cost housing and sizeable government grants, the project for Villa Victoria got underway being managed for its community by the Boston Housing Authority.[4] The overall plan acknowledged the grain and formal block structure of Boston's Back Bay, but incorporated loop roads instead of a straightforward gridiron of streets in order to secure a stronger spatial sense of community. Houses along Tremont Street, a major road on the periphery of Villa Victoria, were maintained and rehabilitated into what became known as Casa Borinquen, although the remainder of the 736 dwelling units was newly constructed. One line of reinterpretation of indigenous circumstances appeared around Plaza Betances, which became framed by six-storey arcaded mid-rise residences and row house units atop a commercial arcade to form something akin to a *zócalo*, or plaza, in a Latin American tradition.[5] Also nearby was the 18-storey Torre Unidad, primarily housing an elderly population and in a manner that broke with the architectural tradition of the South End. The other conspicuous reinterpretation came about with an unmistakable aspirational orientation towards American suburbia and individuated dwellings, although at Villa Victoria in the form of denser row houses. Some of these were duplexes with from three- to six-bedroom units over one- to two-bedroom flats on the lower levels. All incorporated private garden spaces at the back, in common with row houses in the area, and also a common space for children's play and other local activities, insisted on by residents through the participatory process that was employed throughout the project. Despite use of the more urban row house type, the figural expression of the units, with the overlaying of upper floors, window sizes and alignments, prominent pitched roofs, material coloration, and so on, suggested a distinctly different and 'suburban' appearance.

A third form of indigenous reinterpretation took place in Zacatecas, Mexico, at Veta Grande and at Rincón Colonial on the periphery of the inland and arid city, dating from 1990 to 1992. This took the form of an experiment with traditional forms of housing and reinvention of traditional modes of construction using mud bricks. An economic aim was also to reduce the cost of construction with mud brick prototypes, using local materials in place of concrete and steel, which typically accounted for around 80 percent of the construction cost. In fact, this proved to be possible at a twenty percent reduction in cost. Designed by Carlos García Vélez, a partner at the time in GEO, one of the largest producers of low-cost housing in Latin America, the initial prototype at Veta Grande comprised seven small houses of 65 square meters each in a two-storey arrangement with small patios and a common wall and shared service arrangement.[6] Prior precedents involving mud brick construction were investigated, including the work of Hassan Fathy in Egypt and of Pueblo Indians in Taos, New Mexico. Consultation also occurred with the UNESCO research organization in Grenoble, France, who were also investigating and experimenting with mud brick structures. Among the two most generally available approaches for mud brick production, a method involving stationary grinding and sedimentation of blocks was selected over higher-tech pressure systems.

Veta Grande © Carlos García Vélez

Rincón Colonial © Carlos García Vélez

Hutong and *Siheyuan* in Beijing

Lilong in Shanghai

31 Boon Tat Street

This choice proved to be relatively portable and adaptable to local materials, using machines created by Henry Elkins in the United States out of Fresno, California, that were also affordable for the project. A system of brick vaults built in compression spacing between common walls formed the backbone of the construction, with all surfaces covered in stucco. The larger project at Rincón Colonial aimed to build 800 units in clusters of from 50 to 60 units, again enclosing common outdoor spaces. The client for the project was the municipal government of Zacatecas and of the original 800 units, 600 were realized, costing less per square meter to build than comparable low-cost housing and selling at the same price, although 30 percent larger in area. During the process, the mud brick common walls were replaced by concrete block as the scaling up necessary for the larger project proved to be problematic and an episode of highly unusual rainfall hampered the mud brick production. Basic housing units under vaulted roof modules incorporated two-storey layouts of rows and a broad double-height space that could be later filled in with further floor space. The mass wall and mud brick roof construction performed well acoustically and thermally in Zacatecas' arid climate and some 65 percent in savings in steel and concrete also added to the cost savings. In 1993, upon completion of the project, the municipality signed a technical assistance package with Cuba, where some 30,000 units were to be constructed.[7]

In yet other venues, contemporary-looking indigenous reinterpretations are commonly carried out. One such venue is Singapore and the venerable shophouse building typology, with its five-foot ways, vertical orientation to fenestration along street façades, up to four-storey height including use of attic space, and a pancake-like stacking of rooms towards the back and well-proportioned and sometimes double-height rooms at the front. The shophouse at 31 Boon Tat Street of 2003 by Forum Architects, alongside of a renovated original structure is a useful example of this practice.[8] Although using contemporary materials of exposed concrete, broad glass panels, and metal screens, along with unusual angular geometries, this shophouse conforms in almost every other respect to the traditional shophouse form dating well back into the nineteenth century. A top-lit stairway towards the front of the complex departs from the original type, although updating it at the same time through the use of modern materials and methods of construction.

CONTEMPORARY CASES: REFERENCES TO THE PAST IN BEIJING AND SHANGHAI

In the two cases presented and discussed here, the contexts of indigenous reinterpretation are to be found in ubiquitous past dwelling environments and housing types, first in Beijing with the hutong and *siheyuan*, and then in Shanghai with its large blocks and the lilong.[9] Certainly, since the Ming and Qing dynasties, if not before in Beijing, the *hutong* are the lanes or small streets that usually run east-west within the overall gridiron of streets and roads inside the walls of the old city. Indeed, the term *hutong* appears to be derived from the Mongol *hottog*, which means 'well' and ties the *hutong* back to the gridded well-field system of agriculture and cropping division of the Shang dynasty in antiquity. The east-west orientation of the lanes also provides for a north-south alignment of the dwellings and their facing south in accordance to good Confucian and *fengshui* practice. In addition, the *hutong*, which vary in width and local regularity, became defined materially by the adjacent four-sided courtyard houses, or *siheyuan*, that lined them. These dwellings, in turn, usually had a relatively ornate entry gateway at the south-east corner, through which visitors would be ceremoniously received, but the remainder of the façade along the lane would be blank, consisting of the so-called 'reverse' rooms of the *siheyuan,* set aside for service functions. In basic layout, the courtyard houses had open courtyards, surrounded by pavilions and arcades for circulation. Alignment of pavilions was according to a north-south oriented bi-lateral symmetry with occupation according to position in the family. Movement through the *siheyuan*, depending upon one's familiarity with the owners and how far one went, probably involved up to five turns with deliberate pauses and all orchestrated according to the doctrine of *li*, and proprietous and courteous behavior. In other words, the *siheyuan* and *hutong* location facilitated a desirable and preferred form of social interaction. According to the Qianlong Map of 1735, for instance, substantial areas of Beijing, outside of the Forbidden City precinct, were occupied in this manner.[10] Indeed, the first project under discussion, the Ju'er Hutong by Wu Liangyong of 1989 to 1992, was originally a small part of this broader context in the north-eastern Dongcheng District of old Beijing.

From the outset, Wu recognized that it would have been impossible to preserve all the courtyard houses without introducing any interventions, and yet, it would have been unwise to maintain them in an ossified state. In his view, features that have fallen out of pace with demands of contemporary life would have to be adapted, and the rehabilitation of these traditional residential districts in the Old City of Beijing, primarily within the confines of the Second Ring Road, ought to occur as a process of "organic renewal", hinging on "metabolic change rather than total clearance and rebuilding".[11] The Ju'er Hutong project was thus a pilot project in Wu's application of a practical methodology that would "enable the preservation of the historical and cultural value of the Old City as well as promote sustainable development and provide a solution to the housing shortage" the city was then facing in the 1980s and early 1990s.[12] Since the establishment of the People's Republic in 1949, extensive industrial development and the concentration of government offices and commercial enterprises within the Old City resulted in severe congestion and deterioration of the urban-environmental quality. Moreover, the construction of nearly seven million square meters of new housing between 1974 and 1986 alone, or 70 percent of the city's total new housing development since the Communists took power, was associated with uncontrolled infill, often in the form of high-rises that compromised the horizontal character of the Old City and greatly reduced the open spaces and leafy environments.[13]

The Ju'er Hutong is located in what was formerly known as the Zhaohui-Jinggong Fang, a neighborhood block dating back to the Yuan dynasty and built around 1267 and 1290 A.D., and retained the original block layout with nine east-west parallel *hutong* crossed by one north-south street.[14] Since time immemorial, this physical layout of the Old City in the form of neighborhoods composed of courtyards has been integral to the evolution of community life, with a number of Chinese literary works celebrating the socio-cultural life in these communities based on mutual respect and aid. In fact, the courtyard typology lends itself to the fostering of such amiable ties and sense of communal identity with its intimate scale, close relation between the indoor and outdoor spaces, and distinction between the public space of the lane and the semi-public/private space of the courtyard. Further, the attractiveness of the courtyard housing also lies in its union of natural beauty within a man-made environment, incorporating gardens, trees, and plants that offer respite from the hustle and bustle in the lands, and its inherent adaptability to accommodate live-work spaces. The 8.2-hectare block occupied by Ju'er Hutong had deteriorated considerably with poor housing conditions by the time it was selected as an experimental site for renewal by the Dongcheng District in 1989. Despite the overcrowding, poor environmental conditions and utilities, frequent flooding, and its degeneration into a *dazayuan* or "big cluttered courtyard", Ju'er Hutong was home to a close-knit community of some 3,180 residents where neighbors would help each other out.[15] The design team from Tsinghua University led by Wu Liangyong thus resolved to: (i) improve the living conditions of the community through the creation of a new courtyard housing prototype that would attain an ideal balance between insolation and ventilation while increasing the intensity of land use; (ii) "respect, support, and enhance the residents' attachments to each other and their place"; and (iii) to allow them to regain the sense of privacy and spatial control originally afforded by the traditional courtyard environment.[16]

Research and surveys of the area had already been undertaken in 1987, and the rehabilitation was organized to be carried out in four phases, of which only Phases I and II were materialized. From the exterior, the redeveloped neighborhood blends seamlessly into its surrounding fabric of low-rise, grey brick courtyard housing, distinguished by just its white, stuccoed walls rising two- to three-storeys above grade, striated by bands of sliding windows. Crowning these new apartment clusters are roofs that are partially pitched and composed of traditional grey-tiled patterns, inspired clearly by the architectural language of the classic *siheyuan*. Despite the height difference with adjacent one- to two-storey courtyards, these modern additions are not at all imposing. Instead, their presence is softened by setting them back from the *hutong* and incorporating lower garden walls of traditional grey brick and wrought iron on their periphery. From the *hutong*, the courtyard clusters are entered in via an articulated gateway that continues as a system of lanes or public alleyways that later branch off into communal courts before one gains access to the units arranged around the courts, reminiscent of the orchestrated movement in the *siheyuan* of the past which similarly reflected the transitions between zones of differing public-private characters. Old trees were preserved, and serve as departure points for where the communal courts would be located, complete with planter boxes, lamp posts, new trees, and garden furniture like stone benches, tables, and stools.

By way of housing, the apartments were arrayed in two- to three-storey courtyard types that were built within the height restriction of nine meters, allowing for a higher floor area ratio and density comparable to mid-rise residential blocks. In doing so, Wu and his team were able to introduce roof garden terraces, thereby creating more private outdoor space for communal purposes, including planting – an important traditional pastime – as well as opening up views to the Old City and its historic landmarks. Within the clusters, lofts were also made possible under the pitched roofs, providing for more useable space in the attics, and enhancing the rooflines of the project in concert with the rooftop terraces. Besides extending the elevation upwards, additional floor space was created through the introduction of basements in Phase II of the development, once the drainage problems were resolved. With large windows, light-wells, and sunken outdoor patios, these basement apartments were pleasing and well received. Vernacular Chinese architectural elements embellished the courtyard clusters, ranging from ornamented doorways and entrance screens to elaborate door knockers that imbued a sense of belonging and tradition in what otherwise were modern, figural interpretations of the old *siheyuan* typology. In Phase I, 64 bays of old housing made way for 46 new apartment units with a total floor area of 2,760 square meters, the equivalent of 2.5 times the space prior to the renewal.[17] A variety of unit types were included to cater to a range of households, from young or elderly couples, to families and intergenerational living, and the average floor area per person was improved from 7.86 square meters to 20.75 square meters. In Phase II, a collection of individual courts were designed in response to the site conditions around the transistor factory, and included a community center of some 300 square meters in area to complement the modest elderly residents activity centre that doubled up as an after-school youth activity centre. During this second phase 164 new apartment units were built, with a total floor area of 17,897 square meters, and increases in average floor area per person from 11.49 square meters to 26.25 square meters.

It must be said, however, that the project was not a wholesale demolition and redevelopment of a dilapidated neighborhood. In fact, in keeping with Wu's argument for organic renewal, some of the original courtyard houses that were still structurally sound and of notable architectural quality were preserved, including a cluster adjacent to Phase I of the development. In addition, existing buildings such as a small transistor factory dating from the Communist era emphasizing industrial production, as well as a research institute next to Phase II of the project, were retained. To manage the renewal and resettlement of the original residents, a housing cooperative was established during the first phase. As China was undergoing housing reforms, moving away from state-provided free housing to market-oriented conditions, a system of cost sharing was put in place such that the cost of rehabilitation was shared between the local Dongcheng District Government, the residents, and the work units that employed the residents. Under this system, original resident households would pay 350 yuan per square meter, while their employers paid 250 yuan per square meter, and the rest was covered by government subsidies. Residents with the ability to pay thus obtained the use rights to the new units, which could be transacted through the market five years after the purchase; those who were unable to afford the costs or who were unwilling to move back to the new units were provided with good-quality accommodation elsewhere, with the remaining units sold by

the cooperative at market rate to cover the remaining costs while generating a surplus for further work to be conducted.[18] Overall, 13 of the original households in Phase I returned after the renewal, and another 48 of the original households in Phase II, equivalent to 31.7 percent and 23.5 percent of the original total. This system of cost sharing was not just a means of shifting towards a housing market in the early days of housing reform, but also enabled part of the original community to be retained – a highly laudable social goal in and of itself. Given the close ties of the original residents, this gesture allowed the social fabric or at least some parts of it to be preserved, rather than the conventional disintegration of such a community in urban renewal projects. In sum, Ju'er Hutong is not about master plans *per se* but an instance of how the extraordinary *hutong* structure can be redeveloped in Beijing, merging both traditional and modern architecture whilst still maintaining the underlying spatial logic and principles of the traditional courtyard house within contemporary lifestyle and urban demands. In essence, this has given rise to a viable prototype that provided for relatively high-density housing within low-rise, mixed-use circumstances, revitalizing this historic capital's inner-city life even in the modern day.

JU'ER HUTONG

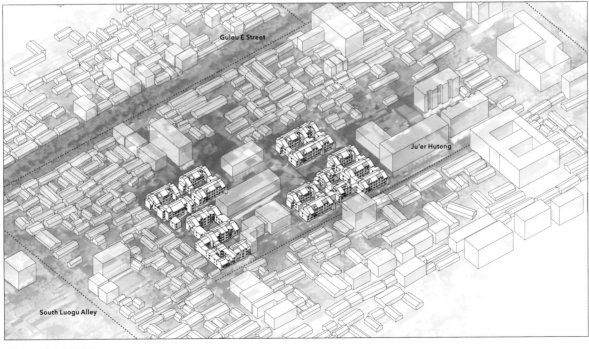

INDIGENOUS REINTERPRETATIONS

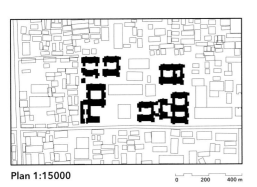

Plan 1:15000

0   200   400 m

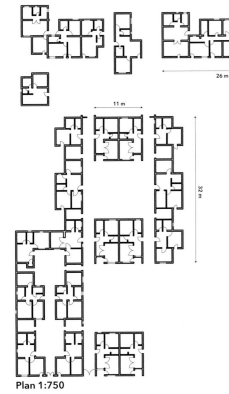

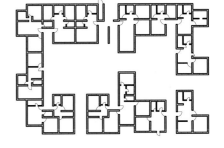

26 m

11 m

32 m

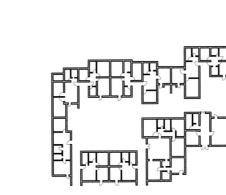

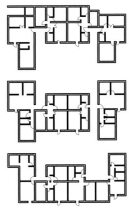

Plan 1:750

0   7.5   15 m

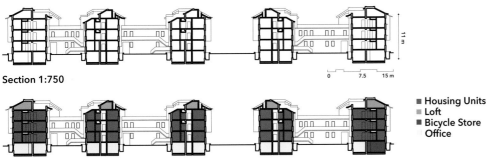

Section 1:750

0   7.5   15 m

11 m

Sectional Variation (Other Uses) 1:750

■ Housing Units
■ Loft
■ Bicycle Store
   Office

Household Types

Unit Types

■ Bedroom/Living
■ Kitchen
■ Bathroom

Unit Type Locations

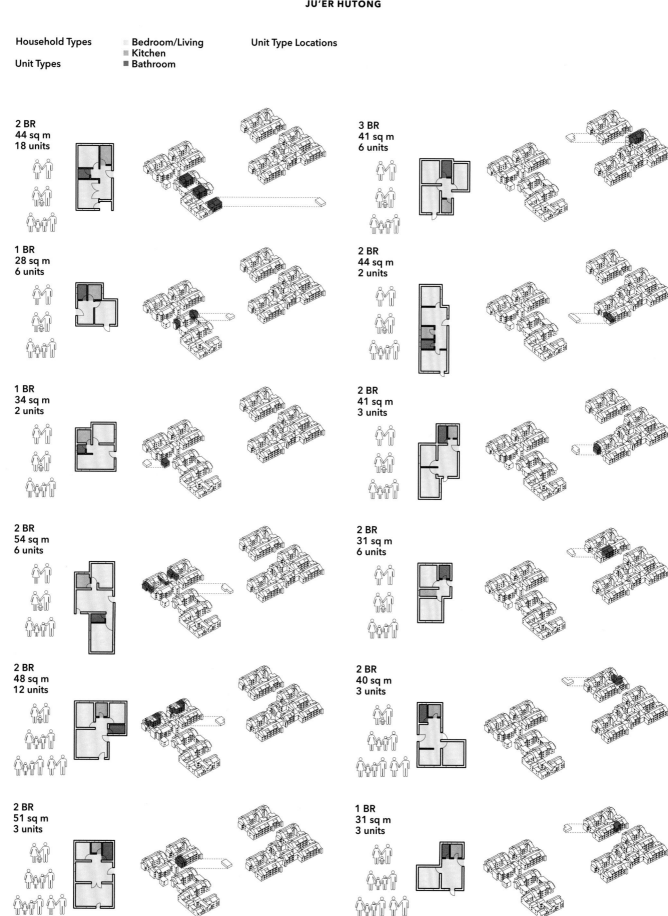

2 BR
44 sq m
18 units

1 BR
28 sq m
6 units

1 BR
34 sq m
2 units

2 BR
54 sq m
6 units

2 BR
48 sq m
12 units

2 BR
51 sq m
3 units

3 BR
41 sq m
6 units

2 BR
44 sq m
2 units

2 BR
41 sq m
3 units

2 BR
31 sq m
6 units

2 BR
40 sq m
3 units

1 BR
31 sq m
3 units

INDIGENOUS REINTERPRETATIONS

Household Types | Bedroom/Living
Kitchen
Unit Types | Bathroom

Unit Type Locations

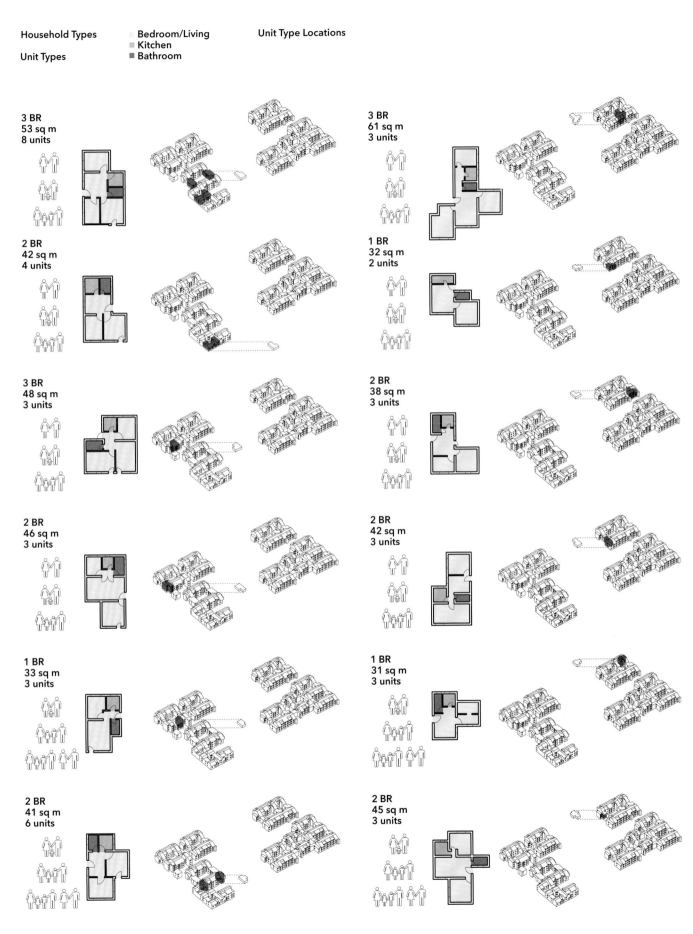

3 BR
53 sq m
8 units

3 BR
61 sq m
3 units

2 BR
42 sq m
4 units

1 BR
32 sq m
2 units

3 BR
48 sq m
3 units

2 BR
38 sq m
3 units

2 BR
46 sq m
3 units

2 BR
42 sq m
3 units

1 BR
33 sq m
3 units

1 BR
31 sq m
3 units

2 BR
41 sq m
6 units

2 BR
45 sq m
3 units

Household Types

Unit Types

■ Bedroom/Living
■ Kitchen
■ Bathroom

Unit Type Locations

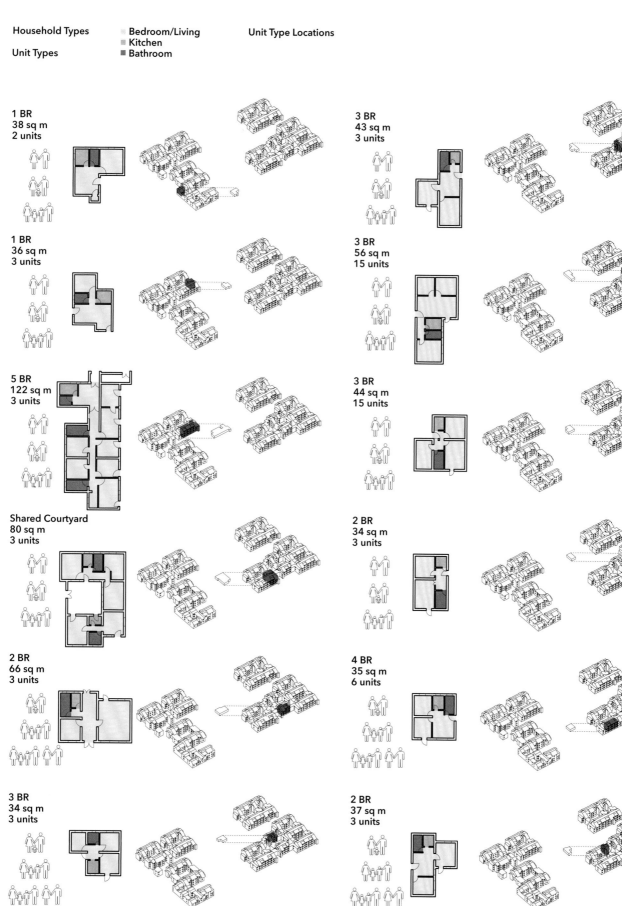

1 BR
38 sq m
2 units

1 BR
36 sq m
3 units

5 BR
122 sq m
3 units

Shared Courtyard
80 sq m
3 units

2 BR
66 sq m
3 units

3 BR
34 sq m
3 units

3 BR
43 sq m
3 units

3 BR
56 sq m
15 units

3 BR
44 sq m
15 units

2 BR
34 sq m
3 units

4 BR
35 sq m
6 units

2 BR
37 sq m
3 units

Household Types

Unit Types

Bedroom/Living
Kitchen
Bathroom

Unit Type Locations

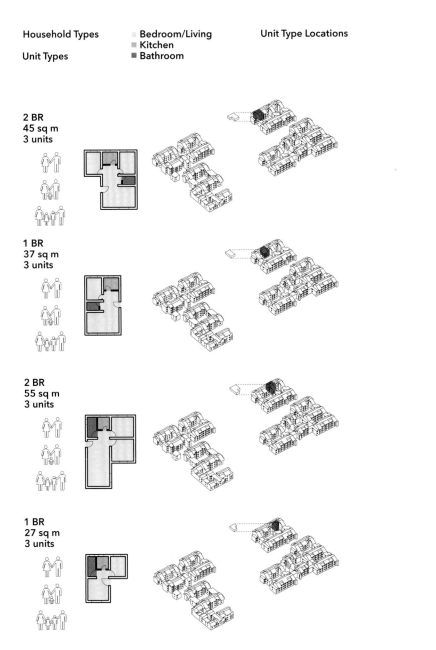

2 BR
45 sq m
3 units

1 BR
37 sq m
3 units

2 BR
55 sq m
3 units

1 BR
27 sq m
3 units

INDIGENOUS REINTERPRETATIONS

In the case of Shanghai, the second case study, the contextual reference is younger, dating from the latter part of the nineteenth century into the twentieth century and the 1920s and 1930s, with the *lilong* or lane housing that became the dominant form of local housing, regardless of background or social standing of the inhabitants. In fact, by 1937, or thereabouts, some 280,000 to 300,000 dwelling units of this type had been constructed, housing well over one million of the city's population. The term *lilong* simply refers to 'neighborhood lanes'.[19] The housing type was a hybrid between a southern *sanheyuan* or three-sided courtyard house and a western terrace or row house. The basic *lilong*, as a housing type, was comprised of a two-storey and sometimes higher dwelling, across a four- to five-meter frontage, built of brick and stucco finish, with a simple arrangement of rooms facing on to a small courtyard at the front and then a lane, and a lane at the back. Aggregations of dwelling units along the lanes varied according to the actual lane structure of the housing development, often referred to as a 'fishbone' configuration or a 'spinal' configuration, and so on. Entry into the lanes from the road outside, which also defined the large urban block in which the lane or *lilong* environments were placed, was through a gateway in the surrounding shophouse alignment along the road.[20] These gateways were often highly ornamented and gave rise to references to *shikumen* houses. In essence, a relatively continuous and multi-storeyed alignment of shophouses encircled a block with an interior lane structure, replete with *lilong*. Unlike the *hutong* of Beijing which were relatively blank with regard to the dwellings, the *lilong* of Shanghai, under the lane space itself, became the site of daily as well as celebratory life. Variations in floor space, height, and width of the basic type were adjusted to meet the needs of different socio-economic groups. Specific developments also varied from a relatively small number of units up to several hundred in some cases. Moreover, the entrepreneurs involved were both Chinese and Western. It is with reference to this context that some of the housing in the Nuova Città di Pujiang by Vittorio Gregotti was designed, although in a context beside the Huangpu River in metropolitan Shanghai which was entirely rural in the early part of the twentieth century.

Developed as part of Shanghai's One City–Nine Towns Plan of 2000, also known as the Comprehensive Plan of Shanghai Metro-Region (1999–2020), these satellite towns were to adopt various international themes in their formal outcomes. While towns like Songjiang, Anting, and Gaoqiao were built in the English, German, and Dutch styles, Pujiang was slated to be constructed in the Italian style. Located some 15 kilometers south of Lujiazui along the Huangpu River, the rectangular site was formerly an assortment of farmlands and villages, criss-crossed by a network of canals. This Italian new town was to house a population of 100,000 inhabitants, and the design brief issued by the city stipulated that the planned settlement would have to be structured around the system of waterways and to introduce hydrological control given its adjacency to the river. The master plan was won by Gregotti Associati International in 2001 in a closed international competition, and was composed of three different grids overlaid on top of each other like a tartan patch: the first was a road network that broke down the site into blocks measuring 300 meters by 300 meters; the second was a system of bicycle and pedestrian pathways, creating a hierarchy of circulatory access as distinct from the vehicular routes; and the third was a grid of canals, some of which are navigable, that provide the landscape connection back to the river, and amplify the hydrological element in the existing site conditions. To accommodate a variation of densities, the plan is further broken down into three districts, increasing in density from low to high along the north-south roadway spine. The plan is bisected laterally by a central axis where the primary public and private urban functions are to be concentrated, including plazas, a university campus, as well as sports and recreational facilities.[21]

The housing project of interest is located in the first sector, covering one square mile or 259 hectares of primarily low-rise residences that broke ground in 2004. Planned also by Vittorio Gregotti and his firm, this first phase was undertaken by a major domestic real estate developer, the Overseas Chinese Town Group, also known as OCT, and completed in 2007. A composition of 'road villas' and 'townhouses', the residences were grouped around loop roads that generated more intimate zones branching off from the arterial streets. Rising two- to four-storeys in height, these contemporary assemblages of cube-like structures in no way resemble the Italian towns they were intended to emulate. Instead of creating the Italian equivalent of Thames Town in Songjiang, Gregotti presented a tasteful, formal reinterpretation of Shanghai's traditional *lilong* fabric. Like some of the old *lilong* neighborhoods, the blocks have through roads that then subdivide into smaller lane structures accessing the individual housing units. Some of the 'road villas' are arranged in a front-back manner, harkening back to the layouts of the hybrid row houses of the past.

In contrast to the Ju'er Hutong, which drew on the architectural language of the *siheyuan*, here, Gregotti makes no material or, indeed, figural references to the *lilong* housing. Rather, the formal qualities are further reified at the scale of each villa, with small entry courts or front yards doubling up as parking spaces just beyond the main entrance, leading to the relatively porous interiors complete with private gardens. The main rooms, such as the living and dining rooms, and bedrooms, typically on the upper floors, unfold along the largest garden, with glazed façades opening up to views of the garden; this visual connection with nature is likewise emphasized for villas or townhouses along the canals. Constructed of concrete, steel, and glass, the minimalist architecture here is clearly modern, although the overall massing and the aggregation of these units side-by-side share volumetric parallels with the *lilong* terraced housing of the past. Each unit is commodious, with 250 to 400 square meters of floor area above grade, and another 120 to 200 square meters in the basement, complemented by a diverse range of outdoor spaces including gardens, skywells, balconies, and terraces. With the exception of the handful of 11-storey high-rise blocks dispersed across this first phase, the overall residential density is low. In Block 6, for instance, there are 39 villas and 30 row houses, yielding around 2,300 people per square kilometer. Ultimately, this well-designed showpiece illustrates how indigenous reinterpretations can occur beyond literal emulations of the figure or *figura*, manifesting themselves through a reference to the form or *forma*, while remaining true to the times of the present or even future in its figure.

NUOVA CITTÀ DI PUJIANG

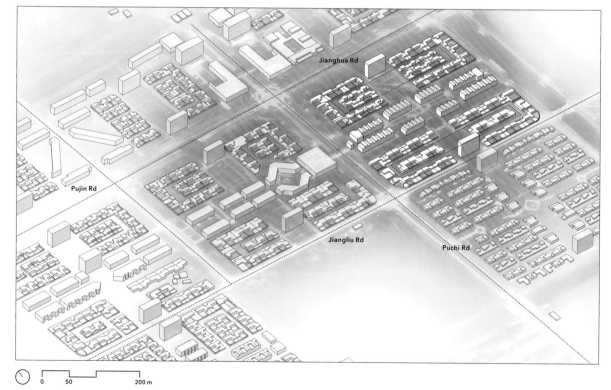

INDIGENOUS REINTERPRETATIONS

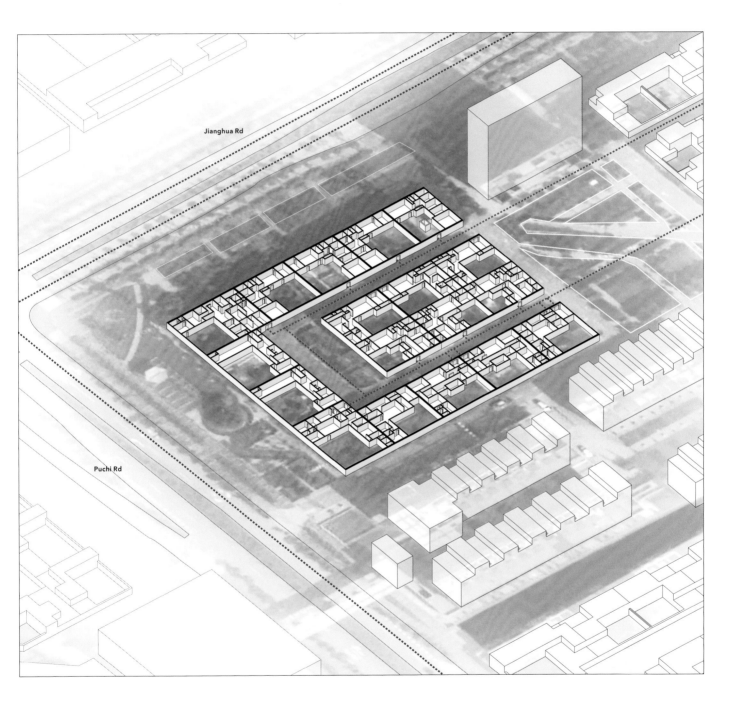

Jianghua Rd

Puchi Rd

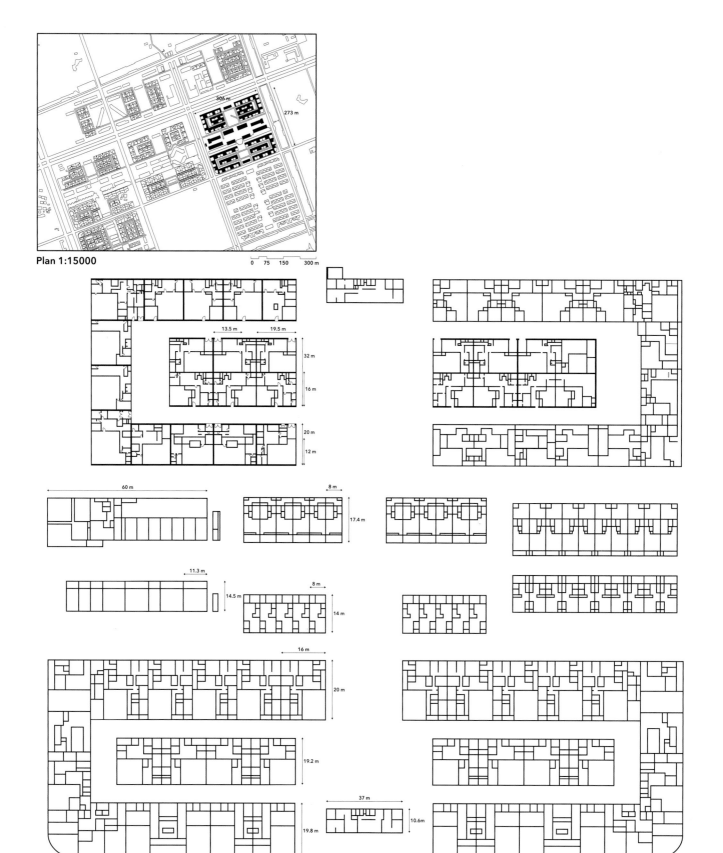

Plan 1:15000

0 75 150 300 m

Plan 1:1600

0 8 16 32 m

INDIGENOUS REINTERPRETATIONS

Key

- ■ Housing Units
- ■ Commercial
- □ Entrance/Courtyard
- ■ Skywell

Sectional Variation (Other Uses)

33 m

6 m

Section 1:1600

0 8 16 32 m

Household Types	Unit Type Locations	**Key**

Unit Types 1:1000

- Bedroom/Living
- ■ Kitchen
- ■ Bathroom

0 5 10 20 m

Courtyard A
492 sq m
40 units

Row House
491 sq m
32 units

Courtyard B
492 sq m
33 units

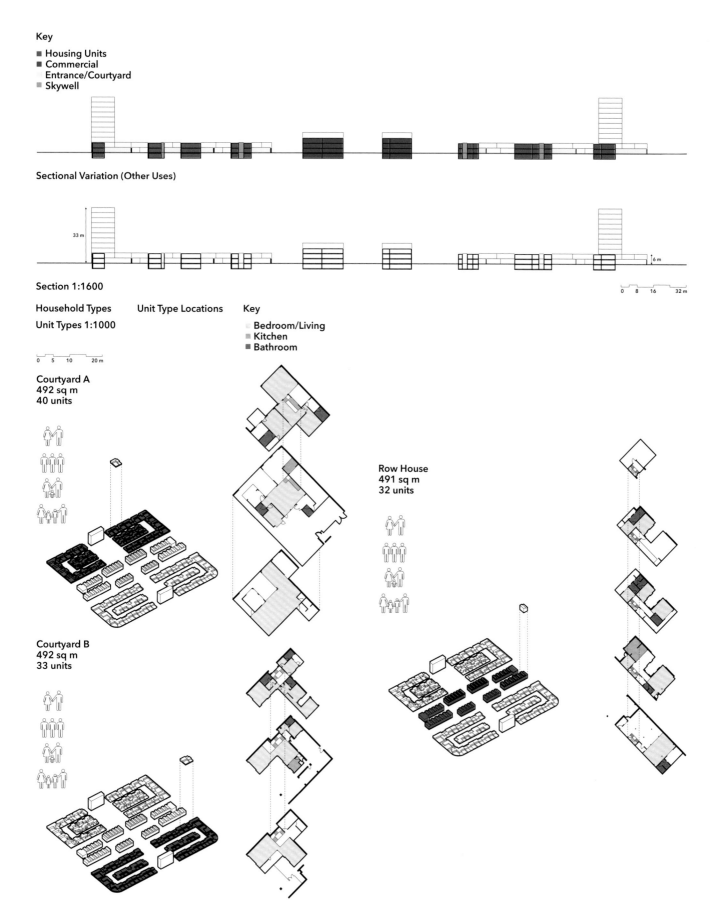

CONTEXTUAL ENGAGEMENTS AND DIFFERENCES BETWEEN FORM AND FIGURE

From the foregoing, the main issue in indigenous reinterpretation as depicted here is two-fold. The first concerns an overall approach in terms of the urban-architectural aims of a project and the interests involved. This may include claims by particular groups, such as heritage officials, or be related straightforwardly to scale requirements in more contextual than historical circumstances. An approach may also derive from a set of interests on the part of a particular architect or builder, regardless of the preserve of a broader institutional context. This, in turn, may be experimental, as with the mud block architecture in Zacatecas, Mexico, or rather more prosaic as in Villa Victoria and the pursuit of a suburban image in an urban context. Built outcomes may be otherwise contemporary, as with the Singaporean shophouses, or backwardly expressive as in the projects in the Saudi Arabian context.

The second aspect of indigenous reinterpretation, closely related to the overall strategy as well as the interests concerned, is the choice of a formal or figural approach to the architecture, including mixtures of both with varying emphases. This pair of qualities derives from *forma* and *figura*, where *forma* refers to the inherent pattern of order of a thing, in Heideggerian terms, while *figura* is its perceptible external boundary. Heidegger in his *excursus* on 'thingness' in *The Origins of a Work of Art* describes a ceramic jug's 'thingness' as being not its physical properties, *per se*, but the void inside it.[22] The jug shapes the void which, in turn, shapes the jug and the form of the jug is its void and its figure is the shape of the void. Much earlier, Aristotle defined form as being not the thing itself but its organizing pattern, while figure, instead, referred to its visual shape. Thomas Aquinas in this *Aesthetics* also took up a similar view. In short, for architecture, form or *forma*, in this kind of discussion, is the layout, spatial organization, its underlying topology or similar, while its figure or *figura* is its actual outward surface manifestations, style, and ornamentation.[23] As for the two principal case studies here, in the Ju'er Hutong, Wu Liangyong was working within the ambit of 'contextual traditionalism', one of the streams of thought associated with China's intellectual period of 'Culture Fever' during the 1980s prior to the Tiananmen Incident. In particular, he was adhering to Li Zehou's formulation of 'modern content with Chinese form', resulting in a figural emphasis.[24] Alongside of this, the use of courtyard housing, albeit at a higher density than the traditional *siheyuan* of Beijing, also further secured an argument in favor of past practices for the project. By contrast, Vittorio Gregotti, with the town villas at Nuova Città di Pujiang, sharply favored a more formal reinterpretation of past practice, in this case with regard to the *lilong* of Shanghai in the 1920s and 1930s. Although somewhat wider to accommodate cars, like the 'new *lilong*' and 'model villages' of Shanghai in the 1930s, the arrangement of entries, small front courtyards, front-to-back layouts

of dwelling, and so on, clearly drew on their earlier precedents. By contrast, there is little if any figural reference, with the exception of the overall massing of building elements and where 'ornamentation' applied by residents is to be found.

An underlying question in all this discussion is, of course, why do it? Why engage in conscious indigenous reinterpretation in the first place? By way of an answer, it seems to make most sense when something about the past way of making housing and the architecture of housing is worthwhile continuing or re-adopting when moving forward. As such, this impetus is certainly consistent with *traditio* in the Latin and Roman sense of 'bringing across'. In other words, it is about deploying dimensions, qualities, or practices from the past that are judged to be useful in the present-future. The manner and mode of the judgment, in turn, reflects back to the interests involved, the strategy being undertaken, and presumably, who or what is being saved. These days, critical accounts of the judgment involved can also be entertained, further relativizing the merit of one approach versus others, as well as making some more apparent than others. All that being said, however, under the colloquial truism that there is very little that is truly novel in this world, reinterpretation of what is there in a place can be a useful point of reference for otherwise highly contemporary architectural production. This is clear, for instance, in several recent Singaporean shophouse-like projects. Also in the spirit of *traditio* and bringing across, the locus of what is being brought across, urban-architecturally speaking, may not be and probably is not complete, fixed, and finished. Further development of typal arguments, as well as work on the language in architecture, is, after all, an ongoing project in itself.

INFILL AND PUNTAL INTERVENTIONS

Elektra House

As intended here, housing as 'infill and puntal interventions' represents at least two kinds of site conditions and two different basic housing types. The first site condition involves the infilling of a prescribed street layout or similar infrastructural armature as new development with a succession of housing units, either completely or partially across the site and where the repetitive infilling may have one or more sequential orders. The second site condition, engaging 'intervention', usually implies redevelopment rather than infill *de novo* and takes place within an existing context of buildings not necessarily of the same vintage. 'Puntal' in this terminology essentially means singular, as in a single building or building complex that can be easily referenced and otherwise understood as a particular point in an urban circumstance from which certain expressive or spatial qualities flow to otherwise reinforce or contradict prevailing urban-architectural situations. In the case of specific houses, such interventions may be responses to different space-making conditions or requirements such as: one house replacing another; one house beside others, with the implication of

shared or different contextual features; a house literally within the framework of another; a house that gives the appearance, rather than the thorough reality of other houses; and even a house under other housing, again with an element of disputation about the expression involved. Over time, puntal interventions may multiply within an urban area to more thoroughly transform it away from an existing condition or, indeed, to reinforce the existing condition still further. Such transformations may also involve regulatory and economic processes that are fundamental to physical outcomes and the kinds of dwellings that replace others on sites. Throughout, the two basic types of housing involved are row or terrace houses, usually on the order of three storeys, sometimes with additional floors and basements, as well as mid-rise unit ensembles of various kinds. Taller structures, such as 'pencil buildings', could also qualify, although they are more usually in the category of tall buildings. In today's contemporary circumstances, especially under the broad rubric of urban intensity, housing as puntal interventions is of more interest than housing as *de novo* infill.

Boston Back Bay bow fronts

New York Brownstones

PRECEDENTS: INFILLS, UNIT ENSEMBLES, AND INTERVENTION PROCESSES

The American row house of the nineteenth century was often built as the more or less coterminous infill of street, block, and lot layouts comprising new sections of cities. The Back Bay of Boston, for instance, was an early version of a public-private joint venture in which the street layout and infrastructure, along with land reclamation, was provided with public support and the neatly-aligned rows of housing came at the hands of private developers. Typically, the row and terrace houses that were built were three storeys in height with additional half basement level and roof dormer accommodations on relatively narrow lots that stretched back to rear gardens and a service alley. In planar arrangement, stairs and services were usually concentrated in the middle with well-made rooms to the front and back, particularly on the *piano nobile* which was largely dedicated to reception, entertainment, and contact with the outside world. The front and sometimes the rear façades of the row houses often bowed out, giving rise to the appellation of '<u>Boston bow fronts</u>', to secure more prominence along the street grid so as to admit more light and air into the dwellings.[1] Raised stairs from the street to the *piano nobile* were also a part of the typology, creating gracious entry into the houses. Mainly built in the 1860s through 1880s, the row offered varied architectural inflections and decorative programs on the façades, reifying particular figural tastes of the time. Similarly, row houses in Philadelphia, built somewhat earlier, show similar conformations, although with more sober façades.

Also, the '<u>brownstones</u>' of New York, built mainly towards the turn of the nineteenth into the twentieth centuries and even later, followed suit with respect to the basic row house type, but often with well-modeled façades and entry stairways, again reflecting architectural tastes of the time.[2]

Among cases of infill housing in the form of singular or puntal interventions, one of the most unusual is the 'house under a house' known as <u>Maison de Verre</u> in the Saint-Germain-des-Prés district of Paris in France. Designed and built by Pierre Chareau in collaboration with Bernard Bijvoet between 1927 and 1932, the Maison de Verre became one of the icons of the modern movement in architecture. Located in a courtyard owned by the Vellay family, the apartment with a doctor's office included was a wedding gift to their daughter on the occasion of her marriage to Dr. Dalsace. However, a renter above would not move out. Hence, the building at the back of the courtyard, facing the entrance, was gutted out below the recalcitrant renter and the Maison de Verre inserted.[3] Three stories in height, the lower floor included the doctor's office, the entrance, and the stairway leading to the apartment complex above. The second floor structured around an airy double-height space was fashioned in a manner that emphasized highly diagonal views and a Japanese sensibility of depth, or *oku*, popular at the time at least in well-informed architectural circles. The third floor housed the family quarters, with a deck overlooking a well-landscaped back garden. The obvious features of the house were the glass block façades that were cast in place on the ground and lifted into place. These were products of

Tsukishima

302 Station Street / Biles Residence
© David Simmons

the Saint Gobain glass company and highly experimental at the time. The screen-like lighting effects, during both day and night, including outside illumination, dramatically lend both a sense of privacy and a capacity for looking out to the apartment complex.

As another example of infill and singular intervention, the Elektra House in London of 2005 by David Adjaye brings a contemporary appearance to a narrow site in a mews setting.[4] Rising two storeys in height, this house is integrated into its surroundings by being literally built within the foundations and outer walls of an earlier dwelling. The new metal framework and cladding, inserted in the space provided, contrasts strongly with neighboring structures to left and right, while poetically projecting a minimalist aesthetic in the dwelling's interiors, topped by skylighting and some side lighting. As a result, this 'house within a house' becomes an experimental essay in the movement of light. Other juxtapositions associated with singular infill interventions include 'houses beside houses' in a manner that evokes architectural qualities of immediate context without replicating or literally emulating them. Juxtaposition can also extend to unexpected and unusual contrivances, like the projection of 'houses that are not there', in order to meet historic heritage or similar requirements within a residential neighborhood. An example of the first category of a 'house beside a house' is 302 Station Street or the Biles Residence in Melbourne, by Graeme Gunn Architects of 2003, constructed on a site sandwiched between old original terrace houses from the nineteenth century and a block of modern flats.[5] The resulting terrace house, typical in overall form of local two-storey terrace house types, reflects expressive conditions to both sides through a fenced-off garden on the front, parallel in dimensions but not in material with its older terrace house neighbor; a second floor protrusion picks up the materiality of the block of flats but comes across as a decorated pediment in the manner of the older terrace house. Neither reference is literal. Rather, the two façade assemblages are roughly equivalent to the older house, but in material qualities and in their lack of decoration they resemble the block of flats. In essence, what is presented is the form of the figure of the old terrace house, not its literal equivalent. In the second category, another example in Melbourne serves as an illustration. At the behest of heritage officials, the glass garage door at the front of a new bungalow dwelling in an old neighborhood built on a vacant site was inscribed with the image of the old bungalow that used to be there. Apparently of interest to the officials was less the building *per se* than some semblance of the original streetscape of the neighborhood.[6]

Moving on to 'unit ensembles' and 'processes resulting in puntal interventions', Space Block in the 36th District of Hanoi, Vietnam, takes on a challenging site in a dense inner-city area. Stretching along a narrow site on the remnants of what was once a strip of irrigated agricultural land, six dwelling units were to be inserted, resulting in a very high dwelling density on the order of 1,000 people per hectare. In collaboration between Tokyo University's Engineering School and local partners, a prototype was constructed in 2001 on the grounds of Hanoi

Space Block © Tomio Ohashi

Maison de Verre

University.[7] Using a methodology involving computer-generated parametric simulation and shape design, shade and ventilation conditions were optimized with functional layout requirements, starting with a four-storey monolith covering the whole site. What emerged were units on the order of 45 square meters in livable area, combining home-office configurations and communal courtyards allowing light to enter the complex from above. Generally, the architectural expression accentuated the play of light and shade across plain white stuccoed walls in a pleasing manner, with sheer glass infill where necessary. More pervasive still, a piece-meal redevelopment and renovation scheme was implemented in <u>Tsukishima</u> in Chūō-ku, Tokyo, beginning in the late 1990s.[8] Of concern in this neighborhood, with a street and land structure dating back at least to the Meiji Restoration period of the nineteenth century, was the legality of housing and other structures on at least two counts. One was the narrowness of the lanes, or *roji*, which were less than the minimum of four meters required by Tokyo's code. The other was earthquake resistance and material vulnerability to fire. A substantial incentive to change existing circumstances lay in the difficulty of transacting property that did not meet code. What transpired was the redrafting of regulations for the affected areas of Tsukishima, reducing the minimum lane width to 3.3 meters, or the width required for two firemen carrying a fire hose.[9] Some bonuses were also included to allow expansion upwards in height, with appropriate setbacks. Under this new regulatory framework, which also included stipulations about building materials and structure, property owners were encouraged to

legalize often dilapidated dwellings by moving their street alignments back along the lanes and constructing with appropriate materials and techniques in the interests of public safety. Over time, this process of incremental adjustment and building transformed areas of Tsukishima but without detracting from the environmental ambience of this otherwise traditional area of Tokyo.

CONTEMPORARY CASES: SINGLE HOUSES AND ENSEMBLES OF UNITS

The phenomenon of small-scale block infills and redevelopment of small sites is probably most commonly found in Japan where the real estate market has been defined largely by countless small landholdings. A result of the strong private property rights and an inheritance policy of keeping the land within the same family across generations by subdividing it, these lots have typically been maintained by the same household or small businesses in the same location over time. Moreover, as documented by Atelier Bow-Wow's "pet architecture", the Japanese have found creative means of maximizing these minute and often unusually shaped parcels, transforming them into a variety of commercial, retail, and residential purposes. Much of this boom in small housing, whether in the form of single-family detached dwellings or collective configurations, occurred after the burst of the 'bubble economy' of the 1980s, gaining traction through the growing attention paid in architectural journals and popular magazines, as well as other types of media. With the dramatic drop in real estate values after the 'bubble' period, some of the relatively larger properties were sold by subdividing them into smaller lots to facilitate the sales, thereby encouraging the proliferation of these small and narrow homes, or *kyōshō jūtaku*. In fact, slightly more than half of all the land transactions in Tokyo between 1991 and 1996 following the burst of the 'bubble' entailed parcels of less than 100 square meters.[10] Working within these tight spatial constraints, homeowners keen on having a comfortable place in central Tokyo rather than a more capacious house in the suburbs were able to hire talented young local architects open to tackling these small homes innovatively. These well-designed, compact houses thus no longer cater to just the budget-conscious, but in fact to clients from all walks of life who seek refined living spaces, even within limited quarters. The Japanese cases of interest here are drawn primarily from the Setagaya ward in Tokyo, one of the major residential suburbs with a population of more than 800,000, well serviced by subway and commuter rail.

Two of the four single-family detached houses showcased here were designed by Atelier Bow-Wow, which seeks to engage with what the architects term 'lively space' through their architecture, while working within the pockets presented in a hyper-dense urban environment.[11] Following on from their earliest deliberations on the *kyōshō jūtaku* as materialized in the Mini House of 1999 to their own House & Atelier Bow-Wow of 2006 are the ACO House and the Sway House completed recently in 2005 and 2008. Occupying a modest corner lot in a low-rise neighborhood composed of single-family houses, the ACO House was designed for a couple working in the music

industry. Working within the building regulations of having a maximum built area of no more than 70 percent and a building height of no more than 12 meters, the architects settled on a building footprint of a modest 35.51 square meters on the 51.26-square-meter site. In reflecting and amplifying the corner location of the house, the façade adjoining the two straight edges of the house is divided into five segments of equal length extending across the full height of the building and tracing the site perimeters, somewhat analogous to the traditional Japanese folding screens or *byōbu* that were used to enclose private spaces. These white, wooden folding panels are punctuated by windows stretching laterally across one or two of the segments at different elevations, allowing views out to the nearby trees and street, as well as permitting adequate light into the interior. A total of five floors with varying ceiling heights and room proportions were accommodated within this 10-meter-high envelope that would conventionally have yielded just three storeys by introducing a stepped section. Within this split-level configuration, Atelier Bow-Wow were able to fit in a sound-proof studio spanning part of the first and second floor, conceal the restroom under the staircase leading from the second to the third floor, provide storage space under the lower floors, and deploy an open space concept for the kitchen-living room complete with two-meter-high windows to let more light into this communal space. In addition, to maximize the floor areas, the vertical circulation is maintained along the outside walls. The arrangement of the rooms also reflects a consideration for the privacy of the owners, moving from the semi-public entryway to the library, the kitchen-living room, and finally to the bedroom and a secluded outdoor terrace.

0   25   100 m

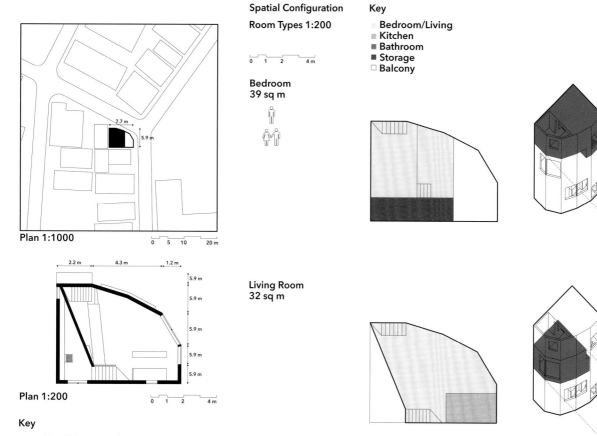

Plan 1:1000

7.7 m
5.9 m

0   5   10   20 m

2.2 m   4.3 m   1.2 m

5.9 m
5.9 m
5.9 m
5.9 m
5.9 m

Plan 1:200

0   1   2   4 m

Key
■ Residential
■ Entrance/Office

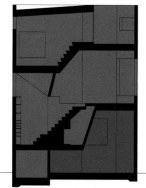

Sectional Variation (Other Uses)

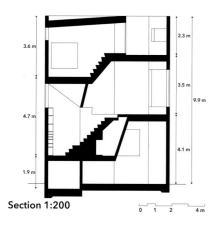

3.6 m
2.3 m
3.5 m
9.9 m
4.7 m
4.1 m
1.9 m

Section 1:200

0   1   2   4 m

Spatial Configuration
Room Types 1:200

0   1   2   4 m

Bedroom
39 sq m

Living Room
32 sq m

Library
23 sq m

Entrance/Studio
39 sq m

Key
░ Bedroom/Living
▒ Kitchen
▓ Bathroom
■ Storage
□ Balcony

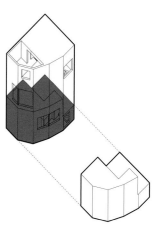

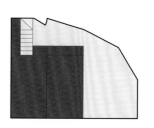

Room Locations

INFILL AND PUNTAL INTERVENTIONS

At the Sway House, Atelier Bow-Wow had a larger site of 78.08 square meters to work with but found themselves in a tight alley sandwiched between houses from the earlier post-war era. To be able to fit a parking lot on the site while also maximizing the solar insolation to this dense pack of residences lined along the alley, the architects bent and tapered the southern and western outer walls of the house, forming an incline and creating a 'sway'-like appearance in the building envelope. In doing so, they were able to maximize the house's overall capacity and at the same time comply with the city's sky exposure regulation to ensure adequate sunlight to the street. The building footprint thus occupied a modest 39.14 square meters, or just barely half the site area. Built of wood and metal, the house is wrapped by horizontal panels of white, galvanized steel, and its slender form is further accentuated by several narrow, rectangular windows of various sizes dispersed in a seemingly random manner on the façades for natural lighting and ventilation purposes. As in the ACO House,

a stepped section was employed to create floors and rooms of optimal heights, including a compressed kitchen and dining area of just 1.92 meters in height, and more commodious work and living areas ranging from 2.23 meters to 4.12 meters in height. The clients are a young couple in the art industry with the flexibility of working from home while taking care of their children, and thus it was important to have a clearer segregation of functions, with two nooks allocated as work spaces for each of them, and a living room as well as a children's room on the top floor that are relatively more open with the elimination of internal walls. Storage spaces are cleverly hidden under benches in the living and dining rooms, while the incorporation of a spiral stairway located at the outer wall further increases the available floor area. Unlike the ACO House where the bedroom was located on the upper level, here the bedroom is situated on the ground floor just beyond the husband's work space, while the rooftop terrace was reserved for an outdoor bathtub.

If the two projects by Atelier Bow-Wow project a sense of distinction between the public and private realms in terms of how the houses relate to the street, then House NA by Sou Fujimoto, completed in 2010, arguably represents their antithesis, blurring the boundaries between outside/inside, public and private. Constructed on a 54.47-square-meter site in the quiet neighborhood of Suginami, this three-dimensional matrix of suspended glass boxes stands as a daring, unconventional take on the *kyōshō jūtaku*. To presume that it was intended as an exhibitionist piece, however, misses its attempt to engage with its environment through the play on transparency. Designed for a working couple in their forties, the house was conceived of as a tree, with the functional spaces extended out from the trunk like branches. According to Fujimoto, this tree is thus akin to "a large single room" devoid of any walls and composed instead of 21 individual floor plates or branches that are situated at various heights, allowing the clients to "live like nomads within their own home".[12] The floating plates are arranged in such a way as to allow for free movement through the loosely defined programs of the house, akin to the *tatami* mats used in traditional Japanese houses in rooms that assumed a range of functions depending on the time of the day or the occasion. At grade, the house is entered through a foyer that branches down towards the guest room, and up towards the kitchen and an attached dining area. The rest of the second floor is composed of different-sized plates to accommodate various living areas, including an adjacent loft floor that is raised, doubling up as a work space when one is seated or perched on the lower branches of the living area. Ascending further up, one finds the library which is adjoined to the master bedroom and the dressing room, before culminating in the bathroom right at the very top of this volumetric assemblage. In-floor heating is installed in some of the horizontal platforms, while electrical outlets are discreetly concealed in the main areas, with other utility areas such as the heating, ventilation, air conditioning, plumbing, and storage located at the rear end of the house. In keeping with the sense of lightness imbued by the extensive use of glazing and the disaggregated floor plates, Fujimoto connected these pieces together with a white,

steel-frame structure with bracings no more than 55 millimeters in width. The cool, minimalistic composition is softened by potted plants placed on the multi-level terraces, as well as the use of wood paneling framing the doors and windows. Despite the project's transparency and openness, this vertical transition from public to intimate spaces reflects an implicit desire to preserve some semblance of privacy. Both in the day and at night, drawn curtains serve as temporary partitions but also as screens defining the personal realm of the household. When the delightful glass boxes are fully revealed, inhabitants are afforded views out to the surroundings while seated within this contemporary interpretation of the Japanese house and the urban landscape beyond, symbolizing a co-existence between architecture and the city, nature and artificiality.[13]

HOUSE NA

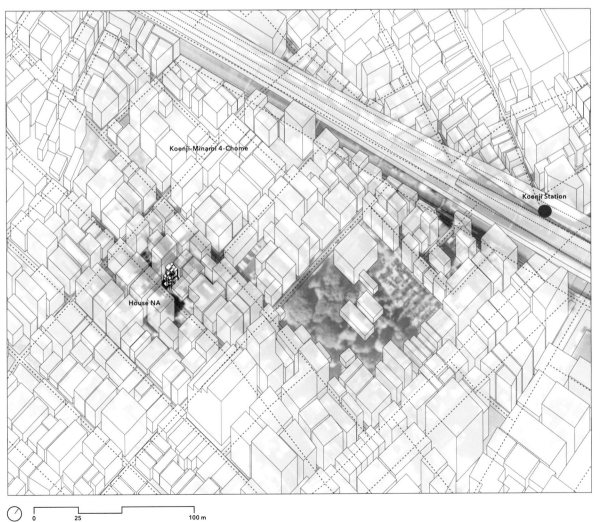

Koenji-Minami 4-Chome

Koenji Station

House NA

0   25   100 m

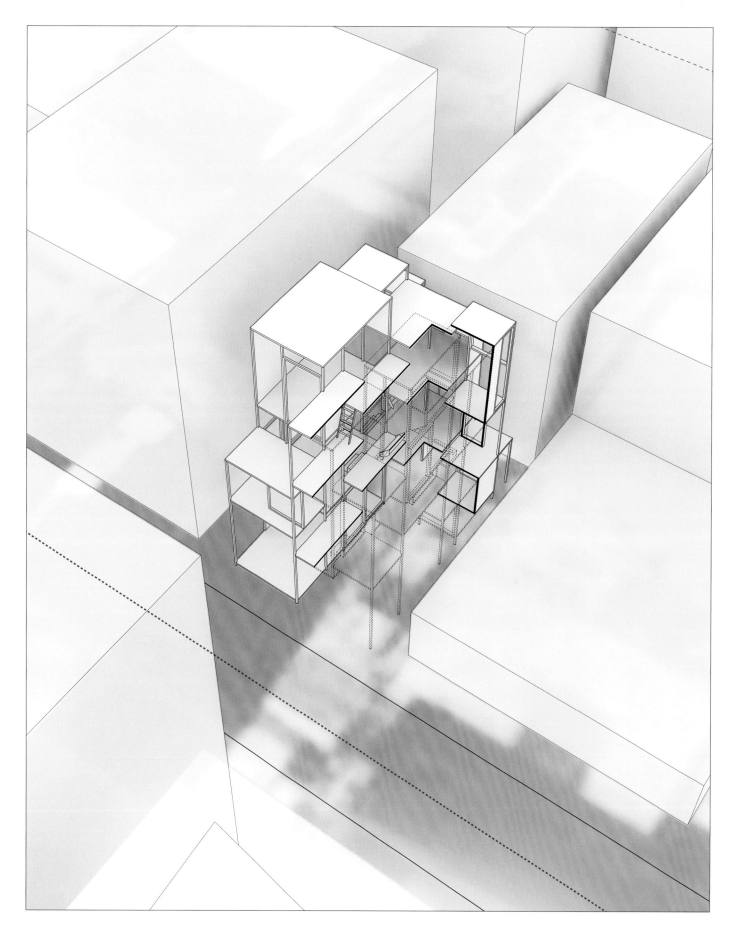

INFILL AND PUNTAL INTERVENTIONS

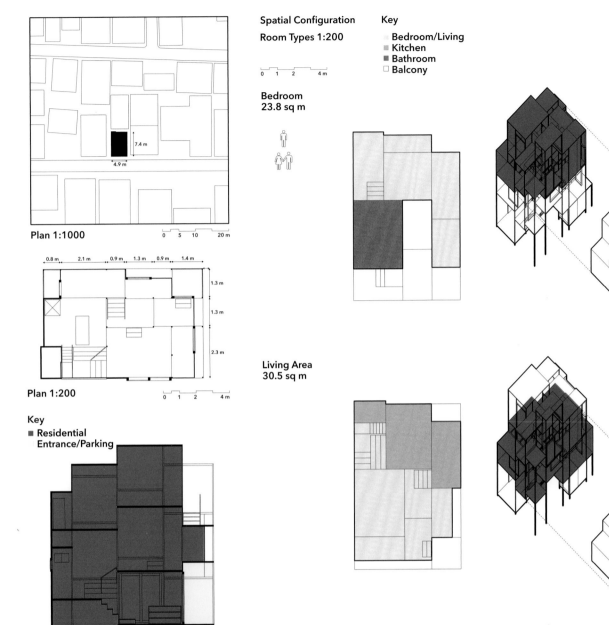

Plan 1:1000

0   5   10   20 m

0.8 m 2.1 m 0.9 m 1.3 m 0.9 m 1.4 m

1.3 m
1.3 m
2.3 m

Plan 1:200

0   1   2   4 m

Key

■ Residential
   Entrance/Parking

Sectional Variation (Other Uses)

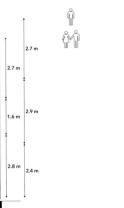

8.1 m

2.7 m
2.7 m
2.9 m
1.6 m
2.8 m   2.4 m

Section 1:200

0   1   2   4 m

Spatial Configuration
Room Types 1:200

0   1   2   4 m

Key

░ Bedroom/Living
▒ Kitchen
■ Bathroom
□ Balcony

Bedroom
23.8 sq m

Living Area
30.5 sq m

Guest Room
20.1 sq m

Room Locations

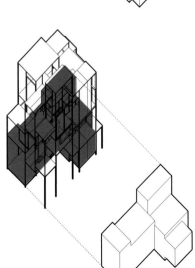

© Iwan Baan

Lucky Drops or Skin House No. 7 by Yamashita Yasuhiro from Atelier Tekuto is another single family detached dwelling, also located in Setagaya-ku. With a building footprint of merely 21.96 square meters, this extraordinary project epitomizes the *kyōshō jūtaku* and the extreme conditions under which these puntal residential insertions are created. Designed for a young couple who had purchased a small plot of land of 58.68 square meters in area and were working with a limited budget, the house maximized the depth of the site, extending up to 19 meters in length to the maximum allowed on the site. The slender, trapezoidal structure tapers from 3.2 meters at its entrance, to a modest 0.7 meters at the back, while the height is correspondingly reduced from 2.5 storeys above grade at the front to 1.5 storeys at the rear end. Apart from taking advantage of the unusually long site, the architect and his team sought to maximize the livable space by extending underground which was not subjected to the same setback regulations in place above ground. As such, what would have been an extremely compressed space was overcome by generating three levels within the house. The upper level accommodating the bedroom and closet space is composed of steel mesh grids adjoining the white-painted steel members that framed each of the drop-shaped panels; the ground floor opens up to a 1.5-storey void with stairs leading to the basement where the rest of the living/dining areas are held, including the living room, kitchen, and bathroom. Given the tapering form of the house, the primary living areas such as the bedroom and living room were stacked at the front where the structural width is the widest, while service areas like the closet and bathroom were tucked away to the back. In addition, to maintain a comfortable passageway through the basement, the service functions were lined up against the eastern walls. Instead of typical glass or wooden exterior walls, fiber-reinforced plastic panels were used to clad the house above grade, thus bringing soft natural light into the deep and narrow interior while maintaining the inhabitants' privacy. Again, white was the predominant color, enhancing the luminosity of the thin exterior skin as well as the visual spaciousness in the interior. At night, the house lights up from within and glows like a jewel box, transforming this thin sliver of a structure into an alluring sight to behold.

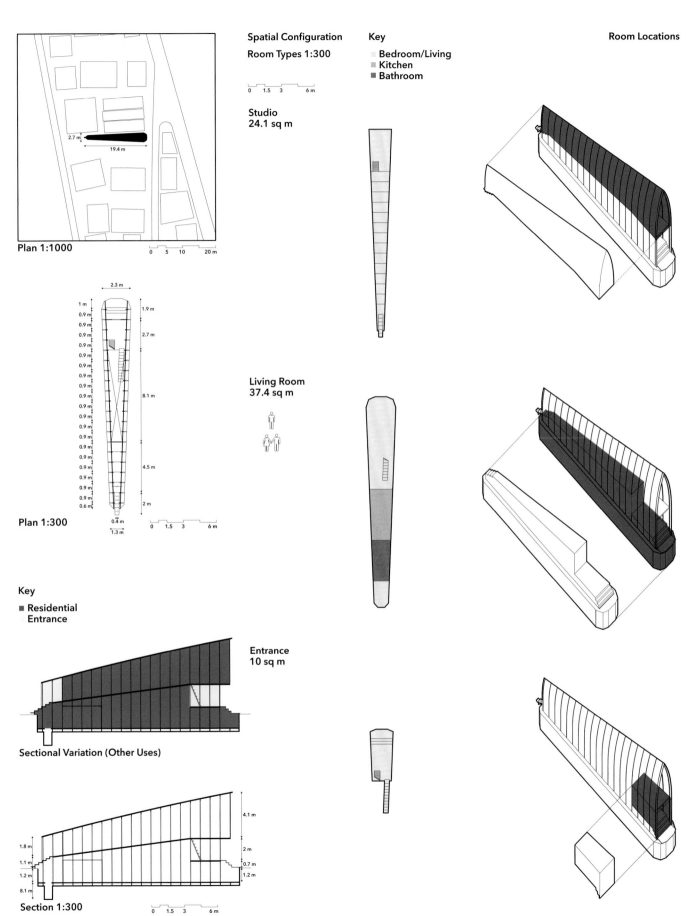

Plan 1:1000

2.7 m
19.4 m

0 5 10 20 m

Spatial Configuration

Room Types 1:300

0 1.5 3 6 m

Studio
24.1 sq m

2.3 m

1 m
0.9 m
0.9 m
0.9 m
0.9 m
0.9 m
0.9 m
0.9 m
0.9 m
0.9 m
0.9 m
0.9 m
0.9 m
0.9 m
0.9 m
0.9 m
0.6 m

1.9 m
2.7 m
8.1 m
4.5 m
2 m

0.4 m
1.3 m

Plan 1:300

0 1.5 3 6 m

Living Room
37.4 sq m

Key

Bedroom/Living
Kitchen
Bathroom

Room Locations

Key

■ Residential
  Entrance

Entrance
10 sq m

Sectional Variation (Other Uses)

1.8 m
1.1 m
1.2 m
8.1 m

4.1 m
2 m
0.7 m
1.2 m

Section 1:300

0 1.5 3 6 m

Besides these standalone architectural gems, small-scale infills can likewise occur through the aggregation of dwelling units into collective housing. In Setagaya-ku, the Seijo Townhouse or the Garden Court Seijo United Cubes completed in 2007 by Kazuyo Sejima is an instance of an experimental undertaking not just by the architect but also by the developer that sought to offer an alternative way of providing condominium apartments within the dense urban fabric of Tokyo. The private developer had organized a competition in search of an architect to design a collective housing project that would attain a "site-specific atmosphere" as well as relate to the city.[14] With a site area of 1,197.6 square meters, which is several times larger than a single-family plot, Sejima was able to propose a large-scale garden in the belief that this agglomeration within a broader environment would be able to generate an urban atmosphere for the city.[15] The outcome was a complex of cubes that were assembled and stacked in an assortment of sequences, interspersed with intimate alleys and communal courtyards and, in essence, constituting a microcosm of the traditional neighborhood communities. This notion of a 'house as a city' was first explored by Sejima's partner, Ryue Nishizawa, in the Moriyama House of 2005 composed of 10 white cuboids of various sizes stacked and arrayed seemingly randomly to form five compact rental apartments with gardens and pathways in between. In this subsequent elaboration, the Seijo Townhouse deployed 20 interlocking block units to form 14 apartment units, with a network of shared interstitial spaces recalling the traditional *roji* in between. Constructed of thinner and longer light-pink bricks laid with white mortar, the complex is visually warm and inviting, and immediately distinguishable from the sea of grey and black pitched roofs. Each of the cubes is adorned with giant windows and is intentionally positioned such that none of the windows are situated directly opposite each other. Apart from letting in plenty of sunlight, this clever offset allows these windows to remain open to the views outside, whether into a private courtyard, communal garden, or alleyway, enhancing the sense of an outward-oriented spatial appreciation intrinsic in the Japanese acumen. Inside, each of the cubes contains a single programmatic function and is linked to the rest of the unit by a hallway, bridge, or courtyard, generating a high degree of unit variation contrary to the standardized types commonly found in Japan's condominium housing market. Unlike the Moriyama House though, this complex is walled and gated, preventing free access by non-residents and retaining a semblance of privacy as well as exclusivity within the community.

Seijo 5-Chome

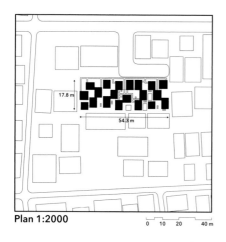

Plan 1:2000

0   10   20   40 m

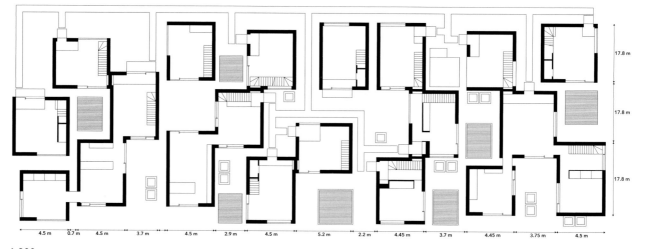

17.8 m

17.8 m

17.8 m

Plan 1:300

4.5 m   0.7 m   4.5 m   3.7 m   4.5 m   2.9 m   4.5 m   5.2 m   2.2 m   4.45 m   3.7 m   4.45 m   3.75 m   4.5 m

0   1.5   3   6 m

Key

■ Housing Units
  Entrance/Parking

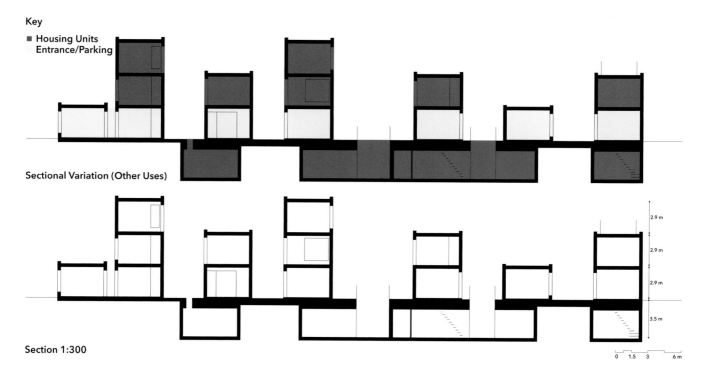

Sectional Variation (Other Uses)

2.9 m

2.9 m

2.9 m

3.5 m

Section 1:300

0   1.5   3   6 m

INFILL AND PUNTAL INTERVENTIONS

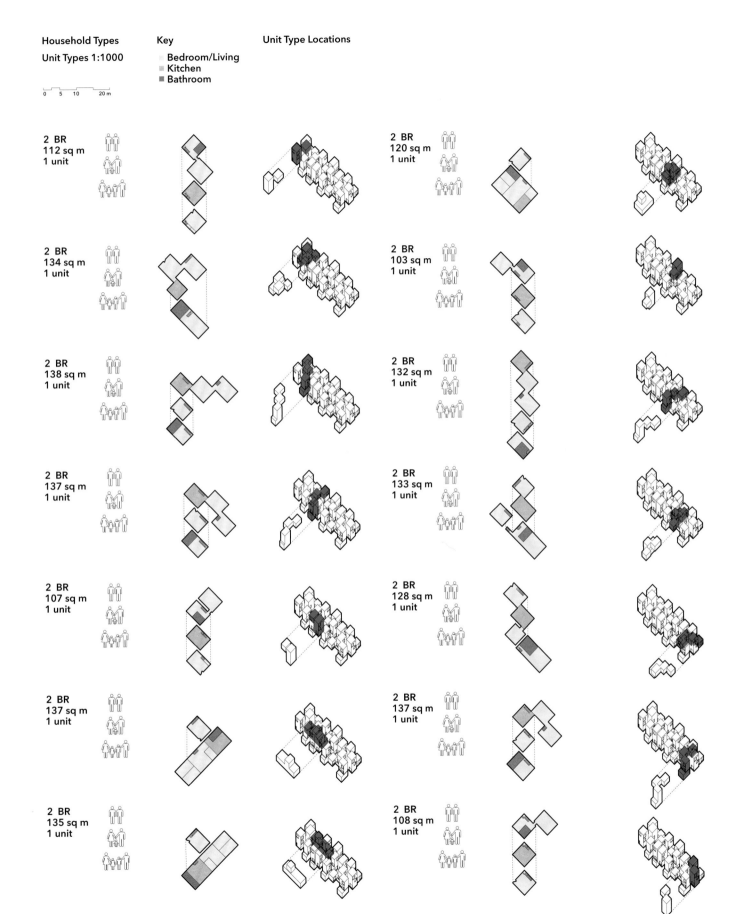

Another collective housing sharing similar unit variation and individuation is the Umegaoka Cooperative Housing ROXI completed earlier in 2003 by Satoshi Sasaki from SGM Architect & Associates.[16] Commissioned by a cooperative with households of differing needs, the architects set about customizing each housing unit within a formally cohesive whole. Located along a main road, the white, reinforced-concrete project crowned with a galvanized steel roof rises up four storeys above grade, setting itself apart from its neighboring residences. Spanning a site area of 417 square meters or the equivalent of nearly four single-family detached units length-wise, the northern façade is relatively closed and sombre, interspersed with several small steel-framed windows and a 1.5-storey screen of steel bars defining part of the G- and K-Units. In contrast, the southern façade is much more playful, with its mosaic-like façade of full-length windows of various shapes and sizes and unadorned white concrete expressing the highly-specialized living conditions and the unit variation within. In fact, seen from afar, the southern façade looks like a section cut through the building, although once further up close, the three-dimensional forms of the projecting balconies and roof terraces reinforce the sculptural effect of this concrete structure with a total built area of 910 square meters. Inside, the project houses a collection of flats, maisonettes, and lofts, with a total of 11 unique units: Units A, D, H, and J were designed by Naoko Tarao from Tarao Hiiro Architects; Units B, E, F, and I were designed by Higa Takehiko from Takehiko Higa Architects & Associates; while Units C, G, and K were designed by Yamamoto Yūsuke from Atelier-YY. Of the four units done by Naoko Tarao, the maisonette in Unit A was for a couple in their forties and can be accessed directly from the main road on the first level as well as from a stairway leading down to the basement terrace court.[17] Unit D was for a couple in their fifties who also had a dog. As the husband works as an illustrator and receives many guests in this live-work apartment, the maisonette is spatially divided into two distinct public and private realms. Unlike the minimalistic, white walls and wooden flooring of Unit A, the interior of Unit D reflects the personalities of its inhabitants with its bright, colorful washes, and playful curved surfaces and slanted lines. In addition, each room is endowed with its own character with unique wall colors and finishing.[18] Unit H located right above Unit D was for a couple in their thirties who desired a small home office environment. Within the apartment, all the service and storage functions are arranged along the walls to create an open space in the center, with continuous lighting and ventilation provided by configuration as a double-height loft.[19] The largest unit in the house, Unit J, was for a couple in their thirties with two young boys and designed with the children's sightlines and movements in mind. More notably, the space under the roof was meant to be flexible, anticipating the future needs of the growing children.[20]

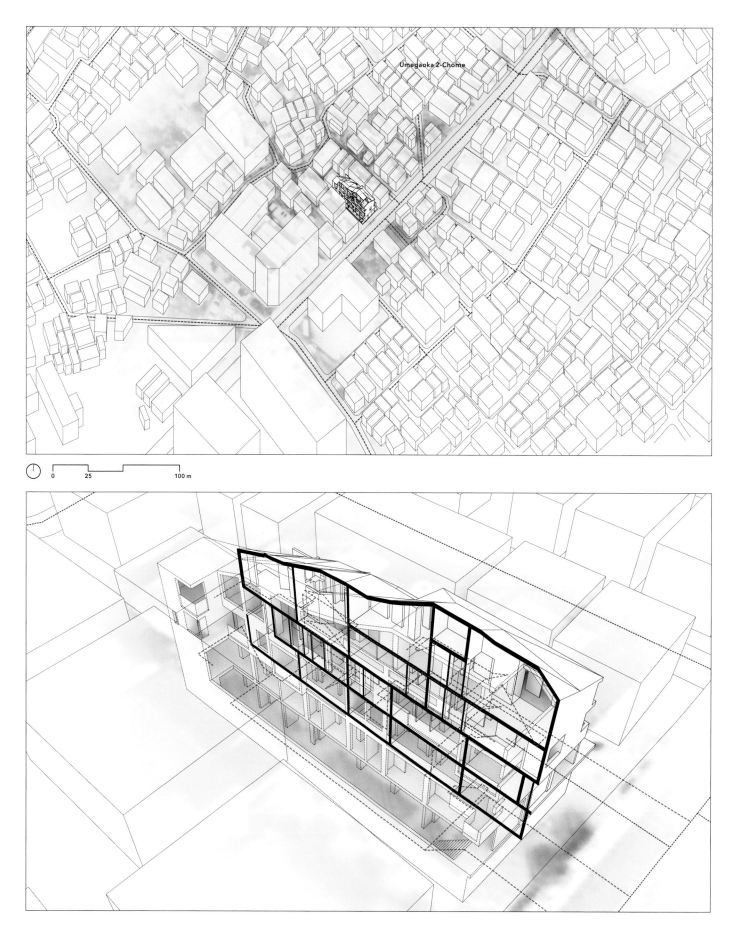

Umegaoka 2-Chome

0   25   100 m

INFILL AND PUNTAL INTERVENTIONS

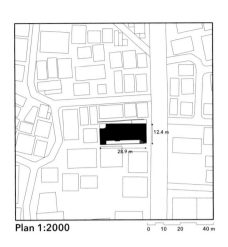

Plan 1:2000

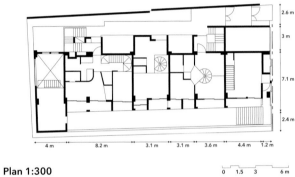

Plan 1:300

Key

■ Housing Units

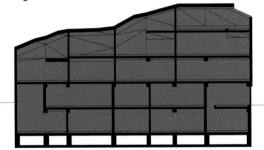

Sectional Variation (Other Uses)

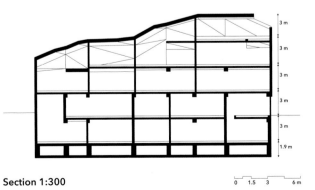

Section 1:300

Household Types

Unit Types 1:200

Key
□ Bedroom/Living
▨ Kitchen
■ Bathroom

Unit Type Locations

1 BR
80 sq m
1 unit

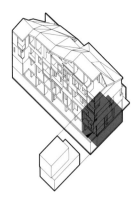

1 BR
92 sq m
1 unit

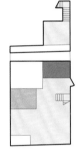

1 BR
77 sq m
1 unit

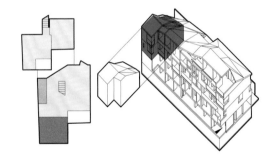

1 BR
76 sq m
1 unit

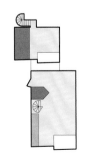

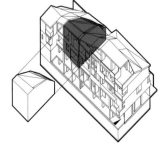

Household Types
Unit Types 1:200

Key

▢ Bedroom/Living
▨ Kitchen
■ Bathroom

Unit Type Locations

0 1 2   4 m

2 BR
127 sq m
1 unit

1 BR
73 sq m
1 unit

2 BR
89 sq m
1 unit

1 BR
96 sq m
1 unit

2 BR
77 sq m
1 unit

1 BR
83 sq m
1 unit

3 BR
102 sq m
1 unit

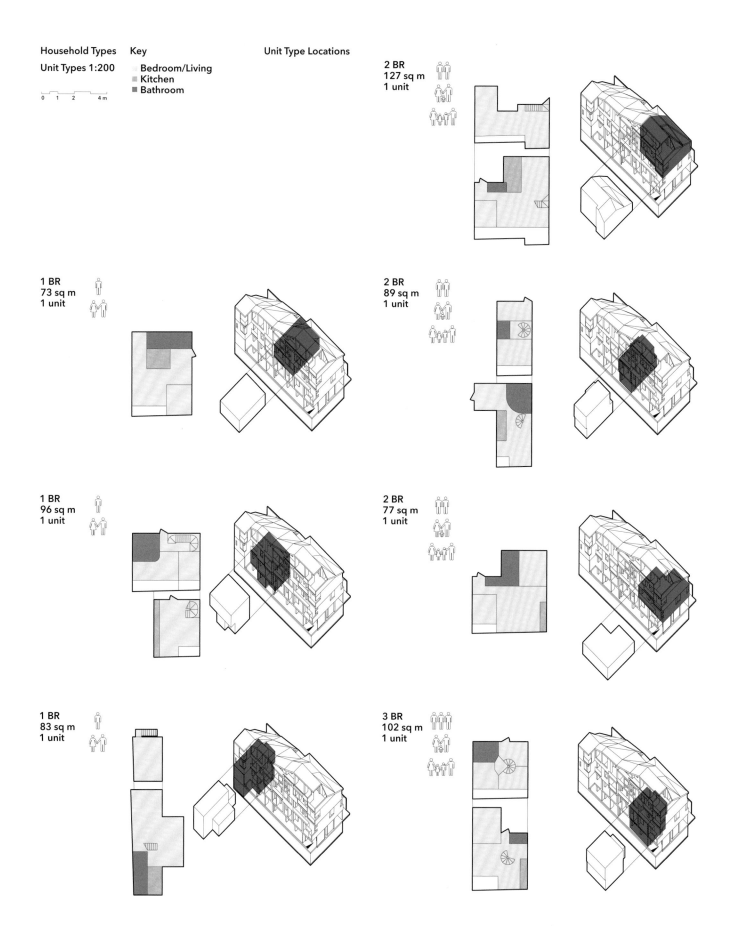

One final infill project that serves as collective housing is the Alfonso Reyes 58, situated in a vastly different context of the Colonia Condesa neighborhood in Mexico City. The dense residential neighborhood itself is an up-and-coming area with an assortment of restaurants and nightclubs popular amongst the young, white-collar professionals, artists, students, and intellectuals. Designed by Dellekamp Architects and completed in 2003, the complex houses seven units with commercial space and parking on the ground floor on a relatively small site of 390 square meters. Located at the edge of a perimeter block comprising traditional Mexican-style row houses, the reflective, aluminum-clad building of stacked boxes rises six storeys above grade. While this contemporary, rectilinear composition might at first glance seem like a stark contrast to the colorful plastered façades and effusive roofs of the low-rise row houses lining the secondary street, it in fact helps to give shape to the arterial road of Avenida Alfonso Reyes, much in line with the bright-red five-storey shophouse and the high-rise commercial building it is sandwiched between. Plan-wise, the architects retained the perimeter block nature of the site, creating a C-shaped structure enclosing a modest courtyard, buffering the high levels of noise emanating from the busy street. Starting from the ground floor, the variously sized boxes are overlapped at various points, creating rectangular and L-shaped voids on the sides as well as along the street façade, separating the apartments while creating interior patios and terraces. All the units are elevator-served and accessed via a central lobby; the four units on the third and fourth floors are configured at mirror opposites of each other, both vertically and horizontally, while the three units on the fifth and sixth floors are each unique in plan. In each of these units, the service spaces are pushed to the back, freeing up the space closer to the street fronts for living areas and allowing for ample light and air to enter through the slim bands of clerestory windows. Façade-wise, these apartments are also materially expressed with dissimilar finishes to their aluminum external cladding, differentiated by the two shades, and either smooth or corrugated surfaces. The floor-to-ceiling height extends 3.2 meters, with the cladding functioning as a screen wrapping around the boxes to retain the internal privacy as well as to block out the noise of the city, punctured occasionally by a few small windows. Overall, this urban insertion deploys a similar strategy to Sejima and Nishizawa, where disaggregated blocks can be assembled in a manner that reflects the individuality of each of the units, attaining a high diversity of unit types in a housing typology that has conventionally been associated with mass production and standardization in the modern age.

Michoacan Ave

Alfonso Reyes

Diagonal Patriotismo

Vicente Suarez

0   25   100 m

Pachuca

Penthouse 1

Penthouse 2

Apartment 3

Apartment 4

Apartment 2

Apartment 1

Alfonso Reyes

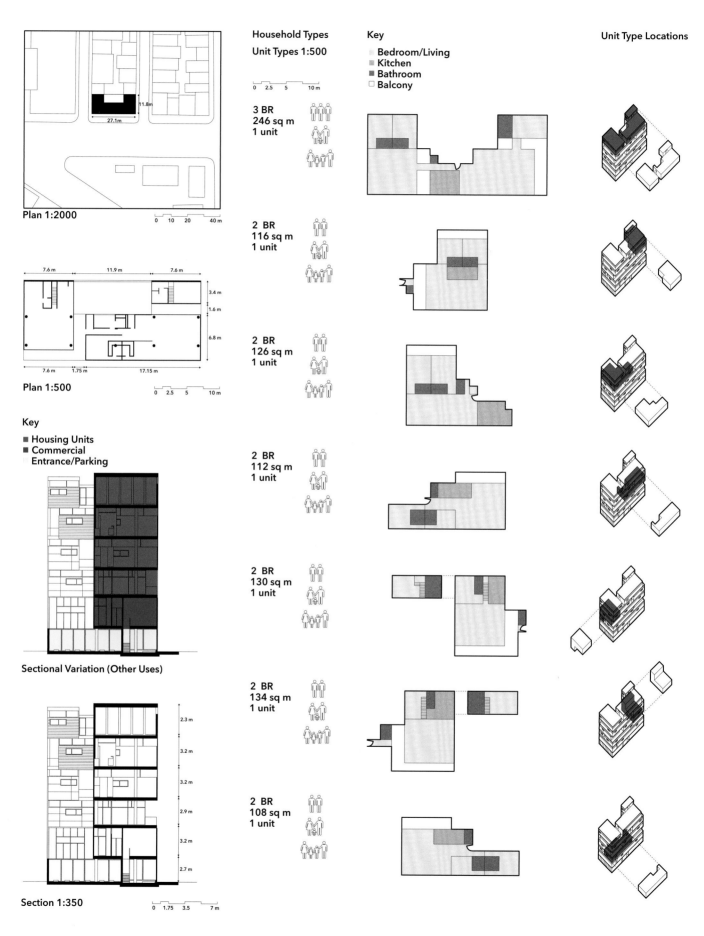

Plan 1:2000

0   10   20   40 m

Plan 1:500

0   2.5   5   10 m

Key
- Housing Units
- Commercial
- Entrance/Parking

Sectional Variation (Other Uses)

Section 1:350

0   1.75   3.5   7 m

Household Types
Unit Types 1:500

0   2.5   5   10 m

3 BR
246 sq m
1 unit

2 BR
116 sq m
1 unit

2 BR
126 sq m
1 unit

2 BR
112 sq m
1 unit

2 BR
130 sq m
1 unit

2 BR
134 sq m
1 unit

2 BR
108 sq m
1 unit

Key
- Bedroom/Living
- Kitchen
- Bathroom
- Balcony

Unit Type Locations

INFILL AND PUNTAL INTERVENTIONS

ANIMATION, COMPLETION, CONTRADISTINCTION, AND OTHER OUTCOMES

The purposes and outcomes of houses and housing deployed as puntal interventions can be varied. One set of outcomes concerns primarily the expressive interchange with adjacent or nearby buildings. Another set has to do largely with functional relationships, again within a neighboring context. A third set involves the relative ease of transferability from a very particular set of relationships to other housing and building types to those that are more general. The first set includes expressive purposes like animation, for instance, where a particular housing context is enlivened by the inclusion of a new addition, the appearance of which has reverberations beyond its immediate boundaries. Certainly, many of Tokyo's small houses described here have this kind of effect. By contrast, another expressive purpose and outcome may be to complete, or sometimes round out, what is already in place, involving direct emulation of the formal and figural composition of adjacent buildings. Many extensions of terraces of row houses in various places have this quality to them. Indeed, the relative ease with which figural aspects of row house architecture can be rather completely changed without interfering unduly with the formal character of the basic housing type makes this sort of outcome possible. Then too, there can be a capacity for contradistinction, whereby sharp differences are drawn with neighboring properties, using basic characteristics that are shared in common, such as materiality, relative openness, and transparency, contemporaneity, or simply style. Again, the row house type can be conducive to this kind of expressive interplay.

A second set of outcomes, involving largely functional relationships with neighboring circumstances, can include facilitation of despecialization over time, where aspects of an original infill of housing become at least partially converted to support, say, storefront activities. This may be very important to the continuing quality of life of an otherwise residential neighborhood, as can conversion in an opposite direction from, say, light industrial to housing and commercial use to loft dwellings. Then, as a corollary to this despecialization of use, entirely new housing types can be introduced, as in Mexico City, with the aim of providing the opportunity to more actively transform a neighborhood. Many work-live arrangements within the broad categories of housing discussed here can have this effect. Provision of higher density is also a functional transformation that can occur with new infill and puntal interventions, as demonstrated in Tsukishima in Tokyo. Further, staying with Tsukishima and other places like it, a function of successive infill projects can be simply to legalize dwelling circumstances through needed construction modifications.

Finally, the third set of aims and outcomes are intertwined with similitude and replicability and concern the degree to which particular kinds of infill and puntal interventions can be made more broadly applicable elsewhere. Often, the sheer specificity of immediate contextual responses, as suggested by the other sets of purposes and outcomes, can limit replicability. Conceptually, replicability requires sufficient similarity between a given set of circumstances and those being potentially emulated. This may take the form of straightforward equivalence and one-to-one correspondence, as in the completion, for instance, of a row of townhouses. In other situations, like the House NA in Tokyo, for example, similitude, in this case concerned with the replication of certain traditional traits in housing, came by way of a certain parallelism and degree of analogy. Rather than a planar conjoint layout of space in the manner of traditional *tatami* mats, an analogous spatial alignment can be seen to be preserved in plan but disengaged vertically via 21 separate floor plates into a three-dimensional format. Similarly, the alley and court spaces in the Seijo Townhouse complex by Kazuyo Sejima were sufficiently reminiscent in scale of lane life in Edo, or pre-modern Tokyo, to essentially replicate it in a contemporary guise. There was also a flexibility in the interweaving of communal and private space which has a resemblance again to arrangements within the lane life of Edo and early Tokyo.

HOUSING SPECIAL POPULATIONS

Simmons Hall

In a perfect world where adequate and workable housing is available to everyone, it would be invidious to single out any particular group with regard to dwelling or accommodation. However, in less perfect yet real worlds, housing for the very poor, for instance, has received focused attention. Among other strategies, sites and services projects amid squatter conditions, evolutionary social housing in response to slum clearance, and heavily-subsidized although otherwise normal-looking housing, all have adherents and practitioners. Certainly, in the last if not other of these circumstances, avoidance of stigmatization of the poor argues for as much 'normalcy' as possible, even if it requires inclusions among subsidized mixed-income housing, intergenerational accommodation and dwelling units that cater to different stages in the life-cycle. Failing this, however, providing roofs over people's heads focuses attention on particular groups in need and dwelling circumstances that fit their needs, with the hope and, indeed, expectation that they might move on to better circumstances. Single-room occupancy hotels, for instance, in the United States for indigent populations on the streets have now become particular building types. Similarly, although more broadly subscribed to, assisted living for the elderly has begun to align certain housing with specific groups. Then too, broad institutional components of society like, for instance, higher education and universities see fit to house students and faculty and to tailor accommodation to the particular needs and, if possible, wants of these groups. Somewhat less commonplace, specific social arrangements of individuals into communities, like collectives for example, have emerged and again tailored housing to their needs and wants. Moreover, given the apparent rise in the diversity of household formations and

195

PREVI © Peter Land

Aranya Community Housing © John Paniker, from "Aranya Community Housing Project Brief" (1995), p. 66

the emphases, socially and otherwise, on the emergence of particular housing types, a category like 'housing of special populations' is understandable. It also comes at a time when individual and social mobility is historically quite high in many places, making the idea of moving from one place to another to suit certain needs more attractive and, ultimately, practical. One result is, of course, more specialized and contingent forms of housing. None of this, however, is entirely without precedent. The almshouses of old, particularly in the wake of the industrial revolution, alongside of institutionalized care for the mentally and physically handicapped, are clear examples. Often, they were built in countryside settings in the belief that clean air and the out-of-doors would serve as a healing balm. Then too, the college houses and even monastic qualities accommodating scholars for periods of time, both have long and ample histories. Clearly a full rendering of all special populations and their housing is far beyond the scope of this narrative. Instead, only broad constituencies like the very poor, the elderly, and student populations will make up the bulk of this account.

PRECEDENTS: RECENT SOCIAL, STUDENT, AND ELDERLY HOUSING

One of the most prominent social housing projects for low-income, primarily immigrant families was the PREVI (Proyecto Experimental de Vivienda)

project in Lima, Peru, that began in 1966 under the United Nations Development Program to devise new concepts and techniques to produce low-cost housing. Work commenced in 1968, largely under Peter Land, with a pilot project and continued well into the 1970s and beyond. The site was eight kilometers north of central Lima with an area of 40 hectares and a target of 1,500 dwelling units of which 467 were built. Early on, schemes were invited for the layout of the master plan, in addition to concepts for the buildings themselves. These included schemes by Atelier 5, a Japanese team of Kikutake, Maki, and Kurokawa, and (probably the most publicized) by Christopher Alexander and his group, based on his 'pattern language' and its movement away from reductive planning practices of the day.[1] In terms of actual construction, a complex was built by various architects in the form of an exposition, somewhat like Weissenhof or IBA, although for low-cost, evolutionary housing. Lot sizes of 80 to 150 square meters were used, of which dwelling units were to occupy from 60 to 120 square meters respectively. Buildings were of one- and two-storeys but with structures able to handle an additional third floor. Most lots were enclosed behind walls or adjacent building. In short, all houses were to comprise a basic or core unit, but be able to expand through planned additions over time. The housing by the Japanese team was row housing in overall configuration, with setbacks on the first storey allowing for addition of a shop or other commercial space. Expansion was planned upwards. Another scheme

202 Island Inn

Housing for the Fishermen of Tyre © Dina Rebbas & Evy Pappas,
Courtesy of Hashim Sarkis Studios

by Charles Correa was comprised of units arranged back to front, again with planned upward expansion and setbacks from the building line along the street. Units by James Stirling, by contrast, involved courtyard housing. In all cases, subsequent additions and modifications were made to units by occupants, especially with regard to the appearance or figuration of buildings.

Another notable social housing project, again for low-income occupants, was the Aranya project by Balkrishna V. Doshi for the Indore Development Authority near Bhopal in central India.[2] Occupying an 85-hectare site, 6,500 plots were divided into 11 types and income levels, with the smallest having an area of just 35.5 square meters for the economically weakest sector of dwellers and up to 600 square meters for the highest income group. The master plan divided the site into six sectors of housing with a central spine of commercial and institutional areas. In proportion, the plots for the economically weakest segment comprised 65 percent of the total, whereas for the high income groups it was nine percent. Circulation through the site was mainly pedestrian with space also for light vehicles. Piped infrastructure was carefully organized to minimize costly runs and several forms of public open space were provided. Housing units began with a plinth across the site with a latrine, water tap, and kitchen space towards the back of lots, on to which rooms were added. In this evolutionary concept, the metrics of additions were established to facilitate building. Further, entrances,

balconies, and other occupiable rooftops provided for views over adjacent streets and open spaces as readily 'defensible' space. Raised sidewalks integral to the plinths provided relief from flooding. More generally, the alignment of architectural elements within dwellings conformed to a shape grammar forming a basic code for construction. The result was a variegated and vibrant environment.

Although not for low-income occupants *per se*, the more recent Housing for the Fishermen of Tyre by Hashim Sarkis evolved over a 10-year period from 1998 to 2008.[3] Built for a special group – the Al Baqaa Housing Cooperative alongside of the Association for Development of Rural Areas in Southern Lebanon – the project occupied a small 0.7-hectare site amid date groves some 80 kilometers south of Beirut. Indeed, the broader site environs were occupied well back into antiquity by Romans and even Phoenicians and almost always by seafarers. The project consists of three different interlocking blocks, more or less around a central court, within which there are three different unit types, nominally of 86 square meters in area with an additional 40 square meters of exterior space; outdoor terraces comprise about a third of the units' total living area. The communal courtyard is spacious and rendered as a safe haven for children's use. The horizontal lines, broad terraces, and fenestration are very much in keeping with the Lebanese modernist tradition, painted in bright colors according to choices by the architect and the fishermen.

In the United States, another aspect of social housing provision is the 'single-room occupancy hotel' and particularly those that were specially built, dating from the 1980s, to house homeless populations in various parts of the country. A well-known complex in San Diego, California, is 202 Island Inn by Rob Wellington Quigley of 1992, built with a subsidy from the Department of Housing and Urban Development on the edge of the city's Chinese district. During this period, Southern California was attractive to itinerant homeless because of its benign climate and access to social services. Rather than appearing as a particular building type, the Inn responded contextually on its block to three very different street façades. Along Island Avenue – the main entrance – it was scaled to adjacent warehouses. Along Third Avenue, contemporary materials were deployed but scaled to the hotel itself. By contrast, the Second Street façade was colorful and varied in form, responding to and counterpointing the nearby condominium towers and hotel architecture. Comprised of 197 units, the four-storey structure also houses 91 parking places in the basement and retail as well as live-work space and Café 22 on its ground floor. Amenities consist of a reading room, a recreation room, lounges, and a laundry as well as vending area. Units in the form of studio apartments are light and spacious. Although distinctive in both form and expression, the New Carver Apartments next to the Santa Monica Freeway in South Park, Los Angeles, by Michael Maltzan of 2007 to 2009, demonstrate similar attempts to move away from any stereotypical and tawdry image of a

single-room occupancy hotel.[4] Its circular shape, with fin-like segments radiating out from the open center, is distinctive and well-scaled to its freeway and warehouse environment. Built for the Skid Row Housing Trust, a long-time supporter of chronically homeless populations, the complex consists of 97 units looping around a 12.5-meter court space, the lower levels of which incorporate non-residential functions, offices, amenities, and a wide stairway as an open communal area. The dwelling units are monastic in quality at 30 square meters in area, but with kitchens. A sixth floor deck at the top of the building is a communal space open to the sky and affording views over the city.

Two prominent contemporary student housing projects are IIT State Street Village by Helmut Jahn of 2004 and Simmons Hall at MIT by Steven Holl of 1999 to 2003.[5] The State Street Village is located literally beside the El Train in Chicago and houses 367 students in suites of apartment-style units within three U-shape building masses linked together under a common roof. The space between the housing is set aside as landscaped courts and the overall structure appears to be almost integral with the elevated train line which provides for dynamic glimpses of passing trains. Constructed of poured-in-place concrete, glass cladding, and corrugated stainless steel panels, the housing projects a quasi-industrial aesthetic, with rooftop decks and airy lounges as communal space. By contrast, Simmons Hall is 10 storeys in height in a single-bar building, reminiscent of an Unité some 117 meters in length and only sixteen

Aranya Community Housing © John Paniker, from "Aranya Community Housing Project Brief" (1995), p.66

New Carver Apartments © Iwan Baan

meters wide. It contains 350 dormitory rooms, along with a multitude of non-residential functions, and features non-orthogonal swooping shafts of space that provide for common areas, light shafts, and an almost Gaudíesque appearance on the inside. The contrast with the insistent orthogonal rhythm of the exterior, as well as other parts of the building, is very striking. The outside skin of the building is a matrix of 0.70-meter square windows, allegedly derived from permeable membranes or sponges, but, in reality, forming an exoskeleton that brings the structural loads together on the outside walls. The dormitory rooms are relatively sparse, with the exception of the gridwork of windows, which on the exterior lends a certain scaleless character to what is a large building.

Living and assisted living for the elderly is in itself a complex and lengthy topic. One project of note is the Wohnfabrik Solinsieme project in St. Gallen, Switzerland, of 2002 by ARCHPLAN AG for the Coop Solinsieme Genossenschaft and its four female founders.[6] This is a cooperative in the manner of many in Europe; 'Solinsieme' designates living alone and together at the same time. The complex consists of the restoration of an embroidery factory

dating from the 1880s, with some additional space, comprising17 flats, each as a freehold unit, with around 20 percent of the residential space set aside for communal spaces, including kitchen facilities, roof terraces, a bar, and two ateliers for pursuing arts and crafts. The flats range in size from 56 to 96 square meters with a variety of floor plans, but all with free-standing sanitary cells placed in boxes in the flats with open kitchens and 3.8-meter-high ceilings, all to add to a feeling of spaciousness. More squarely in the domain of elderly-assisted living is the Kenyuen Home for the Elderly in Wakayama, Japan, by Motoyasu Muramatsu of 2001 for the Tobishima Group in health care.[7] Located on a bluff overlooking the Pacific Ocean and designed specifically for fishermen, the complex is intended both in the siting and in the minimalist abstract quality of the architecture to draw the gaze and experience to the spectacle of the seascape outside. A three-storey wellness and care facility, the home provides facilities for intensive care in hospital-like rooms, in addition to flats for more normal occupancy. In short, it deals with end-of-life experiences from well patients to hospice conditions, provisions for which are not uncommon in Japan with its large and rapidly aging population.

Wohnfabrik Solinsieme © Urs Welter, Courtesy of Archplan AG

Kenyuen Home for the Elderly © Nacasa & Partners Inc

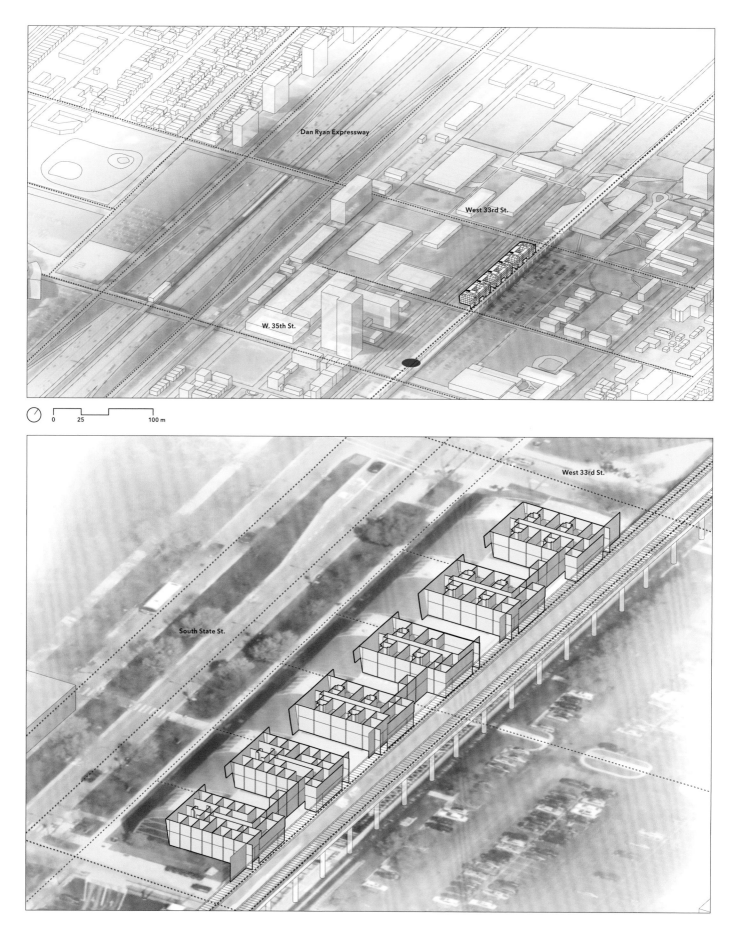

Dan Ryan Expressway

West 33rd St.

W. 35th St.

0 25 100 m

West 33rd St.

South State St.

HOUSING SPECIAL POPULATIONS

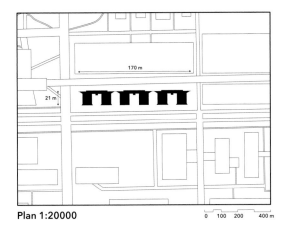

Plan 1:20000

0   100   200   400 m

Level Five

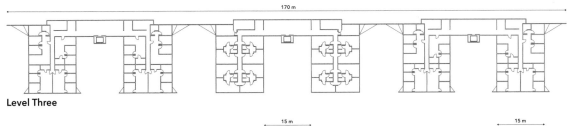

Level Three

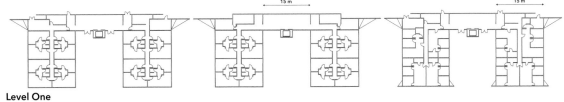

Level One

Plan 1:1000

0   5   10   20 m

Key

■ Housing Units
■ Terrace
  Communal Kitchen

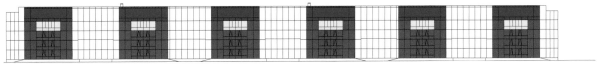

Sectional Variation (Other Uses)

Sectional 1:1000

0   5   10   20 m

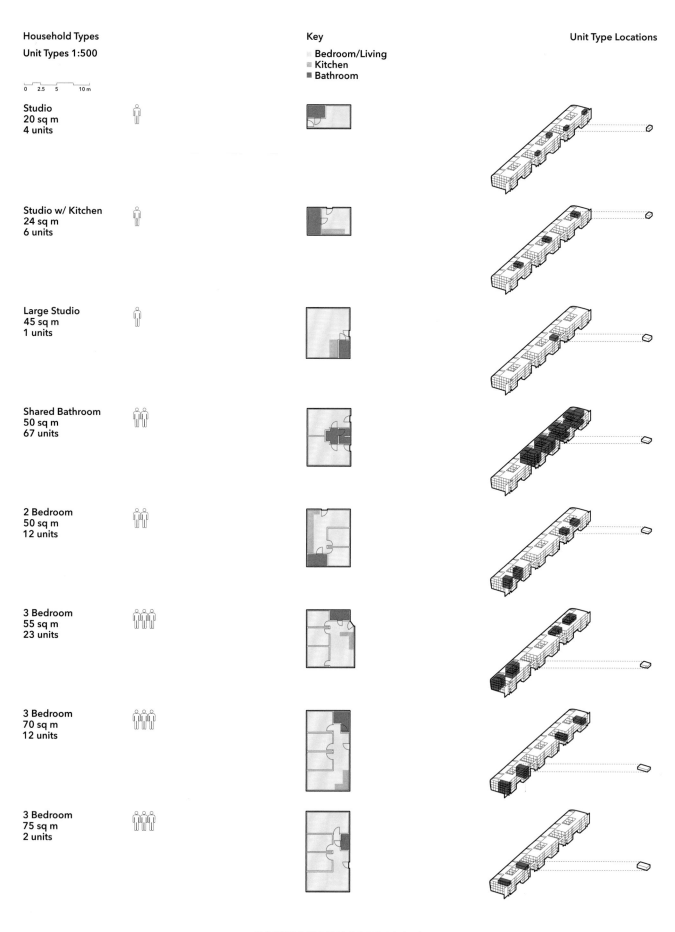

IIT STATE STREET VILLAGE

Household Types

Unit Types 1:500

0   2.5   5   10 m

Studio
20 sq m
4 units

Studio w/ Kitchen
24 sq m
6 units

Large Studio
45 sq m
1 units

Shared Bathroom
50 sq m
67 units

2 Bedroom
50 sq m
12 units

3 Bedroom
55 sq m
23 units

3 Bedroom
70 sq m
12 units

3 Bedroom
75 sq m
2 units

Key

Bedroom/Living
Kitchen
Bathroom

Unit Type Locations

HOUSING SPECIAL POPULATIONS

CONTEMPORARY CASES: FROM SLUM REPARATION TO CO-OP LIFE

Two projects in distinct contexts addressing low-cost housing and housing for a diverse community are Quinta Monroy and Miss Sargfabrik, enjoined by their respective achievements as exceptional experimental prototypes. The former is located in Iquique, the capital of north Chile, which was formerly a part of Peru until 1879. Bordered by the South Pacific Ocean on the west and the Andes mountain range to the east, the city's early development was due in large part to the discovery of metals such as silver and copper, and more importantly, of the nitrates in the Atacama Desert that fueled its boom as a settlement. In 1975, Iquique reinvented itself as a fishing port, and later created the ZOFRI – the Zona Franca or the Duty Free Zone to promote foreign trade in copper mining, tourism, and fishing. Since then,

the population grew from 73,000 to nearly 200,000 in 2000, shrinking slightly to 186,000 in 2012.[8] This zone was developed in the context of the authoritarian political regime that lasted from 1973-1990, and by the time democracy was reclaimed, the country as a whole had a deficit of nearly 1 million affordable housing units. Given that Chile's population at that time was around 14 million people, the deficit implied that close to 20 percent of the country's population was residing in shanty towns, deteriorated housing, or overcrowded houses, and approximately 1.2 million illegal settlements had no access to public utilities such as electricity, drinking water, and sanitation in 1990.[9]

Under the central-leftist Christian Democrat Presidents Patricio Aylwin (1990-1994) and Eduardo Frei (1994-2000), housing programs received a significant increase in government funding and various social programs were launched under a central policy to subsidize housing units and make home ownership affordable even for the poorest of citizens.[10] Frei, in particular, made the eradication of extreme poverty one of his key objectives, and a survey conducted in 1996 during his first term in office revealed that 23.2 percent of the population, or some 3.3 million people, continued to live below the poverty line, of which 800,000 struggled with extreme poverty.[11] A separate study that same year by the Ministry of Housing and Urbanism and the University of Chile's Faculty of Architecture identified 972 squatter camps and informal settlements across the country. 105,888 families, equivalent to more than 500,000 people, lived in these settlements. In light of this, the Chile Barrio or the Chile Neighborhood Program was launched, and became the first public policy intervention focused on populations living in extreme poverty in precarious settlements. Apart from housing and infrastructural improvements, the inter-ministerial program also looked into social inclusion, improving job and productive capabilities, and community development. The implementation of the program extended from 1997 to 2007.

As Iquique's last inner-city *campamento* or informal settlement located along one of the main north-south arteries of Iquique, Avenida Salvador Allende, and surrounded by industries and the desert range to the east, the Quinta Monroy project was a prototype for low-cost dwellings designed by the ELEMENTAL team in 2003, who had been commissioned by the Chile Barrio Program. ELEMENTAL was in fact an unusual partnership that brought together practitioners, universities, and public as well as private agencies. The consortium included the Harvard University Graduate School of Design, the David Rockefeller Center of Latin American Studies at Harvard, the Universidad Católica de Chile, the Housing Ministry of Chile, and a few construction companies. The aim of the collaboration was to design minimum dwelling units that would allow maximum flexibility over time, while maintaining a broader urban, physical, as well as social cohesion. The residents who had occupied Quinta Monroy were initially highly guarded and suspicious of the development. The challenge here then was not just the mere provision of subsidized housing, but to recreate a viable neighborhood of

satisfied homeowners from the *campamento*. Back in the 1960s, the site was in fact an agricultural area and was used for cattle grazing, but with the expansion of the city this peripheral farming land became incorporated into the urban area, and today constitutes part of central Iquique.

By 1995, under the new democratic regime, the land became the subject of dispute among the squatters, the Monroy family who held the original property rights, the city, as well as the official housing organizations. In resolving the deadlock, the Chile Barrio Program intervened and acquired the property with the intention of transforming it into a social housing project for the original occupants. The conditions were decrepit, and 60 percent of the homes in the labyrinthine encampment had no light or direct ventilation, and were devoid of basic utilities such as access to drinking water, sewage, and sanitation. Each home was constructed of waste packaging material discarded from the city's port, and covered an area of around 30 square meters. The community was somewhat socially diverse, and the average monthly income for each household was around US$100 (54,000 pesos). The main breadwinners were more often than not the women, most of whom were single parents.[12] Hence, it was even more critical to retain these households within the original community so that the women would be able to journey to work conveniently and be able to manage their households. Taking advantage of a new housing policy – the Vivienda Social Dinámica sin Deuda, or Dynamic Social Housing Without Debt (VSDsD) – which provided a voucher in the amount of US$7,500 to each low-income family that typically would not qualify for loans, ELEMENTAL worked around this budget to cover the property acquisition, site development, and the physical construction of each dwelling.[13]

The design of the housing departed from urban precedents of the single-family detached house on its individual lot, the row house, and the high-rise, selecting instead a parallel housing typology that is based on the possibility of individual expansion over time. The plan thus was intentionally left somewhat "open" and "incomplete", thereby providing room for growth and self-built additions thereafter, as in the case of PREVI, Lima, which still remains an active construction site. According to Alejandro Aravena of ELEMENTAL, "[they] had to bear in mind that 60 percent of each unit's volume would eventually be self-built and therefore was unknown to [them] in particulars. The initial building had to therefore provide a supporting, unconstrained framework for improvised construction."[14] Further, residents of Quinta Monroy were involved in the design process in the early stages through workshops and meetings organized by ELEMENTAL where they provided their feedback regarding the distribution of the units, their façades, and their preferences for the common areas.[15] The architects thus embarked on the design based on the conformance with two restrictions: (i) each house would have an initial surface area of 36 square meters to ensure that the project would be within the budget, and (ii) each home would be left "unfinished" to allow for future additions in accordance with the needs of each family.[16] A total of 93 low-rise dwelling units were thus arrayed in parallel on the site that occupied an area of 5,722 square meters. The preference for low-rise dwellings was also taking into consideration the seismically active nature of the country as a whole, and the housing units formed contiguous borders interlocked with each other and generally defined four semi-enclosed courtyards or "communities".

ELEMENTAL worked out the most expensive and technically challenging elements of the project, including the basic structure, stairways, service cores, etc., in order to ensure that the self-construction phase would be as easy, economical, and as safe as possible for the homeowners. In fact, the strict building code for the self-construction phase was negotiated with the residents. The houses are thus stacked two levels high on nine-meter by nine-meter lots, with a patio house on the ground floor, and a duplex unit above accessed by stairs above the patio house. The ground floor unit measures six meters by six meters and can expand its width into the adjacent three meters of its lot, and an additional 18 square meters to the back; the duplex which measures three meters by six meters can claim the adjacent three-meters by six-meter-deep bay, yielding a maximum floor area of 72 square meters. In terms of the unit plans, the ground floor primary occupation space for the patio unit is generally open and typically accommodates the living room, dining area, as well as the kitchen and toilet, while the subsequent extension would typically be reserved for more private sleeping quarters. For the duplex, the primary occupation space on the lower level generally opens up to the living/dining area with a kitchen in the area behind the stairs, while the toilets are stacked directly above the kitchen, adjoining the sleeping quarters; the double-storey extensions help to double the living/dining areas as well as serve as bedrooms.

Over time, the other "halves" of the "good houses" were gradually filled in by the tenants. As Alejandro Aravena defines it, what the project tries to attain is a "'porous' architecture that depends and thrives on external inputs".[17] To him, an "ELEMENTAL house is ostensibly a home starter kit, an armature, to be filled out with the homeowners' extensions".[18] This "porosity" translates into a general adaptability where participatory design strategies and layered schemes evolve dynamically, much like Quinta da Malagueira by Siza or the PREVI scheme discussed earlier. After the completion and occupation of the project, the neighborhood is vibrant and retains an overall architectural-urban integrity. The residents, and especially the children, share a close relationship with their collectively owned courtyards that further demarcate a semi-private/public space and one that reinforces a sense of community. These courtyards are in fact not freely accessible to outsiders, and this defined territoriality reinforces the overall safety of the place, furthering the dimensions for family life. In sum, by increasing the building density and retaining the original community as much as possible, Quinta Monroy offers an alternative to the informal settlements endemic to South American cities, ranging from the *campamentoes* to the *barrios*, and *favelas,* and the cheap and substandard housing often associated with low-cost housing. "Social housing," in their approach, was thus "seen as an investment and not an expense".[19] ELEMENTAL thus found ways in which the initial government subsidy can ultimately enhance the value of the property, while keeping the community on the same plot of land close to the centre of the city. Socially speaking, the project thus maintained the emotional ties within the community, as well as the relationship between the place of living and the places of employment.

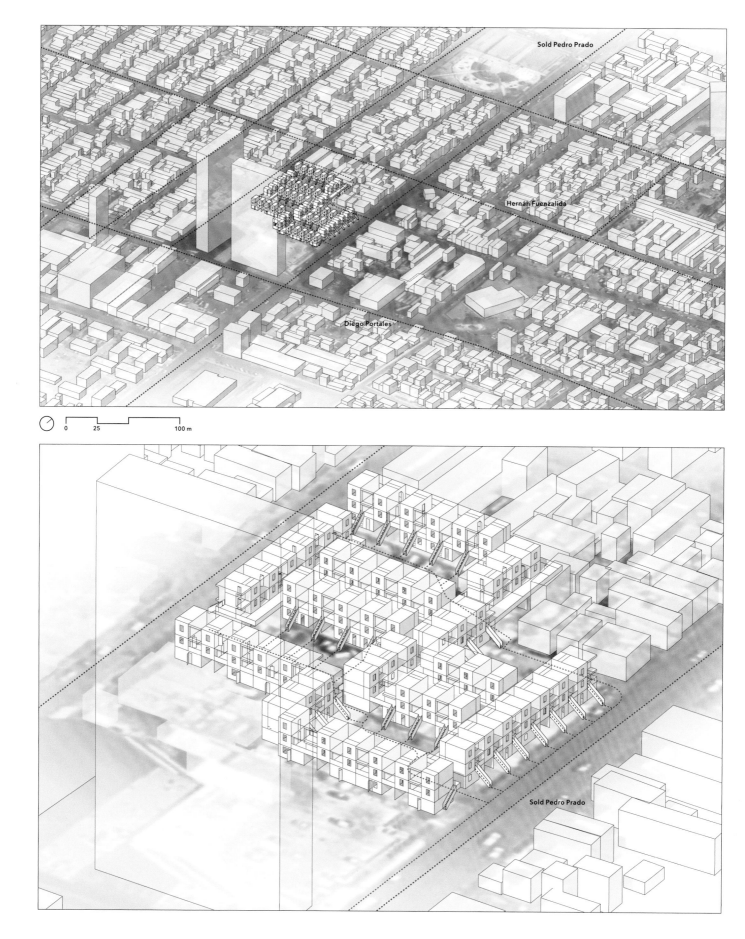

Sold Pedro Prado

Hernán Fuenzalida

Diego Portales

0   25   100 m

Sold Pedro Prado

HOUSING SPECIAL POPULATIONS

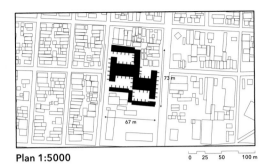

Plan 1:5000

0   25   50   100 m

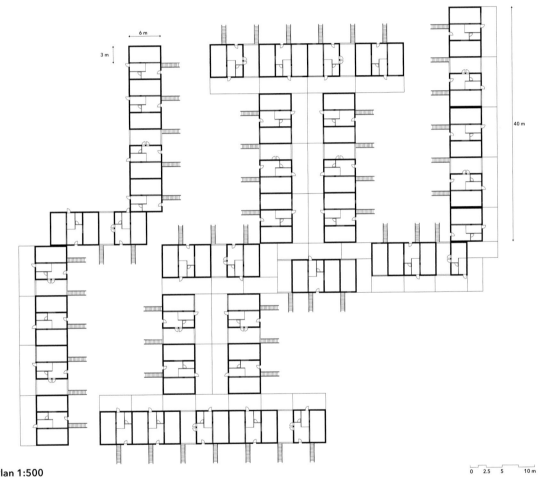

Plan 1:500

0   2.5   5   10 m

Key

■ Housing Units
■ Kitchen
  Bathroom
■ Infill Housing Units

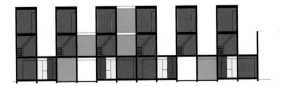

Sectional Variation (Other Uses)

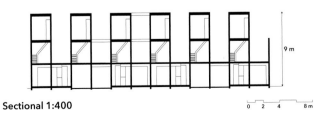

Sectional 1:400

0   2   4   8 m

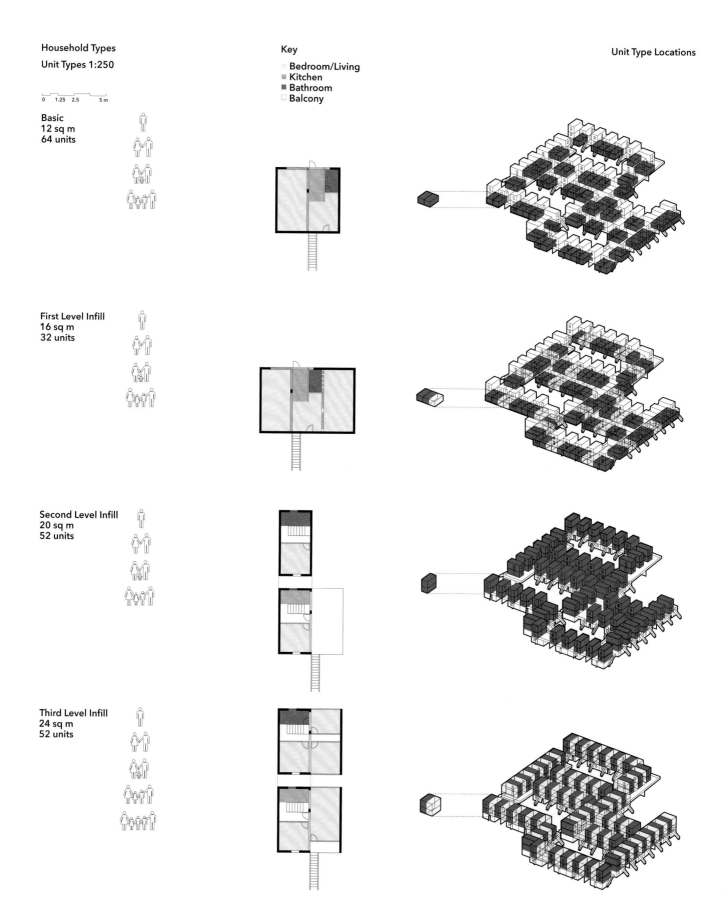

Household Types
Unit Types 1:250

0   1.25   2.5   5 m

Basic
12 sq m
64 units

First Level Infill
16 sq m
32 units

Second Level Infill
20 sq m
52 units

Third Level Infill
24 sq m
52 units

Key
Bedroom/Living
Kitchen
Bathroom
Balcony

Unit Type Locations

The second project, Miss Sargfabrik, is located in Vienna, Austria, which has had a housing history where cost-rent limited-profit housing has played a strong role. The origins date back to the early twentieth century, symbolized by *gemeindebau* projects such as Karl-Marx-Hof where the apartments are rented from the respective municipality. Similar housing schemes gained currency in the post-World War II era despite trends in public policy and mortgage markets that have promoted more individualized forms of housing consumption. Rental housing at present constitutes 45 percent of the housing stock in Austria, largely with the social sector, including limited-profit rental associations, co-operations, and municipal housing providers, overseeing the housing investment, management, and consumption. In Vienna alone, almost 200 municipal and limited-profit providers account for 48 percent of all dwellings, and this is supported by the Austrian Federal Government's provision of grants and public loans for affordable cost-capped housing.[20] The striking Miss Sargfabrik with its bold orange façade is emblematic of the cost-rent limited-profit housing common in Vienna and was designed by BKK-3 in 1998 and completed in 2000. Like Quinta Monroy, Miss Sargfabrik was committed to participatory design strategies and community engagement: during the two-year planning process, BKK-3 initiated discussions and brainstorming sessions with the 30 to 50 potential tenants to find out their personal desires as well as communal aspirations, and ways in which the building would still be functional in 20 years' time.[21] The social element hence was at the very core of this housing collective.

The residential complex of Miss Sargfabrik is located more specifically in the Penzing District (Fourteenth District) on the western edge of the city, within walking distance to Penzing Station and other nearby underground metro stops, and set within a fabric of perimeter block courtyard houses with abundant green spaces in the form of courtyard gardens, parks, and forests. What is notable about the project is that it is the second of collective residential complexes designed by BKK, the first of which was Sargfabrik, meaning coffin factory, and housed 110 units. The original coffin factory buildings on the site were demolished and the site redeveloped

for a communal residential complex which was completed in 1996. Both of these projects were undertaken by the Verein für Integrative Lebensgestaltung (VIL) or the Association for Integrative Living – a body that was founded by a group of people in 1987 who shared a common dissatisfaction with the increasing costs of housing as well as the traditional range of standardized dwellings.[22] They thus set up a cooperative building company that would allow them to create a model of "Living-Culture-Integration", and this autonomy consequently allowed BKK to design and build independently of the real estate market. On joining the cooperative, tenants pay a set amount per square metre as a deposit, which is refunded when they leave. The rental per month includes all the running and heating costs.[23] In May 1989, the VIL purchased what was once the largest coffin factory in the Austro-Hungarian Empire, Maschner & Söhne, a company established at the end of the nineteenth century that had ceased production in 1970. The success and positive experience of Sargfabrik as a "Village within a City" prompted the Association to purchase yet another piece of real estate just across the street along Missindorfstrasse in 1998, which was redeveloped into Miss Sargfabrik.[24]

The project covered an area of 850 square meters, and occupied the corner of a perimeter block construction, housing 45 adults and 12 children. The 12-meter-deep building essentially wraps around the site, retaining the integrity and urban design features of a perimeter block while recreating a courtyard within the building with a shared garden, providing an oasis of calm that harkens back to the old Viennese courtyards that are especially renowned in the city's first district. The covered outdoor entry hall connects the street directly to the courtyard, and stairwells on both ends of the building lead up to the access galleries. In designing the complex, the architects focused on long-term programs, eliminating the notion of sleeping units *per se*, and created apartments around a pattern of sleeping, working and living. In fact, on the ground level, five units have atelier-like features for home offices, and the open spaces of the small units are developed from the external access corridor. Service cores are arrayed to the center of the party walls together with the staircases, thus yielding additional space efficiencies and organizational flexibilities within the units. The variety of unit plans here was derived by the unusual, angular ways in which BKK-3 determined the party walls as well as the introduction of split-levels within the building. Every second party wall is bent like a splayed 'V' so that the apartments are alternately wide at the center and narrower at the glazed front or the other way around, creating a perspective that makes the flats seem larger than they are.[25] The units range in size from 30 to 70 square meters, with the intention of including singles as well as families in the project.[26] In keeping with the goal of accommodating a diverse community, three of the units are adapted for disabled persons in wheelchairs with the access corridor and entrance of the building designed to be barrier-free, and small apartments called "Flex Boxes" are let to students for a period of one year.[27]

There are a total of nine floors, including one underground level with three parking spaces, and penthouses at the very top. The first floor is also raised above ground level. The heights of each floor vary from 2.26 meters to 3.12 meters, which are in fact higher than the low ceilings of conventional buildings.[28] The spatial structure of the interior is expressed on the façade in the form of folded and expanding ribbons of windows, particularly for the split-levels. Apart from the library, the building also houses BKK-3's own office, an apartment for teenagers in the care of the Office for Youth and Family of the City of Vienna, a communal kitchen, laundry room, and computer room. These communal spaces are the focal point within the building complex and are situated on the two levels that interlock with entrances at both levels. Within the broader framework of subsidized housing in Vienna, Miss Sargfabrik and Sargfabrik have earned critical acclaim as radical yet highly successful experiments in the contemporary era, although in the longer history of communal housing, compared for instance to those undertaken in the Soviet Union, they are perhaps not as avantgarde as they might appear.

MISS SARGFABRIK

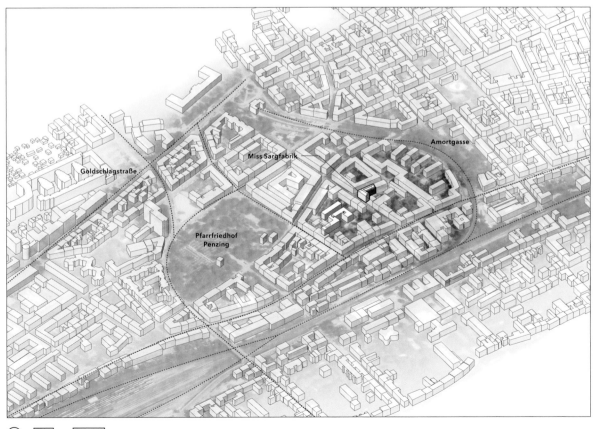

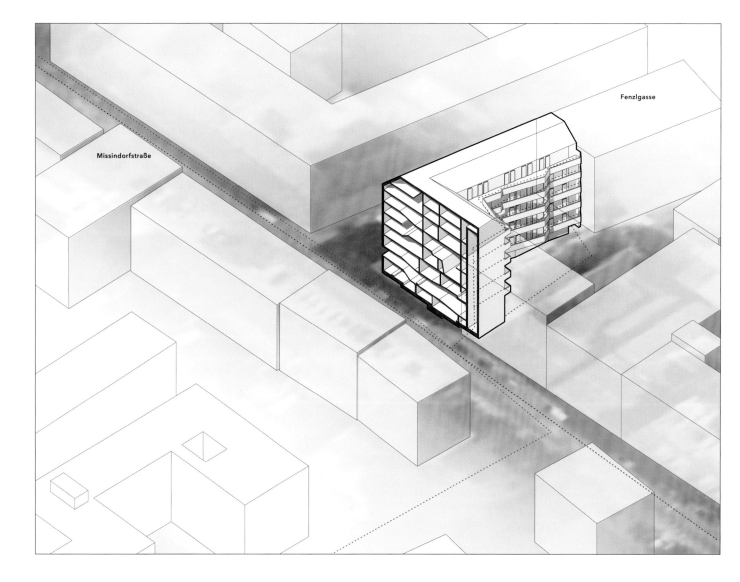

Missindorfstraße

Fenzlgasse

HOUSING SPECIAL POPULATIONS

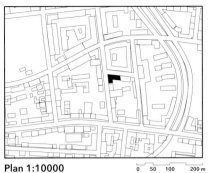

Plan 1:10000

0 50 100 200 m

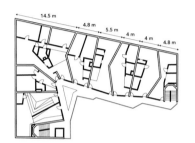

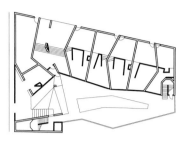

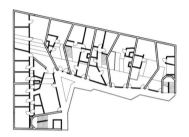

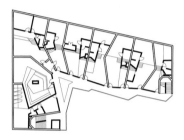

14.5 m 4.8 m 5.5 m 4 m 4 m 4.8 m

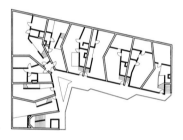

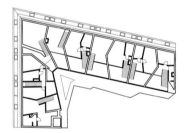

Plan 1:750

0 3.75 7.5 15 m

Key

■ Housing Units
■ Communal Kitchen
  Laundry Room
■ Youth Club Room

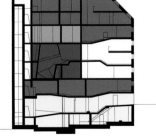

Sectional Variation (Other Uses)

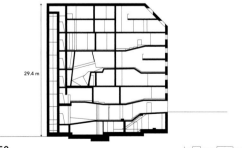

29.4 m

Sectional 1:750

0 3.75 7.5 15 m

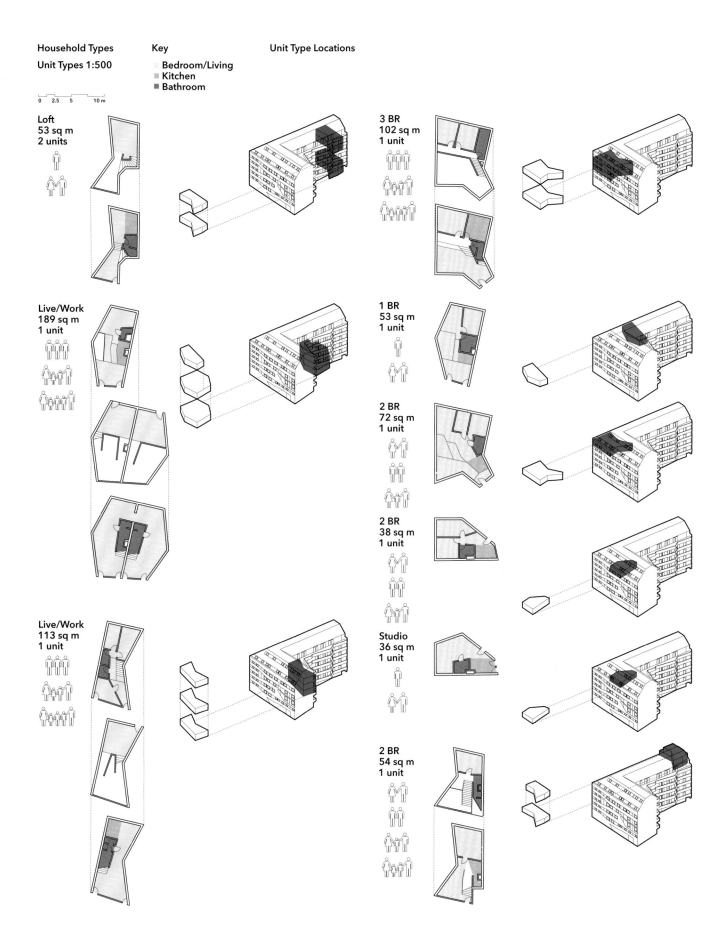

Household Types
Unit Types 1:500

Key
■ Bedroom/Living
■ Kitchen
■ Bathroom

Unit Type Locations

0 2.5 5   10 m

Loft
53 sq m
2 units

Live/Work
189 sq m
1 unit

Live/Work
113 sq m
1 unit

3 BR
102 sq m
1 unit

1 BR
53 sq m
1 unit

2 BR
72 sq m
1 unit

2 BR
38 sq m
1 unit

Studio
36 sq m
1 unit

2 BR
54 sq m
1 unit

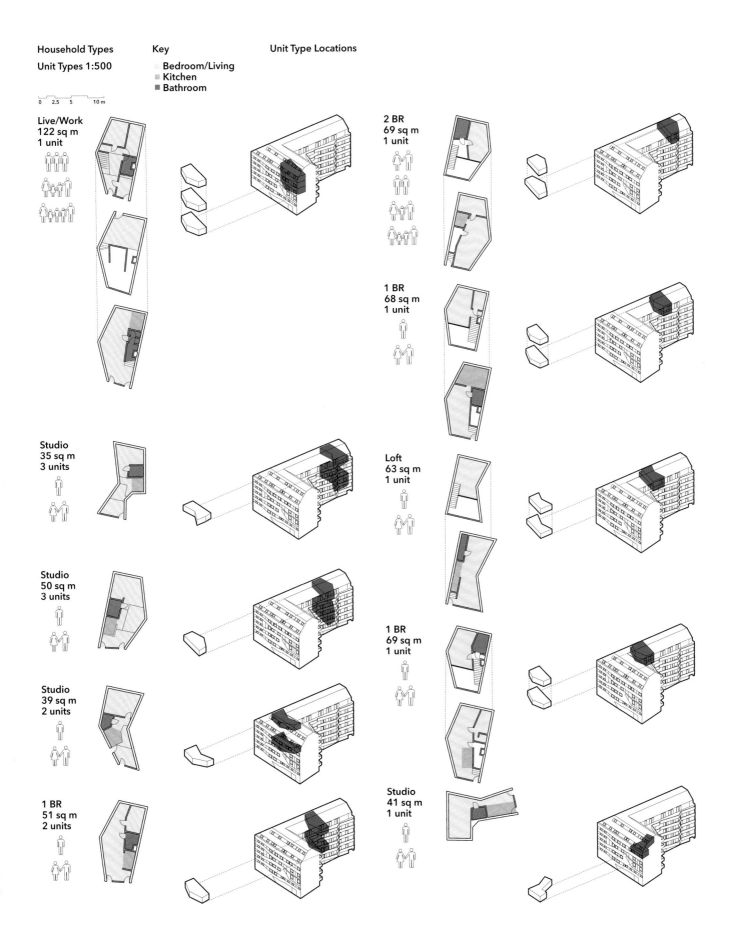

Household Types

Unit Types 1:500

Key
- Bedroom/Living
- Kitchen
- Bathroom

Unit Type Locations

0 2.5 5   10 m

Live/Work
122 sq m
1 unit

2 BR
69 sq m
1 unit

1 BR
68 sq m
1 unit

Studio
35 sq m
3 units

Loft
63 sq m
1 unit

Studio
50 sq m
3 units

Studio
39 sq m
2 units

1 BR
69 sq m
1 unit

1 BR
51 sq m
2 units

Studio
41 sq m
1 unit

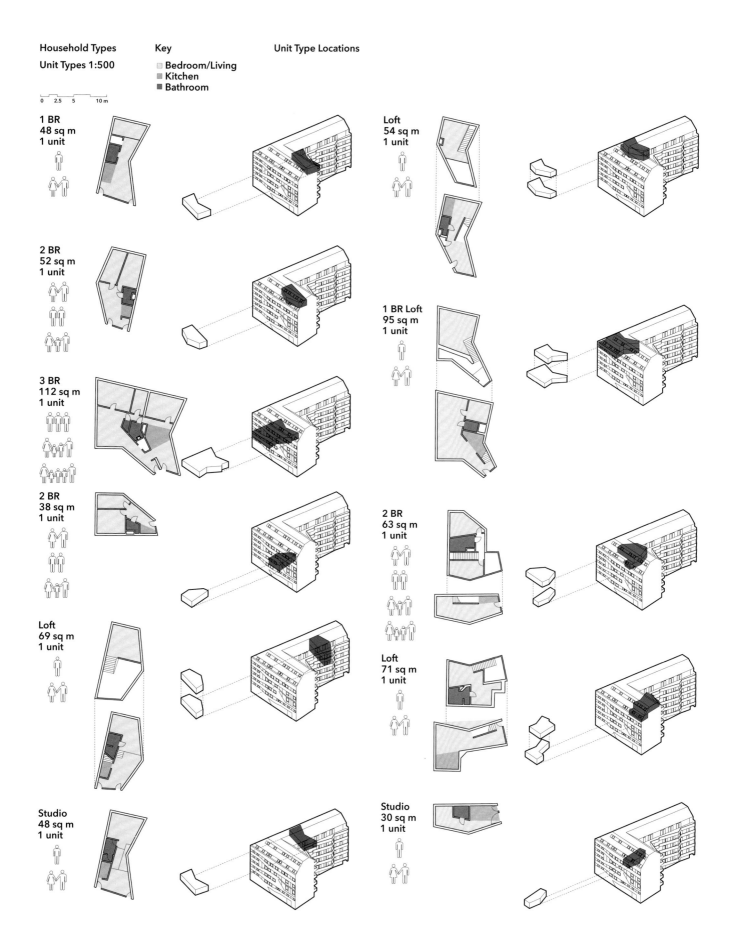

Household Types
Unit Types 1:500

Key
☐ Bedroom/Living
▨ Kitchen
■ Bathroom

Unit Type Locations

0   2.5   5   10 m

1 BR
48 sq m
1 unit

2 BR
52 sq m
1 unit

3 BR
112 sq m
1 unit

2 BR
38 sq m
1 unit

Loft
69 sq m
1 unit

Studio
48 sq m
1 unit

Loft
54 sq m
1 unit

1 BR Loft
95 sq m
1 unit

2 BR
63 sq m
1 unit

Loft
71 sq m
1 unit

Studio
30 sq m
1 unit

Household Types
Unit Types 1:500

Key
Bedroom/Living
Kitchen
Bathroom

Unit Type Locations

0 2.5 5 10 m

1 BR
68 sq m
1 unit

Loft
67 sq m
1 unit

Loft
81 sq m
1 unit

2 BR
50 sq m
1 unit

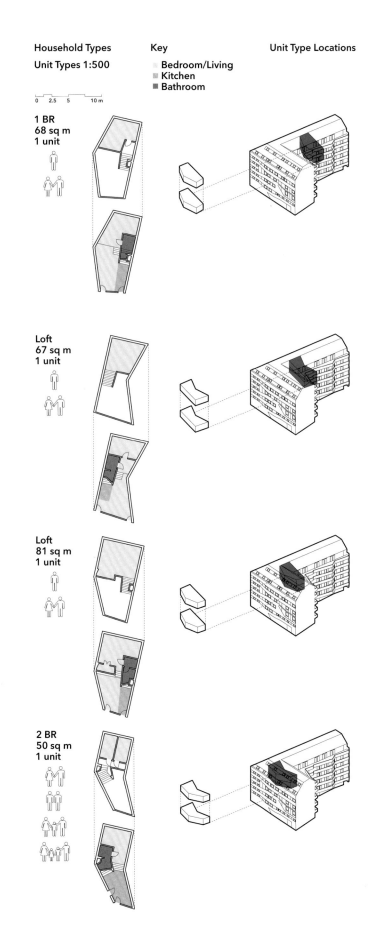

FLEXIBILITY, ACCOMMODATING CHANGE, AND SPECIAL PROGRAMMING

At least three themes run through these examples of housing special populations. They are flexibility, dealing with change, and special programming. Here, flexibility refers to being able to simultaneously accommodate multiple use, often within small spatial confines. It also refers to accommodation of different dominant and subordinate functions through a relatively focused spatial environment like, for instance, work-live circumstances. In addition, it can imply deployment of a number of circumscribed uses and accompanying spaces to be used in various combinations. The more or less constant constraint is the amount of space available, which is typically relatively small. One useful provision is often reasonably capacious, or one might say, over-provided space within a complex, such as large terraces or similar, as in the Aranya low-cost housing or the Fishermen's Housing in Tyre, where otherwise unexpected activities can take place. Similarly, the larger central area in the New Carver Apartments can fulfill that purpose. Communal spaces and wider circulation areas can also fulfill the same sort of function. Accommodation of different dominant functions at different times clearly needs to go beyond simply re-arranging the furniture and take up with carrying over space from one set of activities to another as an important ingredient. As at Simmons Hall and IIT State Street Village, for instance, it can also be shifted out into the communal study areas in live-work circumstances. Then again, it can also be handled by the provision, in both student housing and the single-room occupancy hotels, of an array of specific spaces among communal and associated circulation areas, potentially providing for considerably flexible environments for use by residents. It does require those using them, however, to feel comfortable in moving out into some of the less private spaces of a complex.

Particularly among the examples of social housing presented here, the accommodation of change over time in the spatial composition and size of dwelling units conforms largely to an evolutionary process, whereby an initial core of spaces provided in a dwelling unit can be expanded through planned additions. In the Aranya housing, the Quinta Monroy housing, and most of the PREVI projects, this is a key component and takes place by simply filling in a basic spatial framework or extending it either upwards or outwards. One issue of concern is overbuilding through which the ventilation of courtyard houses, for instance, can be impaired with subsequent deleterious public health effects. Another is creation of problems of access and overshadowing from neighboring units in a tightly-planned complex. A third concern can also occur around the metrics of the core building and its extensions in manners that are either easy or difficult to accommodate with subsequent additions. Efforts must be made in each context to accurately gauge the 'delta function', or likely size and material character of additions, in a manner that facilitates building but without deleterious overbuilding. Both in the Aranya housing and the Quinta Monroy projects, this is an issue and appears to be well handled. Similarly, communal open space needs to be provided and shaped in a manner where there is clear jurisdiction and corresponding responsibility for maintenance. Unfortunately, 'no-person's lands' quickly become that - 'no-person's lands'. Again, the study of circumstances in nearby settlements can prove to be useful, as it was in both Aranya and Quinta Monroy. Then, with regard to the accommodation of change, the matter of what changes and what remains fixed and static rather quickly comes to the fore. The project utility infrastructure in housing for the very poor, for instance, is critical for minimizing both its length

and therefore cost, as well as to ensure that branching and distribution are sufficient to support subsequent phases of development. Again at Aranya housing, this was a very basic and important set of decisions. Indeed, with regard to sites and services provisions of housing, studies as far back as John Turner, Horacio Caminos, and Reinhard Goethert have dwelt heavily on this issue.[29]

In the cases of assisted living and unorthodox cooperative arrangements of housing and community life, as at Miss Sargfabrik, special programming plays a particularly important role. By this is meant inclusion of particular facilities or functional spaces that reach well beyond the normal brief of housing. In the case of assisted living, wellness and care facilities are important components, as are hospital-like rooms and even hospice accommodations for those with terminal illnesses. For the cooperative living complexes, what other programmed spaces are included is often a matter of resident choice and requires substantial dialogue with designers. Among others, the two ateliers at Wohnfabrik Solinsieme in Switzerland are perhaps surprising as are parts of Miss Sargfabrik and particularly the way space was rendered there inside the building, using sloping floors and angled walls. Especially in the Japanese context, where elderly populations and their housing is on the rise, the sheer location of facilities and the environmental ambience they are both placed in and place emphasis upon are significant factors. Clearly, wellness and care extends beyond immediate physical treatment and into the realm of the mind and its respite and serenity. This is particularly evident in the Kenyuen Home for the Elderly and its retired fishermen contemplating the rugged coastline of what was once their domain of active life. Similarly, although very differently realized, the buffering of the rail line at IIT State Street Village offers a particular 'view' or 'scene' that is germane to its student inhabitants, as are its airy lounges and roof decks. A sense of an ambience is also created at Miss Sargfabrik with the angled geometries of rooms, sloping floors, and walls. Although not necessarily for everyone, this very particularized milieu projects a specific version of intergenerational living that is distinctive and deliberately different from more run-of-the-mill examples.

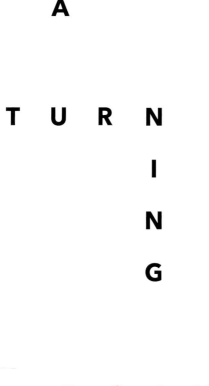

A TURNING POINT

Nearly two decades ago in the early 1990s, the social, cultural, and architectural history of housing over the course of much of the twentieth century served as the focus of the book *Modernity and Housing*.[1] Spanning the post-World War I years and up to around 1990, the narrative explored how the design and production of housing and, more broadly speaking, new urban communities were shaped by two historical moments or turning points that saw the redefinition of social relations and critically questioned architecture's presumed modernity. The first, dating from the 1920s post-World War building boom, was congruent with the emergence of a technological order that underpinned the mass production and standardization of design in the modern housing that was widely adopted in Europe and the United States. The second coincided largely with the re-examination of modernist principles during the 1970s, or commonly referred to as the rise of the post-modern culture. It gave rise to smaller scale and more familiar forms of housing that embraced a different dimension of modernity in which historicism and pluralistic design emphases

opened up possibilities for good modern housing. Since then, much has clearly occurred. This book thus picks up from where *Modernity and Housing* last left off, taking up with the development of housing since the 1990s, and, indeed, exploring three issues identified in the conclusion that have remained pertinent. These include the relationship between collective-individual action and expression in the design of housing, the need to maintain a diversity of housing stock within a locale, and the integration of housing within a city.

Although only partly visible during this account of housing, there were two key underlying assumptions at work. The first was that it is not very useful, nowadays, to discuss urban housing in isolation from its palpable relationships and embeddedness in cities. In fact, many of today's purported problems with urban housing are not really about the buildings *per se* as they are about the manner and making of this embeddedness in cities or the lack thereof. Furthermore, one supposition following on from this underlying assumption was that 'urban intensity', variously defined by dwelling density, several conditions of functional diversity, and high degrees of connectivity to other areas and activities within a city, becomes a more healthy and desirable condition generally as it rises and increases. The second underlying assumption was that 1990, or thereabouts, marked a turning point when the urban-architectural production of housing seen broadly in many parts of the world converted to something else with regard to programmatic intent, shape, appearance, mix, and even aspects of typological evolution. Since then, contemporary urban housing saw considerable investment of architectural energy along with market share, and gave further rise to 'urban intensity' as an outcome. Behind all of this, however, also lurked broader social and cultural forces shaping physical manifestations of the passage of time and urban experience. Beginning in the late 1960s, for instance, there was considerable social upheaval in many parts of the world around rights, justice, access to power, and environmental responsibility. The wrenching impact of the oil embargo of 1973 followed by economic stagflation only exacerbated the situation, at least in the West.[2] As the 1970s wore on, elsewhere in the world China charted a new path forward and the impact of the Second Demographic Shift began to be broadly experienced worldwide. Then towards the conclusion of the 1980s with the end of the Cold War, the unravelling of Bretton Woods and other accords, advances in digital technology, the advent of the World Wide Web in 1993, multinationalism and the rise of what became known as neoliberalism with regard to economic transactions and so-called 'globalization', the world continued to change radically. At the risk of oversimplification, with the experience of these events came widespread concerns for diversity, increases in social pluralism, serious questioning of the hegemony of positivistic interpretations of people and their worlds, a rise in the 'philosophy of differences', a search for gender equality, and profound changes, as mentioned earlier, in demographic profiles and living arrangements in many countries. In short, a tumultuous period in the social and cultural affairs of the world began in the late 1960s, if not before, and resulted in a changed world by the late 1980s going into the 1990s. Now, returning to the two key underlying assumptions of this book,

there are two important ways to assess the impact on urban housing during the post-1990 era. The first is to assess what differentiates contemporary urban housing architecturally from earlier eras much more concerned with narrower production, of putting roofs over people's heads, and with mass housing provision. The second concerns the metrics of 'urban intensity', the *leitmotif* of this book, and resulting empirical measures of the phenomenon itself now as compared to before 1990 or thereabouts.

CONSTANTS AND TRENDS

To begin with, what appears to have persisted from prior periods are certain dimensional and locational regularities. The depth and width of dwelling units arranged serially in plan, as in the 'urban block shapers' or in the more conventional slab buildings, for instance, are nominally 12 meters and seven meters respectively, somewhat larger than earlier examples but not by much. Again, in slab blocks and attached dwellings, there remains general agreement that five floors is a maximum for walk-ups and the use of maisonette units on top floors continues to be pursued. Non-residential functions such as commercial and community services largely remain confined to ground levels and lower floors, although more adventurous locations are also sought more frequently than before at mid-levels in high-rise buildings and on rooftops. If anything, floor-to-ceiling heights are slightly enlarged although again not by a lot. Much of this is perhaps not surprising, given probably only slightly altered ergonometric considerations, sizes of optimal material spans, and the like. Then too, the difficulty in sustaining semi-private or semi-public outdoor spaces, in the absence of high levels of largely independent maintenance, also persists. Indeed, there appears to have been a shift in emphasis to the variety and more tailored provision of private outdoor space integral with units, no matter what the broader building context. Similarly, superblock configurations remained resistant to despecialization of use over time beyond the primary prescription of residential space. Wide roads and coarse-grained street networks commonly associated with superblocks also persist, along with attendant problems of fluid traffic movement and management. There are several notable latter-day exceptions in these regards, however, especially those involving multi-layered 'ground planes' incorporating a variety of movement options such as underground entry, parking, and egress. Also, one persistent aspect of 'slab or tower in the park' arrangements worth clarifying under super-blocks is that the 'park' component belongs to the residential units within the precinct and should not be regarded as public open space, even if it seemingly has that aspect to it. Depending largely on landscape provisions, such ensembles either seem to work or they do not. The tendency for figural and formal separation in the appearance of certain housing typologies also persists, allowing stylistic inflections to be made in keeping with matters of taste and fashionability, and the times. This is particularly the case among 'infill buildings', 'urban block shapers', 'tall towers', and of course, 'indigenous reinterpretations', which as a class of buildings actively trades on this capacity for separation. Finally, cultural conventions, time-honored or not, with regard to aspects of community and privacy in and around dwellings, also persist, although often becoming blurred in the movement towards more singular yet polyvalent layouts, depicting yet another more or less constant feature but one that is fraying at the edges.

By contrast, what appears to have changed or shifted substantially away from the shape, appearance, layout, and so on of prior periods are a number of conspicuous trends. To begin with, there is a proliferation of work-live, hotel-office, or similar programmatic alignments broadening into more exclusive domestic urban housing environments. Certainly, work-live and similar categories are not entirely new. After all, the Maison de Verre, a classic orthodox modernist house from the 1920s was of this ilk. Nevertheless, the occurrence of these categories of dwelling, particularly those housed in special-built complexes, appears to have risen substantially, further underlining changed conditions in the world associated with erosion of differences between daily activities and being home and abroad, as well as assertions of personal autonomy, diversity of lifestyle, and pluralism. Attitudes towards housing and landscape also appear to have shifted substantially, at least with regard to the sensibility involved. To be

sure as discussed here and elsewhere, such attitudes have been shifting for some time, moving generally from 'town-country mergers' to 'dwellings in garden settings' and 'slabs or towers in a park', on to today's 'roofscapes' and similar 'landscape environments'. Likewise, perceptual sensibilities have also shifted with regard to 'the natural' from ones of adjacency and 'being next to', on to 'being within' and actively involved, to 'being removed' and yet empathetically and mentally engaged with potentials. The untouchable grassed roofscape of De Citadel in Almere does not literally have the cows of Lunenberg grazing there, but it can be seen in this light. Moreover, even if nothing much is happening on the sparsely furnished open spaces at Schots, its prolific and active use can be well imagined. Then too, as mentioned in earlier comments about constants, attention to private outdoor space and finding ways to render it effective within otherwise relatively resistant building frameworks, like high-rise towers and slabs, has risen. Again, consistent with social shifts in directions of autonomy, diversity, and pluralism, it is no longer the often weakly-defined community open space that is important as it is the more strictly public and particularly private outdoor realms. Likewise part of one of the earlier constants, indigenous interpretation in various forms and cultural contexts has nevertheless also shifted appreciably away from preoccupations with expressive figuration signaling adherence to a particular tradition. Instead, the question of 'why do it?' appears to have arisen more frequently in contemporary urban housing, suggesting a sharpened cultural awareness and selectivity about what should be brought across, returning to one of the original meanings of tradition and its use. These days, on par, formal interests appear to trump figural preoccupations, clearly switching away from earlier post-modern leanings well prior to 1990 in most places.

More directly affecting contemporary urban housing, though, in the context of this architectural discussion is the presence of a number of spatial strategies with outcomes that are somehow collectively distinctive. The strong manipulation of voids through punctuation of various fields, grounds, and other horizontal datums in buildings is one kind of example. It is evident in places like Beijing's Jian Wai

SOHO, for example, with the literal ground plane punctuated at intervals by open courts clearly revealing commercial, parking, and other functions and effectively thickening the space of a ground plane to advantage with regard to organizational clarity and quality of adjacent indoor and outdoor space. Similarly, active engagement with roofscapes and intermediary levels or datums in building complexes as new grounds and fields for activity has similar effects, on display, for instance, in the De Citadel project in Almere. Also, the manipulation of void spaces within buildings in very deliberate manners, as at Simmons Hall at MIT in Cambridge, or in OMA's Fukuoka project and at the New Carver Apartments in Los Angeles, fits into the same broad category of spatial strategies, as do the 'cut out' voids in a number of projects like Boutique Monaco in Seoul and the Mirador in Madrid. It is not that these are entirely new strategies for they are not. But the sheer élan and forcefulness with which they are deployed and made manifest in contemporary urban housing is novel, at least in degree if not also in kind. Then too, there are other strategies that might be grouped under 'mixed developments' of one kind or another, typically involving the co-existence of components of buildings of different scales and their combination through spatial organizational operations like 'superimposition', 'grafting on', and 'promoting outbreaks'. These are clearly conspicuous at 100 Wozoco in the Netherlands, with displaced and protruding box-like forms, and at 8 Tallet in Copenhagen, with conscious deployment of different building and unit types within an overall assemblage such that they remain relatively distinctive. In both cases, little attempt has been made to entirely homogenize or resolve the different parts together as might have happened in the past. Complex stacking arrangements of dwelling units and other components produce similar outcomes, often embodying processes of arrangement around production of both diversity within an overall dwelling environment, as well as repetition of certain building features. Substantial variations within plans and section of housing, again as at the Mirador in Madrid among other projects described here, can also produce similar alignments. Similar ends of accommodating dwelling diversity and other related functions are accomplished through interlocking operations between and among building compo-

nents, as at the Linked Hybrid in Beijing. Again, the outcome is a formal and programmatic cross-mixing within an overall palette of contemporary housing.

Also at stake appears to have been a broadening and highlighting of manners of appreciating dwelling and living circumstances. Here, two kinds in particular stand out. The first involves the amplification of opportunities presented by the sheer verticality and rise of tall buildings through roof gardens, intermediate-level open spaces of various kinds, community sky decks also with allowances for more public participation, and considerable variation in both private and shared balconies, outdoor terraces, void spaces within buildings, and associated façade treatments. If nothing else, the Pinnacle@Duxton in Singapore is an essay in the deployment of such opportunities, although it is not alone in these regards. The second involves willful playing with formal properties of interior spaces, even going so far as sloping floors and wall sections as at Miss Sargfabrik in Vienna. This is clearly a move away from more strictly utilitarian and even poly-functional provision of unit layouts and accoutrements into the realm of systematic ambience creation, presumably to instantiate some modicum of specialness, difference, and uniqueness to dwelling within grouped or mass housing. Again, the presence and appearance of what is non-standard becomes important. At work, throughout this contemporary era of housing, are more marked and celebrated forms of hybridization away from purer typologies of the past. Moreover, this is hybridization that occurs mainly at the level of ensembles of units. It is a middle-ground procedure, so to speak, involving the mixing and fusing of elements such that aspects remain sufficiently coherent to be recognizable, yet others remain open and malleable, enabling yet some other form to emerge. Moreover, it is the emergence of these 'both-and' outcomes, formally and expressively, that often gives contemporary urban housing its particular and distinctive look. All told and discussed, few except absolutely core constants of urban housing have remained entirely intact from prior periods, often with considerable fraying at the edges of those that even remained relatively coherent. Beyond these relative constants, there was considerable hybridization and trends away from the substance and even program of urban housing in the past.

METRICS AND MEASURES

With regard to 'urban intensity', as used here, its metrics are straightforward. Dwelling density can and is given by the number of dwelling units per hectare of project area. This is not the only measure of diversity that could be used, with, for instance, floor area to site area being another. Nor does it entirely skirt the issue of consistent accuracy implied, for example, given differences between gross and net densities. But, it is a commonly understood measure of at least relative density. As shown graphically here, specific dwelling densities at the immediate project level vary quite dramatically among and across the nine different housing typal-territorial definitions, from lows among the 100 or so projects of below 50 dwelling units per hectare to highs in excess of 700 dwelling units per hectare in the case of 'big buildings', 'tall towers', and 'housing for special populations'. Diversity, moving to the second kind of metric of intensity, is given here via two scales for the larger group of projects. The first is the number of different dwelling unit types in a given project, with ranges all the way up to 20 or more, including some like Boutique Monaco in Seoul where almost all units are, in fact, different to some reasonably discriminable degree. In fact, it is precisely the degree of discriminable difference that makes the metric useful or not. Here, however, commonly accepted measures of difference such as numbers of rooms, including bedrooms; numbers of stories; presence or absence of particular services; livable areas of dwelling space; and so on, have been used.

The second metric is the relative presence of non-residential uses in a housing complex, described as relatively 'high', 'medium', and 'low'. These uses include community services, commercial stores, and other functions, as well as recreational or other facilities present within a complex. Certain uses, like car parking, entrance ways, and lounges, were almost always present and classified projects, in the absence of other non-residential uses, as being 'low' in mixed use. Other projects, by contrast and as can be seen from more specific data sheets, incorporated a range and relatively numerous non-residential uses. The Unité d'habitation in Marseilles, for example, included some 26 stores, gymnasium facilities,

an outdoor auditorium, and a kindergarten. In fact, all submultiples, by definition, presented this kind of array of mixed uses.

Connectivity, a third metric of urban intensity, was given by physical proximity or distance to surrounding and neighboring non-residential functions, including shops, institutional facilities, and available open space, as well as to modes of transportation, like transit. Layouts of the numbers of outlets by category within a walkable radius were used, together with a rough assessment of the likely quality of the walkable experience. The results for the cases central to the chapters are depicted here in the form of pictographs of project environs. In almost all of them, at least proximal association with non-residential uses nearby was relatively high, as was access to public transportation. The likely quality of these environs, as might be expected across such a range of project types and purposes, does show variation. Outside of these examples, the area around the New Carver Apartments in Los Angeles, for instance, is not overly inviting and the deliberate isolation of hospice and elderly care facilities, as at the Kenyuen Home for the Elderly, renders such metrics to be largely irrelevant.

Looking at composite measures, such as the relationship between dwelling unit density and numbers of floors of building rise, there is wide variation particularly beyond thresholds of 100 or more units per hectare. Among the 100 or so project points plotted, there is also clearly not a linear relationship at either the lower or upper ends of the distribution, even if higher-rise buildings are denser in dwelling units than lower-rise structures, as might be expected.[3] Compared to both average and localized 'core' densities of the cities in which most of the projects are located, they are above those magnitudes. Moving on to specific projects of given eras seen in relationship to dwelling density and numbers of unit types, as well as to relative levels of mixed use for each category of types and territory, results are mixed. Nevertheless, they do tend to show contemporary projects as bundles to the higher ends of the two measures of diversity, as well as often being if not entirely denser then comparable in density to others in the same typal-territorial category. More specifically, the 'urban block shapers' tend to exhibit this characteristic, although projects from the 1920s, 1930s, and 1940s show as much if not more use mixture. The category of 'housing and landscapes' by contrast shows contemporary projects to be more dense than examples from prior eras on both measures of diversity as do 'indigenous reinterpretations', whereas contemporary 'tall towers' generally outstrip precedents with regard to density and numbers of unit types but lag behind with regard to use mixture, perhaps suggesting that examples from earlier eras arose out of city contexts rather than being integral through separable parts. For 'big buildings', contemporary projects are more diverse with regard to unit types than the other precedents, with the exception of the Unité d'habitation of the 1950s, and more or less mirror projects from prior eras with regard to relative mixtures of other uses. As with the 'housing and landscapes' category, 'superblock configurations' show contemporary projects to be more mixed on both counts of diversity, although while the same holds for 'infrastructural engagements' with regard to the number of unit types, it does not entirely for the relative mix of uses. For both 'infill and puntal interventions' and 'housing special populations', diversity measures are less relevant due to infill projects being almost entirely about single units of housing here, and examples of special populations bringing with them relatively non-comparable needs with respect to housing diversity. On the whole, however, the examples of contemporary urban housing discussed are more diverse than their precedents and generally as dense or denser. Given that all those examined also fall into the category of being well connected to their larger urban circumstances, the role of contemporary housing in the service of creating conditions of urban intensity also seems to hold, at least empirically.

Looking further forward in time, another phase in the broader turning point referred to here seems to have been reached with the decline of neoliberal orders and the new normals of downturns and slow economic growth, persistently high unemployment, and dampened expectations of further rises in standards of living across the board in most if not all developed countries. While the developing world pushes on, it does so with less of a rush, particularly as it enters middle-income ranges and mounting social pressures with regard to environmental quality, social justice, and economic parity. Indeed, as others join into a club there is likely to be a convergence of interests. Apart from exacerbating adequate provision of housing for all, these sorts of trends would seem to point towards maintaining and increasing dwelling densities and relatively moderate sizes of units for many, including ease of accommodation for life-cycle changes. Changes in household formation and living arrangement, although now relatively stable, seem likely to persist at current levels, sustaining pushes towards diversity among housing units and related uses. All told, if anything 'urban intensity' seems likely to rise objectively, even as making more with less in housing continues to create a more variegated urban residential and architectural landscape.

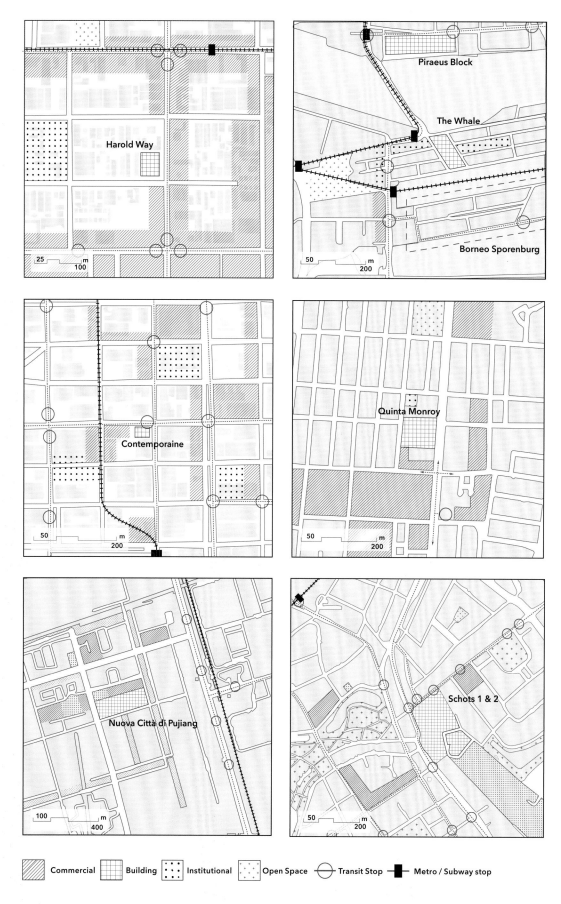

Harold Way

Piraeus Block

The Whale

Borneo Sporenburg

Contemporaine

Quinta Monroy

Nuova Città di Pujiang

Schots 1 & 2

Commercial   Building   Institutional   Open Space   ⊖— Transit Stop   ■— Metro / Subway stop

A TURNING POINT

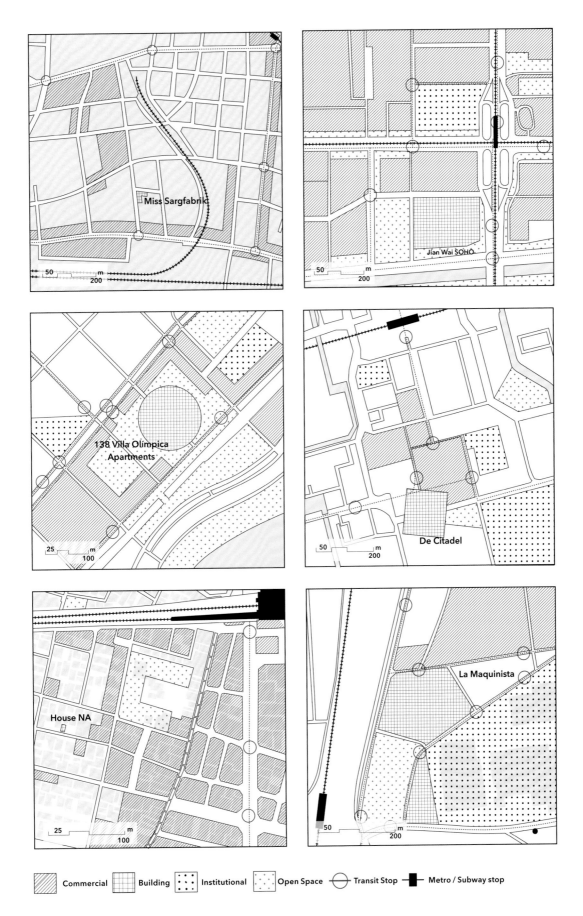

▨ Commercial	▦ Building	⠿ Institutional	⠿ Open Space	⊖ Transit Stop	▮ Metro / Subway stop

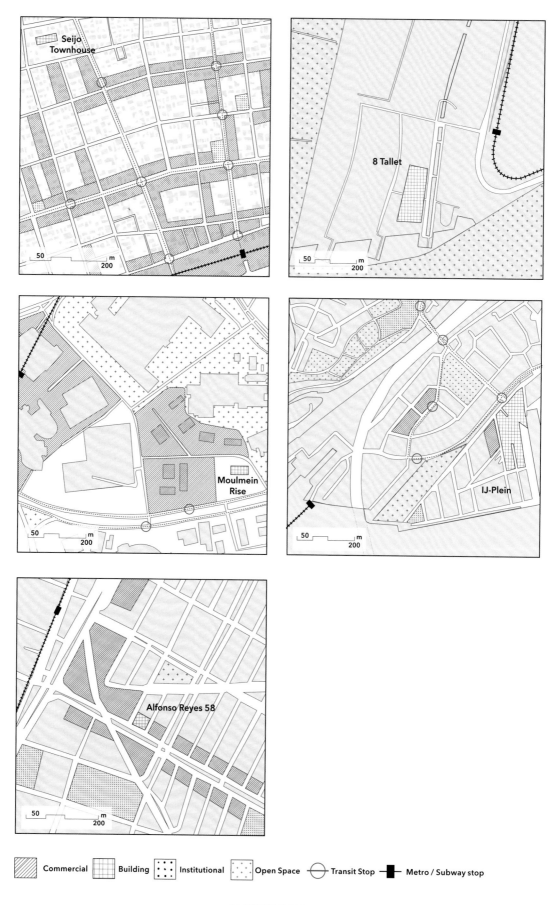

Seijo Townhouse

8 Tallet

Moulmein Rise

IJ-Plein

Alfonso Reyes 58

Commercial   Building   Institutional   Open Space   Transit Stop   Metro / Subway stop

A TURNING POINT

UNITS, TYPES, AND USE MIXES BY CATEGORIES

URBAN BLOCK SHAPERS

Eigen Haard · E
Kiefhoek · K
Spangen · S
Berlin Britz · B
Weisse Stadt · W
El Silencio · El
The Meander · Me
Villa Olímpica · V
La Maquinista · M
Harold Way · H

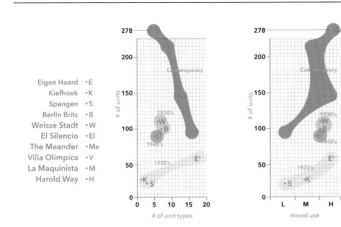

TALL TOWERS

Ritz Tower · Rt
One Fifth Ave · O5
San Remo · Sr
Eldorado · El
Beresford · Br
Broadway Maisons · B
Picadie Apt · P
Villeurbanne · V
Hong Kong Housing Est · HK
Pinnacle @ Duxton · PD
Illa de la Llum · I
Mirador · M
Boutique Monaco · Bm
8 Spruce Street · S8
Moulmein Rise · Mr
Contemporaine · C

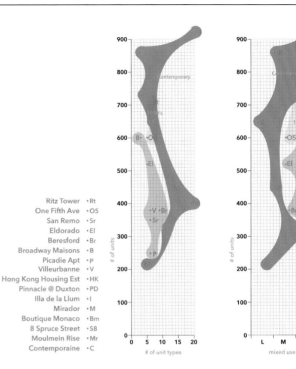

HOUSING & LANDSCAPES

Aniene · A
Sunnyside · S
Radburn · Ra
Römerstadt · Ro
Tiburtino · Ti
Tuscolano · Tu
Roehampton · Roe
Brasilia · Br
De Citadel · Ci
Schots 1 & 2 · Sh
Sanun Maeul · Sm

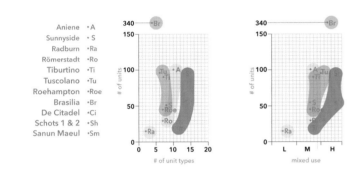

SUPERBLOCK CONFIGURATIONS

Stuyvesant Town · St
Pruitt-Igoe · Pl
Changchun · Ch
Caoyang · C
Sanlinyuan · Sa
Mapo · M
Gangnam · G
Bundang · B
Nexus · N
Shinonome · Sh
Jian Wai SOHO · J
Linked Hybrid · L

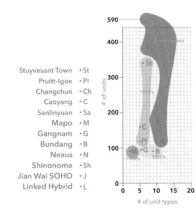
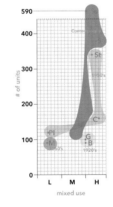

BIG BUILDINGS

Unité d' Habitation · U
Climat de France · Cl
Spinaceto · Sp
Laurentino 38 · L
Corviale · Co
Torrevecchia · T
Gallaratese · G
Edificio Copan · EC
Sewoon Sangga · SS
Via Verde · V
Piraeus Block · P
The Whale · W
8 Tallet · T8

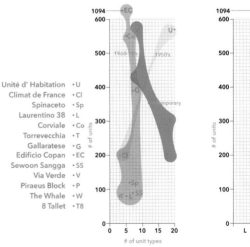
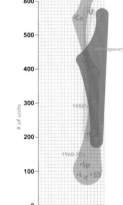

UNITS, TYPES, AND USE MIXES BY CATEGORIES

INFRASTRUCTURAL ENGAGEMENTS

Denenchōfu · D
Euralille · E
Byker Wall · B
Malagueíra · M
Battery Park City · BP
IJ- Plein · IJ
Borneo Sporenburg · BS

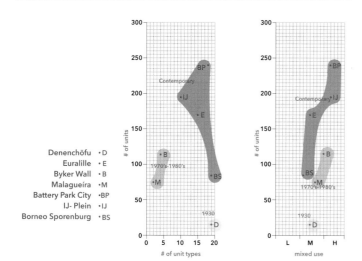

HOUSING SPECIAL POPULATIONS

Previ · Pr
Aranya · A
Fishermen's Houses · F
202 Island Inn · I
New Carver Apts · C
Wohnfabrik Solinsieme · Ws
Kenyuen House · K
Quinta Monroy · Q
Miss Sargfabrik · Sa
IIT State St. · IIT

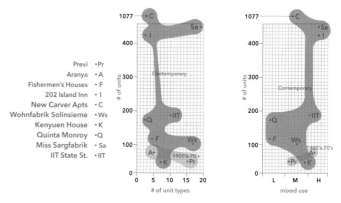

INDIGENOUS REINTERPRETATIONS

Traditional Arab Hsg · Ar
Diplomatic Quarter · D
Villa Victoria · Vv
Veta Grande · Ve
Rincón Colonial · R
31 Boon Tat · B
Ju'er Hutong · J
Puijiang Nuova · P

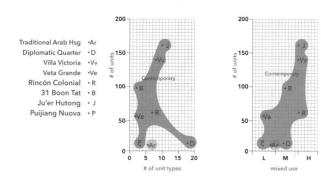

BUILDING RISE AND DWELLING UNITS / HA

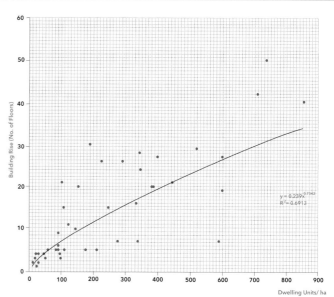

INFILL AND PUNTAL INTERVENTIONS

Boston Bow Fronts,
Phil. Row Houses,
NYC Brownstones · US
Maison De Verre · M
Elektra House · E
302 Station St · S
Space Block · SB
Tsukishma · T
Japanese Sm. Hses · J
Alfonso Reyes · Av

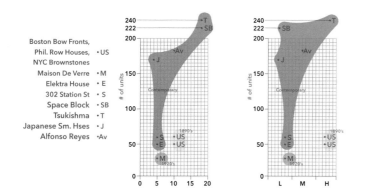

A TURNING POINT

NOTES

INTRODUCTION

1 Bonnie Shelton, Justyna Karakiewicz, and Thomas Kvan, *The Making of Hong Kong: From Vertical to Volumetric* (London: Routledge, 2010).

2 Pietro S. Nivola, *Laws of the Landscape: How Policies Shape Cities in Europe and America* (Washington, D.C.: Brookings Institution, 1999).

3 Manuel Gausa, *Housing: New Alternatives, New Systems* (Barcelona: Actar, 1998).

4 Ron Lesthaeghe, Lisa Neidert, and Johan Surkyn, "Household Formation and the 'Second Demographic Transition' in Europe and the US: Insights from Middle Range Models", accessed August 1, 2013, http://sdt.psc.isr.umich.edu/pubs/online/rl_romantic_unions_paper.pdf (Ann Arbor, MI: Population Studies Center).

5 OECD, "Changes in Demography and Living Arrangements: Are They Widening the Distribution of Household Income?," in OECD, *Growing Unequal?: Income Distribution and Poverty in OECD Countries* (OECD Publishing, 2008), 57-75.

6 Campbell, Gibson, "Figure 6-2. Percent Distribution of Households and Household Population by Size of Household for the United States: 1790 and 1850 to 2010", in *American Demographic History Chartbook: 1790 to 2010*, accessed August 1, 2013, http://www.demographicchartbook.com/Chartbook/index.php?option=com_content&view=article&id=44&Itemid=45

URBAN BLOCK SHAPERS

1 Peter G.Rowe, *Modernity and Housing* (Cambridge, MA: MIT Press, 1993), 186-187.

2 Ministry of Reconstruction and Housing, *Introduction to the Housing Problem in the Netherlands* (The Hague: The Netherlands Government Information Service, 1953).

3 Francis F. Fraenkel, *Het Plan Amsterdam-Zuid van H. P. Berlage: Met Een Catalogus van Uitgevoerde Bouwwerken en Een Register van Architecten* (Alphen aan den Rijn: Vis-druk, 1976).

4 Maristella Casciato, *La Scuola di Amsterdam* (Bologna: Zanichelli Editore, 1987).

5 Department of Housing, *Historical Sketch of Housing in Rotterdam from the Middle Ages to the Present Day* (Amsterdam: Department of Housing, 1950).

6 Rowe, *Modernity and Housing*, 144-157.

7 Norbert Huse, ed., *Vier Berliner Siedlungen der Weimarer Republik* (Berlin: Argon, 1987).

8 Huse, *Vier Berliner Siedlungen der Weimarer Republik*.

9 Ricardo de Sola Ricardo, *La Reurbanización "El Silencio": Crónica 1942-1945* (Caracas: INAVI, 1987).

10 Rob Krier, *Architecture and Urban Design* (London: Academy Editions, 1993).

11 Camillo Sitte, *City Planning According to Artistic Principles*, trans. George R. Collins and Christiane Crasemann Collins (New York, NY: Random House, 1965).

12 In 1981, Barcelona had a population of 1,752,627. See "Número de habitants de la ciudad de Barcelona, 1981", Ajuntament de Barcelona, accessed October 4, 2013, http://www.bcn.cat/estadistica/angles/dades/tpob/ine/a1981/evo02.htm

13 The 1976 General Metropolitan Plan was proposed by Joan Antoni Solans - the Head of Urban Planning for the Corporació Metropolitana de Barcelona - and Manuel de Solà-Morales. The urban renewal program initiated in 1980 was spearheaded by a town-planning commission comprising Josep-Miguel Abad, the vice mayor, Oriol Bohigas, the head of planning since 1979, Jaume Galofré, a lawyer, Albert Puigdomènech, a planner, and Josep-Anton Acebillio, an architect. See Peter Rowe, *Building Barcelona: A Second Renaixença* (Barcelona: Actar, 2006), 48-56.

14 Josep C. Martorell, Oriol Bohigas, David Mackay, and Albert Puigdomènech, *La Villa Olímpica, Barcelona 92: Arquitectura, Parques, Puerto Deportivo* (Barcelona: G. Gili, 1992), 18.

15 Rowe, *Building Barcelona*, 85-86.

16 Martorell et al., *La Villa Olímpica, Barcelona 92*, 188-189.

17 While MBM had established the general urban design parameters, the programmatic decisions like the dimensions and housing types, the location and areas of the commercial uses and car parks, were all determined by NISA. See Martorell et al., *La Villa Olímpica, Barcelona 92*, 114.

18 "Housing for a Compact City", Legacy London, accessed September 28, 2013, http://www.legacy.london.gov.uk/mayor/auu/docs/housing_compact_city.rtf

19 Martorell et al., *La Villa Olímpica, Barcelona 92*, 133.

20 "Barcelona's New High-Speed Train Station Has Its Budget Reduced from €800 to €650 million", Catalan News Agency, July 11, 2013, accessed October 4, 2013, http://www.catalannewsagency.com/business/item/barcelonas-new-high-speed-train-station-has-its-budget-reduced-from-800-to-650-million

21 "La Maquinista" in Ayuntamiento Área de Urbanismo, eds., *Urbanisme a Barcelona: 1999* (Barcelona: Ajuntament de Barcelona, 1999) (Transl. BAU-Barcelona).

22 Julie Eizenberg, *Architecture Isn't Just for Special Occasions: Koning Eizenberg Architecture* (New York, NY: Monacelli Press, 2006), 139.

HOUSING AND LANDSCAPES

1 Jayme A. Sokolow, *The North American Phalanx (1843-1855): A Nineteenth-Century Utopian Community* (Lewiston, NY: Edwin Mellen Press, 2009).

2 Leonardo Benevolo, *The History of the City*, trans. Geoffrey Culverwell (Cambridge, MA: MIT Press, 1980).

3 Italo Insolera, *Roma Moderna: Un Secolo di Storia Urbanistica, 1870-1970* (Turin: Piccola Biblioteca Einaudi, 1993).

4 Peter G. Rowe, *Modernity and Housing* (Cambridge, MA: MIT Press, 1993), 114-121; City Housing Corporation, *Sunnyside: A Step Towards Better Housing* (New York, NY: City Housing Corporation, 1927); and Clarence S. Stein, *Towards New Towns for America* (Cambridge, M.A.: MIT Press, 1966).

5 Rowe, *Modernity and Housing*, 128-144; and John R. Mullin, "German City Planning in the 1920s: An American Perspective of the Frankfurt Experience," *Occasional Paper No. 16* (Faculty of Environmental Studies, University of Waterloo, Canada, 1975).

6 D. W. Dreysse, *Ernst May Housing Estates: Architectural Guide to Eight New Frankfurt Estates, 1926-1930* (Frankfurt: Fricke Verlag, 1988).

7 Heike Risse, *Frühe Moderne in Frankfurt am Main 1920-1933* (Frankfurt: Societäts-Verlag, 1984), 275.

8 Barbara Miller Lane, "Architects in Power: Politics and Ideology in the Work of Ernst May and Albert Speer," in *Art and History: Images and Their Meaning*, ed. Robert I. Rotberg and Theodore K. Rabb (Cambridge: Cambridge University Press, 1986), 293; and Ernst May, *Das Neue Frankfurt* (Frankfurt, 1926), 2-11.

9 Giovanni Astengo, "Nuovi Quartieri in Italia," *Urbanistica*, 7 (1951): 9-25.

10 Manfredo Tafuri, *History of Italian Architecture, 1944-1985* (Cambridge, MA: MIT Press, 1989), 13.

11 Piero Ostilio Rossi, *Roma: Guida all'Architettura Moderna, 1909-1991* (Roma: Laterza, 1991), 176.

12 Bunting Bainbridge, *Houses of Boston's Back Bay: An Architectural History, 1840-1917* (Cambridge, MA: Belknap Press, 1967); Agnes Repplier, *Philadelphia: The Place and The People* (New York, N.Y.: Macmillan, 1898); and Charles Lockwood, *Bricks & Brownstone: The New York Row House, 1783-1929* (New York, N.Y.: Abbeville Press, 1972).

13 Nikolaus Pevsner, "Roehampton: LCC Housing and the Picturesque Tradition," *Architectural Review* 126 (July 1959): 21-25.

14 Farès El-Dahdah, *CASE Lucio Costa: Brasilia's Superquadra* (Munich: Prestel, 2005).

15 Sandra Bernades Ribeiro and Marta Litwinczik Sinote, "A Post-Occupancy Assessment of the Neighborhood Unit," in Farès El-Dahdah, *CASE Lucio Costa: Brasilia's Superquadra* (Munich: Prestel, 2005), 91-96.

16 Lucy Bullivant, "Working the Programme: Designing Social and Affordable Housing in the Netherlands," *Architectural Digest* 73 (July-August 2003): 13.

17 These housing associations were first established as private organizations subject to varying degrees of government influence during the twentieth century, and were key players in resolving the housing shortages after World War II. Their funding and operations were supported by the state from 1945 to the 1990s. See Gerard van Bortel and Marja Elsinga, "A Network Perspective on the Organization of Social Housing in the Netherlands: the Case of Urban Renewal in The Hague," *Housing Theory and Society* 24 (2007): 32-48.

18 "Amsterdam - UNESCO Report", UNESCO, accessed October 13, 2013, http://www.unesco.org/most/p97adam.rtf

19 "Groeikernen (growth centres)", iMURp (Integrated Mobility and Urban Planning), accessed October 13, 2013, http://imurp.nl/portfolio/groeikernen-centres-of-growth/#

20 Michelle Provoost, Bernard Colenbrander, and Floris Alkernade, *Dutchtown: A City Centre Design by OMA* (Rotterdam: NAi Publishers, 1999), 2.

21 Elena Cardani, "Stratificazione e Differenze: The Citadel, Almere," *L'Arca* 228 (Sept 2007): 24-33.

22 "The CiBoGa Terrain, Groningen", S333, accessed October 13, 2013, http://s333.org/projects.43.html?no=true&projectFK=105#

23 "Schots 1 + 2, The CiBoGa Terrain", S333, accessed October 13, 2013, http://s333.org/projects.43.html?no=true&projectFK=3&cameFrom=/projects/

housing_+_mixed_use.2.html. Also see "What We Do", Nijestee, accessed October 13, 2013, http://www.nijestee.nl/ikzoekinfo_nijestee/watwijdoen/160

24 "Schots 1 + 2, The CiBoGa Terrain", S333, accessed October 13, 2013, http://s333.org/projects.43.html?no=true&projectFK=3&cameFrom=/projects/housing_+_mixed_use.2.html.

25 "Schots 1 + 2, The CiBoGa Terrain", S333, accessed October 13, 2013, http://s333.org/projects.43.html?no=true&projectFK=3&cameFrom=/projects/housing_+_mixed_use.2.html.

26 "Pangyo Sanuntown Humansia Terrace-Type Apartment 7", Archiworld Magazine 199 (2011): 114-121.

SUPERBLOCK CONFIGURATIONS

1 Sarah Whiting, "The invisible Superblock," SOM, accessed September 30, 2013, https://www.som.com/publication/invisible-superblock

2 Johann Friedrich Geist and Klaus Kürvers, Das Berliner Mietshaus: 1862-1945 (Munich: Prestel, 1984).

3 Peter G. Rowe, East Asia Modern: Shaping the Contemporary City (London: Reaktion Books, 2005), 121-126.

4 Arthur R. Simon, Stuyvesant Town, USA: A Pattern for Two Americas (New York, N.Y.: New York University Press, 1970).

5 Richard Plunz, A History of Housing in New York City: Dwelling Type and Social Change in the American Metropolis (New York, N.Y.: Columbia University Press, 1990), 255-261.

6 David Bray, Social Space and Governance in Urban China: The Danwei System from Origins to Reform (Stanford, CA: Stanford University Press, 2005).

7 H. Wang, "Our Self-Criticism on Residential Planning for a Factory in Northeast China," Architectural Journal (Jian Zhu Xue Bao) 2 (1955): 20-40. (in Chinese)

8 Yuxue Shi, Housing in Shanghai: 1951-1996 (Shanghai:

Architecture and Construction Press, 1998), 81-87.

9 Shi, Housing in Shanghai, 289-297.

10 Inha Jung, Architecture and Urbanism in Modern Korea (Honolulu: University of Hawai'i Press, 2013), 74-76.

11 Jung, Architecture and Urbanism in Modern Korea, 55-62.

12 Jung, Architecture and Urbanism in Modern Korea, 65-69.

13 Wolfgang Förster, Housing in the 20th and 21st Centuries (Munich: Prestel, 2006), 124-125.

14 "Riken Yamamoto: Shinonome Canal Court Block 1," Japan Architect 51 (Autumn 2003): 98-107.

15 Phases I, II, III, and VI of Jian Wai SOHO were completed by 2004. Phases IV, V, and VII were completed later in 2007.

16 "Jian Wai SOHO", SOHO China, accessed October 20, 2013, http://jianwaisoho.sohochina.com/en

17 "Jian Wai SOHO - Design & Architecture", SOHO China, accessed October 20, 2013, http://jianwaisoho.sohochina.com/en/design

18 Riken Yamamoto, "Beijing Jian Wai SOHO," Japan Architect 51 (Autumn 2003): 108-109

19 Steven Holl, "Linked Hybrid," Domus 928 (September 2009): 14-26.

20 Holl, "Linked Hybrid," 14-26.

21 Híbrido Enlazado, "Linked Hybrid," El Croquis 141 (2008): 226-241.

TALL TOWERS

1 Theodore Turak, William Le Baron Jenney: A Pioneer of Modern Architecture (Ann Arbor, M.I.: UMI Research Press, 1986).

2 Rosella Vantaggi, San Gimignano: Town of Fine Towers (Milan: Phingraf, 1979).

3 Robert A. M. Stern, Gregory Gilmartin, and Thomas Mellins, New York 1930: Architecture and Urbanism Between the Two World Wars (New York: Rizzoli, 1987), 212-215.

4 Stern et al., New York 1930, 214-215.

5 Hugh Ferriss, The Metropolis of Tomorrow (Princeton, N.J.: Princeton Architectural Press,

1986); and Dennis Sharp, ed., Alfred C. Bossom's American Architecture, 1903-1926 (London: Book Art, 1984).

6 Richard Plunz, A History of Housing in New York City: Dwelling Type and Social Change in the American Metropolis (New York: Columbia University Press, 1990), 194-195.

7 Plunz, A History of Housing in New York City, 195-196.

8 Plunz, A History of Housing in New York City, 196-200.

9 Edward Denison and Guang Yu Ren, Building Shanghai: The Story of China's Gateway (Hoboken, N.J.: Wiley-Academy, 2006), 128-193.

10 Chisong Qu, Gemischt-funktionale Hochhäuser in China und Deutschland (TU Darmstadt: Fachbereich Architektur, 2003).

11 Anne-Sophie Clémençon, Les Gratte-Ciel de Villeurbanne (Besançon: Editions de l'Imprimeur, 2004).

12 Clémençon, Les Gratte-Ciel de Villeurbanne.

13 Manuel Castells, L. Goh, and R. Y-W Kwok, The Shek Kip Mei Syndrome: Economic Development and Housing in Hong Kong and Singapore (London: Pion, 1990).

14 Peter G. Rowe, "Hong Kong - New Territories, New Towns," Arbitare 450 (May 2005): 118-125.

15 Constance Mary Turnbull, A History of Singapore, 1819-1988 (Singapore: Oxford University Press, 1989), 288-327; and Giok Ling Ooi, "Singapore's Changing International Orientations: 1960-1990," in Singapore from Temasek to the 21st Century: Reinventing the Global City, ed. Karl Hack and Jean-Louis Margolin, with Karine Delaye (Singapore: NUS Press, 2010), 323-344.

16 David Cohn, "ARC Plans Mega-Structure for Singapore," World Architecture 108 (July-August 2002): 19-24.

17 Matteo Poli, "MAD Absolute Towers: Mississauga," Arbitare 527 (2012): 42-49.

18 Aurora Fernández Per, Javier Mozas, and Javier Arpa. DBook: Density, Data, Diagrams, Dwellings: A Visual Analysis of 64 Collective Housing Projects (Vito-

ria-Gasteiz: a+t ediciones, 2007), 344-349.

19 Michele Costanzo, MVRDV: Works and Projects, 1991-2006 (Milan: Skira, 2006), 158-167.

20 "Boutique Monaco," Space 491 (October 2008): 76-91.

21 "Minister Mah launches Draft Concept Plan 2001 Exhibition," Urban Redevelopment Authority, April 28, 2001, accessed October 26, 2013, http://www.ura.gov.sg/pr/text/pr01-20.html

22 Aga Khan Award for Architecture, "Moulmein Rise Residential Tower, Singapore" in Intervention Architecture: Building for Change (London: I. B. Tauris & Co Ltd., for the Aga Khan Award for Architecture, 2007), 102.

23 "Building", New York by Gehry, accessed October 27, 2013, http://www.newyorkbygehry.com/#!new-york-by-gehry

24 David Dunlap, "Tower Would Create Residences, And Space for Pace University," New York Times, April 20, 2004, accessed October 27, 2013, http://www.nytimes.com/2004/04/20/nyregion/tower-would-create-residences-and-space-for-pace-university.html

25 David Dunlap, "Pace Pulls Out of Expansion Project, Citing Builder's Price Increase," New York Times, November 4, 2004, accessed October 27, 2013, http://www.nytimes.com/2004/11/04/nyregion/04pace.html?_r=0

26 "HDC Board Approves Financing for Two Major Projects," NYC HDC, accessed October 27, 2013, http://www.nychdc.com/pages/pr_02%252d27%252d20081.html

27 "8 Spruce Street", accessed October 27, 2013, http://ominy.org/media/projects/Spring11_8Spruce_web.PDF

28 Pippo Ciorra and Marco Biagi, "Beekman Tower, New York," Casabella 797 (January 2011): 8-19.

29 Meghan Drueding et al., "Residential Architect Design Awards '05: Project of the Year - Contemporaine, Chicago," Residential Architect (May 2005): 42.

30 Drueding et al., "Residential Architect Design Awards '05: Project of the Year - Contemporaine, Chicago," 42.

BIG BUILDINGS

1 David Jenkins, Unité d'Habitation, Marseille: Le Corbusier (London: Phaidon Press, 1993).

2 Stanislaus von Moos, Le Corbusier: Elements of a Synthesis (Cambridge, MA: MIT Press, 1979), 204.

3 "Unité d'Habitation à Nantes-Rezé, France," Architecture d'Aujourd'hui 66 (July 1956): 2-11.

4 Bernard Félix Dubor, Fernand Pouillon (Paris: Electa France, 1986).

5 Piero Ostilio Rossi, Roma: Guida all'Architettura Moderna, 1909-1991(Rome: Laterza, 1991), 258-261; and Italo Insolera, Roma Moderna: Un Secolo di Storia Urbanistica, 1870-1970 (Turin: Piccola Biblioteca Einaudi, 1993), 264-277.

6 Rossi, Roma, 262-265.

7 Rossi, Roma, 314-317.

8 Rossi, Roma, 321-323.

9 Rossi, Roma, 333-336.

10 Yukio Futagawa, Global Architecture: Carlo Aymonino/Aldo Rossi, Housing Complex at the Gallaratese Quarter, Milan, Italy, 1969-1974 (Tokyo: ADA. EDITA, 1977).

11 Joann Gonchar, "Affordable's New Look, New York City: With Via Verde - a Mixed-use Complex in a Rapidly Changing Bronx Neighborhood - Dattner & Grimshaw Reimagine City Dwelling," Architectural Record 200 (July 2012): 97-101.

12 Michael Kimmelman, "In a Bronx Complex, Doing Good Mixes With Looking Good," New York Times, September 26, 2011, accessed October 15, 2013, http://www.nytimes.com/2011/09/26/arts/design/via-verde-in-south-bronx-rewrites-low-income-housing-rules.html?pagewanted=all&_r=0

13 Kimmelman, "In a Bronx Complex, Doing Good Mixes With Looking Good".

14 Jaap Evert Abrahamse, "Amsterdam on the sea: The historic development of the Eastern Harbour District,"

in *Eastern Harbour District Amsterdam: Urbanism and Architecture,* ed. Jaap Evert Abrahamse et al. (Rotterdam: NAi Publishers, 2006), 9.

15   Allard Jolles, "Tail Winds," in *Eastern Harbour District Amsterdam: Urbanism and Architecture,* ed. Jaap Evert Abrahamse et al. (Rotterdam: NAi Publishers, 2006), 25-26.

16   Allard Jolles, "Tail Winds", 27.

17   Marlies Buurman, "KNSM Island," in *Eastern Harbour District Amsterdam: Urbanism and Architecture,* ed. Jaap Evert Abrahamse et al. (Rotterdam: NAi Publishers, 2006), 58.

18   Buurman, "KNSM Island", 59, 61, 63.

19   Hans Kollhoff, "Against the Taboos of an Urban Architecture," *Domus* (April 1995): 107.

20   "'The Whale' residential complex, Amsterdam", Cie, accessed November 2, 2013, http://www1.cie.nl/projects/projects/residential/the-whale,-amsterdam.aspx

21   "Facts on Ørestad," Ørestad, accessed November 2, 2013, http://www.orestad.dk/Fakta.aspx

22   1994 Competition Stipulation cited in "Copenhagen Growing: The Story of Ørestad," Ørestad, accessed November 2, 2013, http://www.orestad.dk/Fakta/~/media/Orestad/pdf/Copenhagen-Growing_web.ashx

23   Bjarke Ingels, cited in "Copenhagen's BIG Architects Complete 8 House Landmark Residential Project," by Alma Kadragic, *World Property Channel,* accessed November 2, 2013, http://www.worldpropertychannel.com/featured-columnists/uae-watch-big-bjarke-ingels-group-8-house-guinness-book-of-records-emaar-burj-khalifa-stfredeikslung-holding-per-hopfner-hopfner-partners-3367.php

24   Bjarke Ingels, cited in "8 House, Village Gigantesque = 8 House, A Giant Village," by Marie-Douce Albert, *Architecture d'Aujourd'hui* 380 (November-December 2010): 155.

INFRASTRUCTURAL ENGAGEMENTS

1   Jeffrey E. Fulmer, "What in the World is Infrastructure?," *Infrastructure Investor* (July-Aug 2009): 30-32, accessed October 20, 2013, http://www.corridortrust.com/uploads/Infrastructure_Investor.pdf

2   Ken Tadashi Oshima, "Denenchōfu: Building the Garden City in Japan," *Journal of the Society of Architectural Historians* 55 (June 1996): 140-151, 218.

3   "Euralille, Lille, France", *GA Document* 41 (November 1994): 36-65; "Xaveer de Geyter, 1992-2005", *El Croquis* 126 (2005): 44-49.

4   Colin Emery, "Byker by Erskine: Housing, Byker, Newcastle upon Tyne," *Architectural Review* 156 (December 1974): 346-362; and Peter Buchanan, "Landscaping at Byker, Newcastle upon Tyne," *Architectural Review* 156 (December 1974): 334-343.

5   Pierluigi Nicoli, "Quinta da Malagueira, Évora," in *Álvaro Siza: Poetic Profession*; Kenneth Frampton, Nuño Portas, Alexander Alves Costa, Pierluigi Nicolini (New York: Electa/Rizzoli, 1986), 10-23; Jean-Paul Rayon, "Il Quartiere Malagueira a Évora," *Casabella* 478 (March 1982): 2-15; Peter G. Rowe, *Byker Project, United Kingdom and Malagueira Quarter, Portugal* (Cambridge, MA: Harvard Graduate School of Design, 1988); Brigitte Fleck, Günter Pfeifer (eds.), *Malagueira. Álvaro Siza in Évora* (Freiburg: Syntagma, 2013).

6   Eric Firley and Katharina Grön, *The Urban Masterplanning Handbook* (Chichester, UK: Wiley, 2013), 62-75.

7   Allard Jolles, Erik Klusman, and Ben Teunissen, *Planning Amsterdam: Scenarios for Urban Development, 1928-2003* (Rotterdam: NAi Publishers, 2003).

8   Bernard Leupen, *IJ-Plein, Amsterdam: Een Speurtocht Naar Nieuwe Compositorische Middelen: Rem Koolhaas, Office for Metropolitan Architecture* (Rotterdam: Uitgeverij 010, 1989), 109.

9   Thomas Fisher, "Logic and Will," *Progressive Architecture* 71 (March 1990): 98-99.

10   Leupen, *IJ-Plein, Amsterdam,* 110.

11   Leupen, *IJ-Plein, Amsterdam,* 111.

12   Jan de Waal, "Living in the Eastern Harbour District," in *Eastern Harbour District Amsterdam: Urbanism and Architecture,* ed. Jaap Evert Abrahamse et al. (Rotterdam: NAi Publishers, 2006), 85.

13   Allard Jolles, "Tail Winds," in *Eastern Harbour District Amsterdam: Urbanism and Architecture,* ed. Jaap Evert Abrahamse et al. (Rotterdam: NAi Publishers, 2006), 27.

14   Ton Schaap, "Collective Curiosity, the Development of Borneo/Sporenburg in Amsterdam, 1992-1995," *A+U* 380 (May 2002): 56.

15   Marlies Buurman, "Borneo and Sporenburg." in *Eastern Harbour District Amsterdam: Urbanism and Architecture,* ed. Jaap Evert Abrahamse et al (Rotterdam: NAi Publishers, 2006), 131.

16   Schaap, "Collective Curiosity, the Development of Borneo/Sporenburg in Amsterdam, 1992-1995," 58.

17   Graham Smith, "Design coding in Amsterdam - Borneo and Sporenburg," *rudi.net,* accessed November 2, 2013, http://www.rudi.net/books/15907

18   "Borneo 12," MVRDV, accessed November 2, 2013, http://www.mvrdv.nl/projects/BORNEO.12/ ; "Borneo 18, MVRDV, accessed November 2, 2013, http://www.mvrdv.nl/projects/BORNEO.18/

19   Christian Schittich, *High-Density Housing: Concepts, Planning, Construction* (Munich: Edition Detail, 2004), 86-95.

20   Hans Ibelings, *Claus en Kaan: Building* (Rotterdam: NAi, 2001), 80-85.

INDIGENOUS REINTERPRETATIONS

1   Françoise Choay, *The Invention of the Historic Monument,* trans. Lauren M. O'Connell (Cambridge, U.K.: Cambridge University Press, 2001).

2   Peter G. Rowe, "Dual Aspects of Tradition in Saudi Arabian Housing," in *Housing, Culture and Design: A Comparative Perspective,* ed. Setha M. Low and Erve Chambas (Philadelphia: University of Pennsylvania Press, 1989), 303-334.

3   Arthur Clark, "Riyadh's New DQ," *Saudi Aramco World* (September-October 1988): 8-21.

4   John Sharratt, "Urban Neighborhood Preservation and Development," *Process Architecture* 14 (1980): 28-32; and Mildred E. Schmertz, "Housing," *Architectural Record* 163 (February 1978): 78-94.

5   Peter G. Rowe, *Modernity and Housing* (Cambridge, MA: MIT Press, 1993), 244-252.

6   Carlos García Vélez, *La Morada: Low Entry Level Housing in Mexico* (MDes Thesis, Harvard University Graduate School of Design, 1995).

7   *Proyecto 2000* (Mexico: Grupo Editorial InterBooks, 2000), 146-147; and Luis Al Sousa Ramírez and Martín Gómez-Tagle, "Geomoradas en Zacatecas," *Entre Rayas* 27 (October 1998): 30-35.

8   Wong Yunn Chii, et al., "31 Boon Tat Street," *Singapore 1:1 City* (Singapore: URA, 2005), 313-317.

9   Shouyi Zhang and Ting Tan, "An Important Period for the Early Development of Housing in Modern China," in *Modern Urban Housing in China: 1840-2000,* ed. Junhua Lü, Peter G. Rowe, and Zhang Jie (Munich: Prestel, 2001), 48-102.

10   Peter G. Rowe and Seng Kuan, *Architectural Encounters with Essence and Form in Modern China* (Cambridge, MA: MIT Press, 2002), 8-15.

11   Liangyong, Wu, *Rehabilitating the Old City of Beijing: A Project in the Ju'er Hutong Neighbourhood* (Vancouver: University of British Columbia Press, 1999), xix.

12   Wu, *Rehabilitating the Old City of Beijing,* xx.

13   Wu, *Rehabilitating the Old City of Beijing,* 51.

14   Wu, *Rehabilitating the Old City of Beijing,* 77.

15   Wu, *Rehabilitating the Old City of Beijing,* 104-115.

16   Wu, *Rehabilitating the Old City of Beijing,* 114.

17   Wu, *Rehabilitating the Old City of Beijing,* 140.

18   Wu, *Rehabilitating the Old City of Beijing,* 140 and 144; "Ju'er Hutong Courtyard Housing Project, Beijing," World Habitat Awards, accessed November 24, 2013, http://www.worldhabitatawards.org/winners-and-finalists/project-details.cfm?lang=00&theProjectID=119

19   Bo Guo, *The Fast Vanishing Shanghai Lanes* (Shanghai: Shanghai Pictorial Publishing House, 1996), 119-125.

20   Junhua Lü, Peter G. Rowe, and Zhang Jie, *Modern Urban Housing in China: 1840-2000* (Munich: Prestel, 2001), 64-76.

21   Guido Morpurgo, *Gregotti & Associates: The Architecture of Urban Design* (New York: Rizzoli, 2008), 250.

22   Martin Heidegger, "The Origin of the Work of Art," in *Martin Heidegger: The Basic Writings* (New York: HarperCollins, 2008).

23   Umberto Eco, *The Aesthetics of Thomas Aquinas,* trans. Hugh Bredin (Cambridge, MA: Harvard University Press, 1988).

24   Rowe and Kuan, *Architectural Encounters with Essence and Form in Modern China,* 137-160.

INFILL AND PUNTAL INTERVENTIONS

1   Bunting Bainbridge, *Houses of Boston's Back Bay: An Architectural History, 1840-1917* (Cambridge, MA: Belknap Press, 1967)

2   Agnes Repplier, *Philadelphia: The Place and The People* (New York: Macmillan, 1898); and Charles Lockwood, *Bricks & Brownstone: The New York Row House, 1783-1929* (New York, NY: Abbeville Press, 1972).

3   Dominique Vellay, *La Maison de Verre: Pierre Chareau's Modernist Masterwork* (London: Thames & Hudson, 2007).

4   Rowan Moore, "Una Casa Per Elektra," *Domus* 835 (March 2001): 60-71.

5 "302 Station Street," in *Infill: New Houses for Urban Sites*, Adam Mornement and Annabel Biles (London: Laurence King, 2009), 20-23.

6 "Old House," in *Infill: New Houses for Urban Sites*, 154-159.

7 Aurora Fernández Per, Javier Mozas and Javier Arpa, *DBook: Density, Data, Diagrams, Dwellings: A Visual Analysis of 64 Collective Housing Projects* (Vitoria-Gasteiz: a+t ediciones, 2007), 340-343.

8 Tokyo-tō Chūō-ku, "New Rules for Determining the Street Widths in the Tsukishima's *Machi* Area", (Tokyo: Tokyo-tō Chūō-ku Government, 1999) (in Japanese).

9 Personal conversation with Yoshida-san, then the Planning Director for Chūō-ku, Tokyo, March, 2003.

10 "Japan: Market Situation," National Association of Realtors, accessed November 16, 2013, http://www.realtor.org/intlprof.nsf/92bf-c17e61d4b650862568110 04d5632/11b2499831c0a1d-b8625681000680edb?Open-Document

11 "Atelier Bow-Wow - Japanese Pet Architecture," designbuild-network.com, accessed November 16, 2013, http://www.design-build-network.com/features/feature49404/

12 Sou Fujimoto, "Sou Fujimoto: House NA, Tokyo, Japan," *GA Houses* 121 (May 2011): 146; "House NA/ Sou Fujimoto Architects," archdaily, accessed November 16, 2013, http://www.archdaily.com/230533/house-na-sou-fujimoto-architects/

13 Fujimoto, "Sou Fujimoto: House NA, Tokyo, Japan," 146.

14 Stefano Casciani and Kazuyo Sejima, "Kazuyo Sejima, Seijoville," *Domus* 915 (June 2008): 35.

15 Casciani and Sejima, "Kazuyo Sejima, Seijoville," 35.

16 "Umegaoka Cooperative House ROXI: SGM Architect & Associates, Tarao Hiiro Architects, Takehiko Higa Architect & Associates, Atelier-YY," *Japan Architect* 56 (Winter 2005): 88-89.

17 Tarao Hiiro Architects, "Umegaoka Cooperative House ROXI A-unit," accessed November 17, 2013, http://www.taraohiiro.co.jp/umegaoka/A-unit/A-unit.html

18 Tarao Hiiro Architects, "Umegaoka Cooperative House ROXI D-unit," accessed November 17, 2013, http://www.taraohiiro.co.jp/umegaoka/D-unit/D-unit.html

19 Tarao Hiiro Architects, "Umegaoka Cooperative House ROXI H-unit," accessed November 17, 2013, http://www.taraohiiro.co.jp/umegaoka/H-unit/H-unit.html

20 Tarao Hiiro Architects, "Umegaoka Cooperative House ROXI J-unit," accessed November 17, 2013, http://www.taraohiiro.co.jp/umegaoka/J-unit/J-unit.html

HOUSING SPECIAL POPULATIONS

1 "PREVI/Lima: Low Cost Housing Project," *Architectural Design* 40 (Apr 1970): 187-205.

2 "Aranya Community Housing," Aga Khan Award for Architecture, accessed November 20, 2013, http://www.akdn.org/architecture/pdf/1242_Ind.pdf

3 "Houses for the Fishermen of Tyre," in Andres Lepik, *Small Scale Big Change* (New York, NY: MOMA, 2010), 43-52.

4 Mimi Zeiger, "New Carver Apartments," *Architect* 99 (May 2010): 53-59.

5 Sarah Amelar, "Steven Holl Experiments with Constructed 'Porosity' in His Design for Simmons Hall," *Architectural Record* 191 (May 2003): 204-215.

6 Eckhard Feddersen and Insa Lüdtke, *Living for the Elderly: A Design Manual* (Basel: Birkhäuser, 2009), 146-149.

7 Feddersen and Lüdtke, *Living for the Elderly*, 152-157.

8 "Iquique City", ZOFRI El Corazón del Norte, accessed December 1, 2013, http://www.zofri.cl/index.php/en/why-have-to-establish-it-/iquique-city.html

9 Rodrigo Salcedo, "The Last Slum: Moving from Illegal Settlements to Subsidized Home Ownership in Chile", *Urban Affairs Review* 2010, 46(1): 90-118.

10 Salcedo, "The Last Slum", 90-118.

11 Patricia Frenz, "Innovative Practices for Intersectoral Action on Health: A Case Study of Four Programs for Social Equity - Chile Barrio, Chile Solidario, Chile Emprende, Chile Crece Contigo", Ministry of Health Chile, August 31, 2007, http://www.who.int/social_determinants/resources/isa_4progs_so-social_equity_chile.pdf, 12.

12 "Quinta Monroy, Iquique: Elemental - Alejandro Aravena", *Verb: Architecture Boogazine* 6 (2008): 55-57.

13 Mario Ballesteros, "Elemental - Lessons in Pragmatism", *Perspecta* 42 (2010): 83-84.

14 Irina Verona, "ELEMENTAL Program: Rethinking Low-Cost Housing in Chile", *Praxis: Journal of Writing & Building* 8 (2006): 56.

15 "Quinta Monroy, Iquique: Elemental - Alejandro Aravena", 283.

16 "Quinta Monroy, Iquique: Elemental - Alejandro Aravena", 279.

17 Ballesteros, "Elemental - Lessons in Pragmatism", 87.

18 Ballesteros, "Elemental - Lessons in Pragmatism", 87.

19 Verona, "ELEMENTAL Program: Rethinking Low-Cost Housing in Chile", 56.

20 Julie Lawson, "Path Dependency and Emergent Relations: Explaining the Different Role of Limited Profit Housing in the Dynamic Urban Regimes of Vienna and Zurich", *Housing, Theory and Society* Vol. 27, No. 3 (2010): 205-211.

21 BKK-3, Haig Beck, and Jackie Cooper, "BKK-3 Architects: Miss Sargfabrik Housing Collective, Vienna, Austria", *UME* 14 (2002): 20.

22 "Sargfabrik - Das Projekt", Sargfabrik, accessed December 1, 2013, http://www.sargfabrik.at/docs/verein/index.htm

23 BKK-3 et al., "BKK-3 Architects", 20-22.

24 "Sargfabrik - Das Projekt", Sargfabrik, accessed December 1, 2013, http://www.sargfabrik.at/docs/verein/index.htm

25 Rory O'Donovan, "Sargfabrik and Miss Sargfabrik, Vienna-Penzing, Austria", *Irish Architect* 185 (March 2003): 47-48.

26 "BKK-3", *26: Revista Internacional de Arquitectura* 36 (2005): 27.

27 "Miss Sargfabrik: BKK-3 Vienna, Austria 1998-2000", *A+U* 380 (May 2002): 128.

28 "Miss Sargfabrik", 128.

29 Horacio Caminos, John F.C. Turner, and John A. Steffian, *Urban Dwelling Environments: An Elementary Survey of Settlements for the Study of Design Determinants* (Cambridge, MA: MIT Press, 1969); and John F.C. Turner and Robert Fichter, eds., *Freedom to Build: Dweller Control of the Housing Process* (New York, NY: Macmillan, 1972).

A TURNING POINT

1 Peter G. Rowe, *Modernity and Housing* (Cambridge, Mass.: MIT Press, 1993).

2 Peter G. Rowe, *East Asia Modern: Shaping the Contemporary City* (London: Reaktion Books, 2005), 59-163.

3 A similar comment can be found in Aurora Fernández Per, Javier Mozas, and Javier Arpa, *DBook: Density, Data, Diagrams, Dwellings: A Visual Analysis of 64 Collective Housing Projects* (Vitoria-Gasteiz: a+t ediciones, 2007).

Editorial Note
The written scales indicate the scales at which the drawings were produced. In the book the drawings have been slightly reduced in size. The precise dimensions are indicated by the measured scales.

ABOUT THE AUTHORS

Peter G. Rowe is the Raymond Garbe Professor of Architecture and Urban Design and a Harvard University Distinguished Service Professor at Harvard University where he has taught since 1985 and served as Dean of the Graduate School of Design between 1992 and 2004. He is an author or editor of numerous books, several of which deal with housing, including *Making a Middle Landscape*, *Modernity and Housing*, and *Modern Housing in China, 1840–2000*.

Har Ye Kan is a Research Associate and Post-Doctoral Fellow at the Graduate School of Design, Harvard University, where she recently completed her doctoral degree. The author of several articles and book chapters dealing primarily with Chinese urbanism, she also served as an instructor with Peter Rowe in a graduate seminar on housing.

ACKNOWLEDGMENTS

Much of the research involved in the book was generously supported by the Eugene Group in Seoul, Korea, through the Korean and East Asian Urban Research Program Fund they established at the Harvard University Graduate School of Design. In particular, key aspects of the case study material appearing in the book and bearing on East Asia, along with the book's graphical material, benefited from this support. Early on, Michael Sypkens participated in the book's planning and laid the foundation for the book's drawings. Saehoon Kim, now at Seoul National University, was also helpful in bringing several Korean projects to our attention, as were John Hong and Jinhee Park. Joan Busquets shared some valuable insights, particularly regarding his own work and that of others in Europe and Barcelona. Two classes of extraordinary graduate students enrolled in a seminar titled "Modern Housing and Urban Districts: Concepts, Cases, and Comparisons", at Harvard, and contributed their insights and knowledge during the fall terms of 2012 and 2013 respectively. Finally, Andreas Müller as editor for the publisher and by now a dear friend, stayed with the project through ups and downs, as did Reinhard Steger, the book's graphic designer, always bubbly with creative energy.

CREDITS

The illustrations, drawings, and graphs that accompany the text are the creative productions of a talented team of students from the Harvard University Graduate School of Design. This publication was made possible with the exceptional graphic materials crafted by Matthew J. Conway, Yun Fu, Amy Garlock, Cheng He Guan, Christopher Johnson, Jae Hyoung Kim, and Dingliang Yang. To them, we extend our deepest appreciation. We thank the various photographers and members of architectural firms who have kindly provided the images of the individual projects. Any photographs that are not credited in the publication were taken by the authors or sourced from the public domain.

Graphic design and layout:
Reinhard Steger
Deborah van Mourik
Proxi, Barcelona
www.proxi.me

Editor for the publisher:
Andreas Müller, Berlin

Library of Congress
Cataloging-in-Publication Data
A CIP catalog record for this book has been applied to at the Library of Congress.

Bibliographic information published by the Deutsche Nationalbibliothek
The Deutsche Nationalbibliothek lists this publication in the Deutsche Nationalbibliografie; detailed bibliographic data are available in the Internet at http://dnb.dnb.de.

© 2014 Birkhäuser Verlag GmbH, Basel
P.O. Box 44, 4009 Basel, Switzerland
Part of De Gruyter

Printed on acid-free paper produced from chlorine-free pulp. TCF ∞

Printed in Germany

ISBN
978-3-03821-477-9

9 8 7 6 5 4 3 2 1

www.birkhauser.com